Partition, Bengal and After: The Great Tragedy of India

Kali Prasad Mukhopadhyay

Ess Ess Publications

4837/24, Ansari Road, Darya Ganj,
New Delhi-110002
✆ : 23260807, 41563444
Fax : 011-41563334
E-mail: info@essessreference.com
url:http://www.essessreference.com

First Published 2007

ISBN : 81-84050-34-8

Price : Rs. 575/-

Published by :

Ess Ess Publications

4837/24, Ansari Road, Darya Ganj,
New Delhi - 110 002
✆ : 23260807, 41563444
Fax : 011-41563334
E-mail: info@essessreference.com
url:http://www.essessreference.com

Laser Typesetting:

Mukesh Graphics

T-1264, Mangolpuri, New Delhi
Ph. : 9899079035, 20106135
E-mail:mukeshgraphics29@yahoo.com

Printed at :

Print Line

Dedication

To all innocent hapless minorities who lost their life, liberty, property and due to atrocities and humiliation had to quit their hearth and home and became destitutes overnight as the victims of the Independence and Partition of India.

FOREWORD

Generations born in India since 1930 have scanty knowledge about what happened in Indian Sub-Continent in the years of 1946 and 1947 leading to the partition of India. In the Western world, particularly in Europe hundreds of novels and memoirs have been published and almost equal number of movies were produced depicting the tragedy of Jews in Germany and its adjoining European countries and some movies even won the OSCAR awards. But how many human beings were involved in that tragedy? Certainly not more than two million Jews. As a fellow human being I share the tragedy. But who will share my tragedy, our tragedy, our sorrows and tears of at least one hundred million people of India who fell victims to the Great Indian Tragedy that was the Partition and Afterwards? Shri Kali Prasad Mukhopadhyay who to my mind eminently knowledgeable on the subject has tried to depict and paint the pangs and pathoes of those human beings. Though many Scholars and Historians, of them the most outstanding are Leonard Mosley and Michael Edwards have painted many human tragedies, but the tragedy of the Bengali Hindus of earstwhile East Bengal have not been placed in proper perspective by any of the authors of fame. That is another tragedy poured on them. Leonard Mosley in his book *The Last Days of the British Raj* has rightly painted the year 1947 as the "Year of Vultures", because their most favourite food the human flesh were in abundance in Indian streets and fields! Those authors whom I have mentioned had the fabulous financial backing in their effort to write on the subject, which Shri Mukhopadhyay has done single handed without the least financial backing from elsewhere. It has surprised me to a considerable extent that without being an academician sheer passion has motioned him to embark upon the voluminous work which produced the *Partition, Bengal And After: The Great Tragedy of India*, which carried the

Tragedy to whom he fell victim personally in 1947, the "Year of Vultures"! Generations which I have mentioned earlier, shall be benefited I feel fondly, if they go through the well documented Annal.

Sukharanjan Sengupta
Block – P, Flat-8 (MIG)
Belgachia Villa
Kolkata-700037

ACKNOWLEDGEMENTS

I am indebted to Prof. Gautam Bhadra of the Centre of Social Studies who has encouraged me to write my first book about refugees *Sikarer Sandhane*. He has very kindly written the Foreword also. Having seen the book Prof. Arun Kumar Dasgupta of the University of Calcutta encouraged me to write such books and referred me to the historians who were working on this subject. Though I am not their student yet I am blessed to receive their affection and sympathy. After going through my book the ex-Justice Brigadier D. M. Sen of Assam High Court also encouraged me to write the history of the Partition. I am indebted to Dr. Jayanta Kumar Ray, presently the Chairman of Maulana Abul Kalam Azad Institute of Asian Studies, to whom I always seek his valuable advice on this subject. He has presented me a copy of his book, *Democracy and Nationalism on Trial – A study of East Pakistan* for my study. Besides writing many features as a freelance writer and contributed to many esteemed newspapers I have taken it a mission to explore the truth behind the reasons for partition and its aftermath.

I am grateful to Dr. Dinesh Chandra Sinha who was awarded Sir Ashutosh Gold Medal and Griffith Memorial Prize for his outstanding work on the '*Role of the Calcutta University for spreading education through Bengali language*' and author of two books '*Shyamaprasad – Bangabi Bhag O Pashchimbanga*' and '*Noakhalir Mati O Manush*' and Shri Subir Kumar Sen, Reader of the Calcutta University Library and Information Science, who has reviewed and edited my manuscript and always advised me for improvement of the write up. I have also every respect to Dr. Jayati Ghose, ex-Librarian of the Commercial and Intelligence Library, Calcutta.

I must acknowledge my deep debt of gratitude to Prof. L. S. Ramaiah, University Librarian (Ret.) Central Institute of English and Foreign Languages, Hyderabad and a good friend who has suggested the many facets of the book and rearranged the manuscript, making the pages for formation of the book, edited, corrected even the punctuations. More so, he has selected the publisher for which I am once more thankful to him. I am really grateful to Late Kalidas Dey, Late Gourhari Saha, Sri Krishna Banerjee, Librarians of the Secretariat Library, Calcutta; Sri Binod Behari Das, Librarian, Dr. D. K. Roy Ex-Associate Librarian, Sri Pulak Saha of Jadavpur University Central Library; Sri Asim Mukherjee of National Library; Sri Sandip Sarkar, Librarian, Srijukta Godhuli Ghosh, Assistant Librarian, Sri Jayanta Dhara of Maulana Abul Kalam Azad Institute of Asian Studies.

I will, however, express my heartfelt gratitude to Sri Arun Kumar Das Gupta, ex-Librarian, Administrative Staff Training College, Hyderabad, who has gone through the manuscript and conveyed his valuable instructions. I express my gratitude to Dr. Pulak Narayan Dhar of Abul Kalam Azad College who has very kindly gone through the manuscript inspite of his busy schedule. I also share the worries, anxieties and sufferings of the victims of the partition especially to those who struggled hard for settlement of the colonies. I am indebted to Late Santiranjan Sengupta, Late Dhirendra Nath Roychoudhury (nee Kalabhai), Sri Himangshu Majumdar, Sri Moni Pal, Sri Bikramjit Dutta, Sri Kanchan Basu Thakur of Bijoygarh and Sri Pranab Sen Sharma of Jadavpur University Alumni Association..

I also express my gratitude to the writers of the books from which the extracts and illustrations have been taken. Last but not the least, I am personally thankful to Shri Sumit Sethi of the ESS ESS Publications, New Delhi for publishing this book keeping standards of excellence.

Kali Prasad Mukhopadhyay

CONTENTS

INTRODUCTION

The Partition of India is the greatest tragedy of mankind. It has ruined our life, liberty and unity. Penderel Moon said - "The dawn of Indian independence was marred by massacres and migrations in the Punjab on a scale unparalled in world history in time of peace"[1]. Likewise Frank Moraes said – "The Freedom of the country brought Partition as well as 'a holocaust of blood and fire".[2]

In 1888, Sir Syed Ahmad, the greatest Muslim leader of the nineteenth century laid down the idea of separation of India. He said – Is it possible that the Hindus and the Mohammedans being two nations – could sit on the same throne after the British left India. As such he suggested to divide.

The Premier Sir Sikander Hyat Khan said that there were several schemes of Pakistan, the first of which was of Maulana Jamat-ud-Din Afghani. Next was the scheme of late Allama Iqbal. Then there was Chaudhuri Rahmat Ali's scheme. Rahmat Ali's scheme was P for Punjab, A for Afghanistan including, Pathanistan, i.e the North-West Frontier Province, K for Kashmir, S for Sind and the last three letters 'tan' of Baluchistan. Towards the end of March 1940, the Muslim League held its annual session at Lahore. Jinnah in his presidential address said Islam and Hinduism are different and distinct social orders. Hindus and Muslims can never evolve a common nationality and democracy is unsuited to India. The Muslims "must have their homeland; their territory and their State."[3] Thus the seeds of seperation were laid and the British took the advantage of 'Divide and Rule'.

In 1947 after the transfer of Power there was a great holocaust. "From East and West Pakistan and from India to the two wings of her new neighbour flared a two-way trail of blood which mounted to monstrous and angry dimensions."[4]. Thus within an area of 30,000 Square miles on India's Western flank some nine million people moved between India and Pakistan and vice-versa. No one could tell how many people perished in that tragic two-way trek and no one could calculate exactly which is no less than 750,000. Till June 1948 some nine million non-muslims moved into India while in the reverse direction over four million Muslims migrated to Pakistan.

While India was divided the Western Zone was effected by an exchange of population and the West Pakistan refugees within two years were settled and integrated into the main stream of economic life in India. But in the East Pakistan, Jawaharlal Nehru made Nehru-Liaquat Ali Pact in 1950 which Pakistan treated as a waste paper. As a result the Hindus were fallen in immense misery and distress which knew no bounds. In the East Pakistan, now Bangladesh, the condition of the non-muslims remain unaltered and rather going to be an ethnic cleansing operation gradually. This book is written in an attempt to highlight the recurring exodus and holocaust on the minorities in the Eastern Pakistan now Bangladesh.

Dr. Triguna Sen wrote that "how passively West Bengal accepted after partition the uprooting and the near-extermination of an entire people who participated almost to a man in the Indian struggle for freedom. True, the uprooting did not occur in East Pakistan in one swift swipe. It was like a wasting disease. But it was thus slow and surer process which ensured the steady expulsion of a completely denuded the Hindu population through riots sponsored by an Islamic State and social, economic and religious persecution of the Hindus by Muslims in collusion parternership with the bureaucracy, which caused anger in West Bengal but did not provoke the Hindus to retaliatory reprisal. Only in 1950, in the wake of brutal massacres in different districts of East Bengal, did the Hindus retaliate and immediately a two-way exodus began which might have brought about an unofficial transfer of population and a natural solution of the communal problem in West Bengal.

But Nehru had reasons of his own to stop this natural solution of the problem and he bestirred himself immediately to stop this two-way movement by the Delhi Pact of 1950 which is also known as Nehru-Liaquat Ali Pact. The Pact stopped this two-way movement effectively and the Muslims who had left West Bengal returned and Nehru saw to it that their property was restored to them. But the exodus of the Hindus continued and lingers down to this day. Even the Buddhists and the Chakmas of the Chittagong Hill Tract are now being hounded out of the recesses of their hills."[5]

Sir Jadunath Sarkar, while delivering his presidential address at a conference held on 16 August 1948, in the University Institute Hall, Kolkata, emphasised that the migration was due to religious persecution and distrust and dishonest, discriminatory legislation setting one such sect above the law. He compared the migration from the East Bengal to the flight of English Puritans to Holland and thence to Massachusetts and of the French Huguenots in the time of Louis XIV to Holland, Prussia and England. He regarded this influx as one of the most tragic migrations in history. He also said that the "Hindus leaving East Bengal are the very best portion of the local population, in brain, wealth, organising capacity and indomitable spirit, however crushed and benumbered they may look, when they are unloaded from their third class wagons on the Sealdah station yard. They are the most valuable portion of the population and a greatness of a country depends on exactly men of this type." Can anybody imagine at Bikrampur of Dacca district the famous Dutta family of Tongibari Sonarang village could produce seven I.C.S. There were many other famous joint families like the Basu family (ancestral house of the Writer Buddhadeb Basu) of village Malkhanagar Sirajdigha, the Bhuia family and the Mukherjee family, Somesh Basu of village Bajrajogini. Ex-Police IG Dhar family, Zaminder of Outshahi were all cultural famous joint families crushed by Partition. Marcus Franda observed that the West Bengal intelligentsia shied away from any description of communal violence and uprooting of the Hindus in East Bengal.[6] Nobody, not even the superior Calcutta intelligentsia, had anything to say about these unfortunate humans, Writers and painters remained unmoved by this spectacle of misery. ... No big rallies or protest demonstrations were organised by any political party to force State and Central Governments to take more meaningful steps for the relief and rehabilitation of the refugees until the emergence of a new protagonist which the refugees threw up themselves.[7]

Saroj Chakrabarti (P.A. to Dr. B. C. Roy the Chief Minister of West Bengal) stated – "Then one evening when he (Dr. Roy) returned from the Secretariat, news reached him from the Sealdah station that some *boggies* (railway compartments) from border areas had reached without any passengers. They were filled with broken conchshell bangles, shreds of wearing apparel of women and men with blood-stains.[8] He contacted the Prime Minister, and those of us who were on the ground floor could hear his excited voice on the telephone. In a high-pitched voice he told the Prime Minister that it would no longer be possible for him to protect the minorities. Only a war could end this human suffering. His patience was exhausted."[9] Sri S. P. Guha of Valley Park, Garia, Kolkata, who was then a student of Ripon College confirmed the incident. Another friend of this author Sri Khagendra Mohan De who hails from a remote village Barali of P.S. Faridgunge, Sub-division Chandpur District Tipperah in undivided Bengal, who was a victim of the Noakhali riot now residing at Tollygunge described the horrors he had experienced when their villages were torched and attacked by the Muslims led by the Moulavis who declared *'Jihad'*. Can anybody imagine after the Lakshmi Puja day the muslims attacked their villages in the evening and all of a sudden all the villagers – men, women, old, frail and infirms, pregnant ladies and children being panicky ran for safety and in the melee how many old and infirms, pregnant ladies delivered children on the way and were wounded. An old man Shri Nishikanta Majumder died by heart failure. About 150 villagers took shelter in the Dak Bungalow. Sri De had witnessed while rescuing the destitutes from the Police Station premises by a launch to Chandpur, a small country boat with the dead bodies of the miscreants was tug with their launch which was also carried to Chandpur for post mortem. The exodus of 1950 brought the administrative machinery virtually to failure. The Chief Minister of West Bengal Dr. B. C. Roy to check the retaliation called upon the Editors and Journalists of the Media and asked them not to publish the facts of atrocities in East Pakistan. Thus the news were censored before publication.

The distinguished Journalist Khwaja Ahmad Abbas told - on June 3, 1947, when he and Sathe were at the house of the Maharashtrian actor-director-producer, the late Master Vinayak, discussing about a film project, heard the radio announced that in a few minutes the speeches of Lord Louis Montbatten, Pandit Jawaharlal Nehru, Mr. M. A. Jinnah and Sardar Baldev Singh would be broadcast. Hence millions of people all over India, sat glued to the radio sets to hear the fate of India . He said "never before in the history of the world would the destiny of so many depend upon the words that would fall from the mouths of so few."[10]

Pakistan and partition had been in the air for too long for any one to be surprised by the content of these speeches. The 'special correspondents' and their 'sources close to Whitehall' had for once been quite correct in their forecasts. "When we sat down to listen in we knew exactly what was coming. And yet when it came, one could hardly believe one's ears. And, as one after another, the four speakers of the evening reiterated their acceptance of the fact of partition, the thought kept hammering at one's mind : can these four people, or even greater ones than they, conjure away the oneness of India and divide it into two separate countries – Pakistan (truncated) and Hindustan (*non-akhand*)?"[11]

"Lord Louis Mountbatten was confident, complacent, patronizing. He knew he had achieved a rare miracle .... Jawaharlal Nehru was choked with emotion, rhetorical rather than (as was usual with him) conversational, indulging in the professional writer's weakness to cloak inconvenient facts with a pretty turn of phrase. He talked of Indians 'being on the march', of 'the goal' and 'the journey's end, of 'months of sore trial, difficulty, anxiety and, sometimes, even heartbreaks' and of his abiding faith 'in the great destiny of India which takes shape, even though with travail and suffering'; he commended 'the vital change affecting the future of India'. And he concluded with the salutation that would sound hollow at least on that day: *Jai Hind*![12]

"It would have been all so amusing, even funny, if it were not for the tragic implications of what was said. Jawaharlal Nehru's words might well have been the theme song of the moment – 'With no joy in my heart!' There was no joy even in the hearts of his listeners. I saw tears in the eyes of the people listening in along with me. Death is final, inevitable, yet every time someone dear to us passes away, human sentiment, protests, revolts, bursts out in a flood of tears. How does one mourn the death of a country, one's country?"[13]

But why did Jawaharlal the secularist, Maulana Azad, the apostle of unity, and Sardar Patel, the nationalist, agree to this partition? According to Durga Das, the author of *India from Curzon to Nehru and After*, they were old men who 'were too weary to carry on the struggle any further and were, in their heart of hearts, anxious to grasp power and enjoy its fruits without further delay.'[14]

Another theory which K. A. Abbas have heard advanced by a knowledgeable person is that Nehru, when questioned about partition, said, 'It is either that – or back to jail!'[15]

Leonard Mosley also recounted a conversation with Nehru that rings true. The Prime Minister told him in 1960: "The truth is that we were tired men, and we were getting on in years too. Few of us could stand the prospect of going to prison again – and if we had stood out for a United India as we wished it, prison obviously awaited us. We saw the fires burning in the Punjab and heard everyday of the killings. The plan for partition offered a way out and we took it.....we expected that Partition would be temporary, that Pakistan was bound to come back to us."[16]

Prof. Bimal Prasad who is the Former Dean of School of International Studies, JNU, and presently the Honourary Director of Rajendra Prasad Academy, New Delhi, while delivering Maulana

Azad Memorial Lecture, 2005, said – "Actually, Nehru had in the course of a private conversation indicated to a retiring British Civilian, Malcolm Darling, even before this, on 24 April 1940, shortly after the adoption of the Pakistan Resolution by the League, that while he was opposed to Partition, he would accept it if the alternative to it was continuation of British Rule."[17]

At the end of his lecture he said that the historical and social background of Indian politics between 1885 and 1947 have so far been generally ignored by most historians, who have generally chosen to concentrate on the period 1937 to 1947 and therein on the role of Jinnah on one side and Gandhi, Nehru and Patel on the other in order to explain the onset of Partition. There has also been a tendency to add certain Viceroys, like Linlithgow, Wavell and Mountbatten, to this list. The authors who have done so are apparently ignorant of the fact that Viceroys did not make policies, but only implemented policies made by their superiors in London. All this has naturally let to a quite distorted view of the background of Partition, some accusing or defending Jinnah and others accusing or defending Gandhi, Nehru and Patel. Actually, the purpose of history is neither to accuse nor to defend any one but to explain why a certain development took place at a given time....... Partition was an event, which can be understood or explained only by taking a long view, and without making any value-judgement or praising or blaming a particular leader for it.

On the face of it, it is not easy to understand why Partition took place. "In spite of the presence of general mutual dislike between Hindus and Muslims over a long period of time, the two communities were bound together by innumerable ties over the same period and it is unimaginable that mutual animosities among them should in course of time become so strong as to break the old ties as under and make the Muslims finally decide to have a separate, sovereign State for themselves even though it involved living behind in the rest of India a fair number of the members of their community."[18]

The British Governor of Bengal Sir Frederick Burrows who

was former president of the Railwaymen's Union, warned that "Calcutta ... will become a battleground after our departure" if Bengal was, in fact, partitioned. "I have sufficient troops, if I am allowed to utilize maximum fire-power ... to deal with any situation likely to arise in Calcutta. I have not sufficient troops ..... to deal with widespread rising in East Bengal."[19]

As is evident from the British Policy of *Divide and Rule*, Prof. Bimal Prasad also mentioned in his lecture – "Since long Churchill had not made a secret of his belief that it was not in British interests to try to bring the Hindus and the Muslims together, who once united would show them the door."

The fact is that after the Second World War when Germany surrendered on 5 May, 1945, Prime Minister Winston Churchill had a top secret appraisal report for the long-term policy which was required to safeguard the strategic interests of the British Empire in India and the Indian ocean. The main theme of the report was that Britain must retain its military connection with the Sub-Continent so as to ward off the Soviet Union's threat to the area. Thus the idea of partitioning India in some form or other had started to circulate in the Whitehall in Churchill's time. The British Cabinet reported that Russia is the most potential enemy since Soviet Policy appears to extend her influence to further strategic areas. Really it was a big game of the Imperialist powers which our leaders could not foresee. But Netaji Subhas broadcast to Gandhi on July 6, 1944, over the Rangoon Radio that "the British will never surrender to persuasion of moral pressure or non-violent resistance. .... Britain's only effort is to exploit India to the fullest degree in her endeavour to win the war. ....They have already hatched a plan in London for crushing the nationalist movement in India once for all - as I know of these plans from a secret but reliable source I feel it my duty to bring it to your notice."[20]

In a recent publication – *The Untold Story of India's Partition : The Shadow of the Great Game* by Narendra Singh Sarila wherein in the Preface he has stated that "The USSR's powerful victory over Germany in 1945 had increased Joseph Stalin's ambitions to extend his country's influence into territories on its periphery; indeed, he had already started to do so in Eastern Europe. To the Soviet Union's southern border lay the region of the Persian Gulf with its oil fields – *the wells of power* – that were of vital interest to the West. Under the circumstances, Britain could ill afford to lose control over the entire Indian sub-continent that had served as its military base in dominating the Indian Ocean area and the countries around the Persian Gulf for more than half a century and which also the main source of manpower for the Imperial Army."[21] Thus we in India suffer in the midst of big game of the Imperialist powers.

Winston Churchill was much concerned to hear on July 1, that the proposed 'India Bill' was called "the Indian Independence Bill," writing Attlee to complain that "the essence of the Mountbatten proposals and the only reason why I gave support to them is because "they establish the phase of Dominion Status. Dominion Status is not the same as Independence. It is not true that a community is independent when its Ministers have in fact taken the Oath of Allegiance to the King."[22]

Churchill was not as easily fooled as most Indians were made by Mountbatten. He never forgave him for being so 'tricky and angrily snubbed' him after he returned to London. When Anthony Eden gave a big party to welcome Mountbatten home, Churchill "glowered and pointed a threatening finger at him" as he strode toward Winston with outstretched arms : "Dickie, stand there! What you did to us in India was like whipping your riding crop across my face!" Then Churchill turned on his heel and walked away, not speaking to Mountbatten again for seven years.[23]

It is observed that while the cross-border terrorist activities in Kashmir and series of bomb-blasts in New Delhi/Mumbai continues unabated there are instances of greetings by the people of India and Pakistan border where both sides welcome each other by showing lamps on Festive occasions. The Bus service, Cricket match, liberal trade facilities extend further goodwill missions. The recent visit of some of the relations of Pervez Musharraf to India could not conceal their nostalgia. It cannot be denied that how India played a joint operation in the liberation of Bangladesh. The continuing communal violence since 1947 has forced millions of Hindus to migrate from East Pakistan and Bangladesh to India. The pauperised, landless Muslims from Bangladesh since mid-1970's have been infiltrating India on a massive scale and the flow continues even today. Still then it is observed that for the medical treatment, for higher education, trade and commerce hundreds of Pakistani and Bangladeshi nationals flock to different Hospitals for treatment, Centrally administered Institutions for higher education etc. in India. By opening the five points along the Line of Control at the Chakothi-Uri crossing point enabled the distribution of relief to quake-affected people on both sides of the divide and also to meet the relatives on the other side. Their exposition after meeting with their kith and kin discloses the accumulated feelings of human relations. Abul Kalam Azad said "If we put a stick in the water, it may appear that the water has been divided but the water remains the same and the moment the stick is removed, even the appearance of division disappears."[24] On the contrary it is learnt that the "Bangladeshi Islamic hardliners got a new impetus when they came in touch with the highly trained and sophisticated foreign Islamic terrorists."

The Unification of North and South Vietnam into the Socialist Republic of Vietnam took place on July 2, 1976. The Federal Republic of Germany (West Germany) and German Democratic Republic (East Germany) merged on October 3, 1990. Even if the Republic of Lebanon where the Christians (42%) and Muslims (57%), after prolonged civil war can maintain peace and shared power jointly according to their constitutional conventions then why our progressive intelligentsia of twentyfirst century cannot come to a settlement and devoid the barrier?

The author who was born in East Bengal in undivided India lost their house at 20 Faridabad Lane, Dacca had bitter experience and witnessed the plight of their relatives and the refugees of East Pakistan. He has visited the Sealdah Railway Station, Ranaghat and other border towns, witnessed the destitutes living on roadsides under the sky, saw the pathetic condition of the uprooted persons, the people who were forced to become beggars overnight. In the Sealdah Railway station about six thousand refugees men, women and children were spending their days and nights. If a man falls ill there was none to look out. 'If a woman is in birth-pangs she can expect no other help except those offered by her neighbours.' They were offered free *chira* (puffed rice) and *gur* (molasses) which was distributed by non-official relief organizations. Can anybody imagine with so many refugees in the platform there were only three taps, two latrines for women and about 12 latrines for men. One day at Sealdah Station he found an Octogenarian old man wearing a 'Sengupta' brand milk white Dhoti just completed his lunch at 4 O'clock and washing his mouth. A beautiful lady wearing a rose coloured Benarasi sari with matching ornaments weeping continuously. She was requesting her father to go to her residence leaving the side way of the road island of the Route 36 Bus terminus. But the gentleman denied and said why I have been forced to be a begger for no fault of us. He also said when God has allotted such sufferings to us I must admit. The author also visited the Sqatters' colonies and witnessed one of his relatives committed suicide who was suffering from TB. His maternal uncle who used to enjoy landed property of their joint family at the village Kulla, Police Station Dhamrai, District Dacca and lived well but coming over to West Bengal died in starvation. One of his eldest daughter who married to a widower gentleman of 60 years old and saved herself. In another instance he found an unmarried educated lady took up a job of an attendant in a rich family and maintained her young brothers. Another gentleman from Dacca who was a poor paid employee of Sakti Oushadhalaya used to sell potato in the footpath of Lake market. Such lists are inexhaustive. After giving option many collegues of his father took shelter in their house then at Burdwan and after finding an accommodation brought their family from Dacca. While they stayed in their house his mother had to bear all the burden of cooking. He has already wrote two books in Bengali on the refugees (*Sikarer Sandhane* and *Desh Bivajaner Antarale*). He has observed that the incidents of atrocities in many occasions have been suppressed because of civil war in this part. Even when in 1950 due to atrocities fleeing refugees flooded the border town of Bongaon, thousands of refugees were stranded at railheads, steamer stations and Dacca Airport, Dr. B. C. Roy sent immediately sixteen chartered planes to airlift the stranded passengers from Dacca Airport. Fifteen big steamers were sent to rescue stranded refugees from districts like Faridpur and Barisal.

The author has taken the pains to write this book and attempts to write the background of Partition and its upheavals. Apart from the authors of various books and documents to whom he has been grateful, he has taken the details of information from *the Report of the Indian Commission of Jurists by its Committee of Enquiry, 1965.* They had undertaken a strenuous Job of finding the reasons for the refugees leaving East Pakistan and the hardships they had undergone on their way. The Committee have enquired into the causes of the recurrent large-scale migration into India from East Pakistan of Pakistani citizens of Hindu, Christian and Buddhist persuasion, to report whether and to what extent and in what manner such migrations are occasioned by violation of human rights and fundamental freedom enshrined in the *Universal Declaration of Human Rights 1948* and by the practice of genocide as defined in Article II of the *Genocide Convention of 1948*. The book also covered the details of Holocaust, Contrast of dealings of Pakistan and India, The great Blunder, Islamisation, Sense of realisation, Emergence of Banglabhai, The Tragedy and Jinnah's wrong conception of two-nation theory.

NOTES AND REFERENCES

1. Moon, Penderel, Divide and Quit, p-7.
2. Moraes, Frank, Nehru – Sunlight and Shadow, p-73.
3. Menon, V.P. , The Transfer of Power of India, p-83.
4. Moraes, Frank, Nehru - Sunlight and Shadow, p-74.
5. Chakrabarti, Prafulla K, The Marginal Men, p-XV.

6. Franda, Marcus, Radical Politics in West Bengal, p-38.
7. Chakrabarti, Praulla K, The Marginal Men, p-25-26.
8. Bandopadhyay, Hiranmoy, Udvastu, p.88-89.
9. Chakrabarti, Prafulla K, The Marginal Men, p-27.
10. Abbas, Khwaja Ahmmad, Who Killed India?, Hasan Mushirul, Ed. India Partitioned: The Other Face of Freedom, Vol.II, p-234.
11. Ibid.
12. Ibid, P-234-35.
13. Ibid.
14. Ibid, p-236. Durga Das, India from Curzon to Nehru (London:Collins), p-255.
15. Hasan, Mushirul, Ed. India Partitioned: The Other Face of Freedom, p-237. Abbas, Khwaja Ahmmad, Who Killed India ?
16. Mosley, Leonard, The Last of the British Raj, p-248.
17. Prasad, Bimal, Maulana Azad Memorial Lecture, 2005, India's Partition in Historical Perspective, p-51-52.
18. Ibid, p-88
19. The Transfer of Power, Vol.X, p-772-773.
20. Bhattacharyya, Sushil Kumar, Gandhism in Indian Politics, P. - 207-8.
21. Sarila, Narendra Singh, The Untold Story of India's Partition: The Shadow of the Great Game, p-9.
22. The Transfer of Power, Vol.XI, p-812-13.
23. Wolpert, Stanley, Nehru : A Tryst with Destiny, p-401.
24. Azad, Maulana Abul Kalam, India Wins Freedom, p-177.

The June 2, 1947 meeting accepting the independence and partition of India. Clockwise after Patel are Nehru, Mountbatten, Jinnah, Liaqat Ali, Abdur Rab Nishtar, Baldev Singh and Kriplani

By Courtesy : *Film Division 4 : The June 2, 1947 meeting accepting the independence and partition of India*

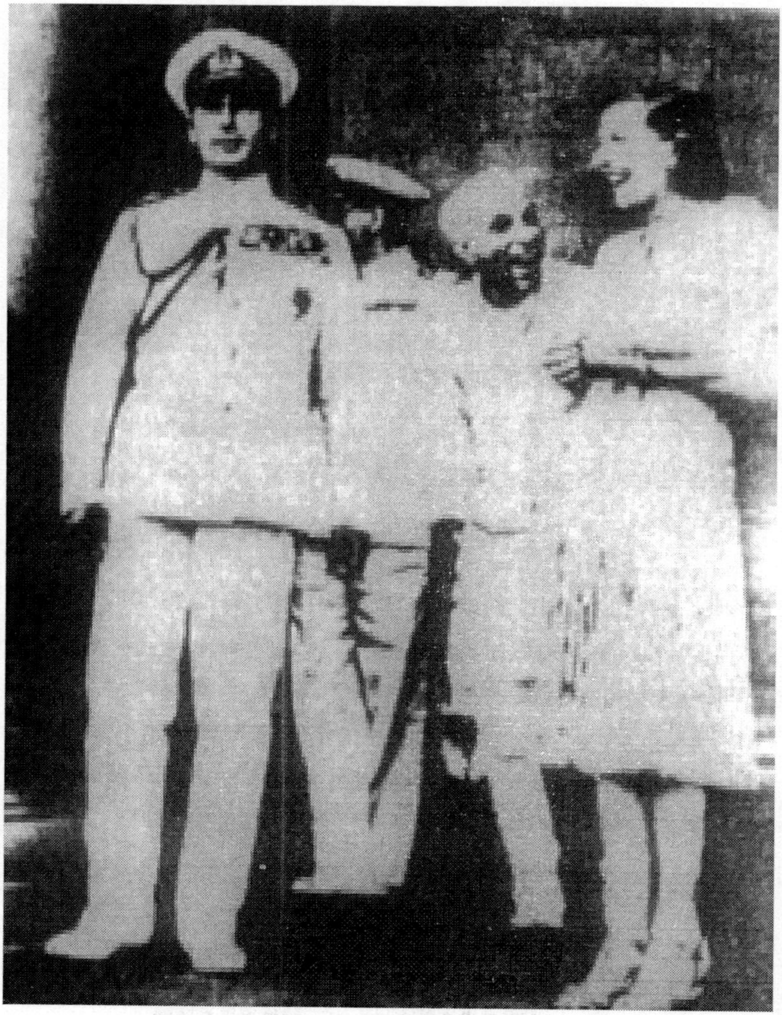

Edwina Mountbatten and Pandit Jawaharlal Nehru Share a joke outside Viceroy's House

By Courtesy : *Philip Zeiglar*

In November, 1943 Netaji addressed the Greater Asia Co-operative Sphere Conference at Tokyo. It was at this conference that Japan gifted the Andaman and Nicobar Islands to Netaji's Azad Hind Provisional Government to provide it with territory.

By Courtesy : *V.R. Adiraju*

S.C. Bose meeting Adolf Hitler, 27 May 1942

By Courtesy : *V.R. Adiraju*

Attacking the Historical Dhakeswari Temple, Dacca

By Courtesy : *Salam Azad*

NOSTALGIA – Pujor Shei Smriti

By Courtesy : *Dainik Statesman*

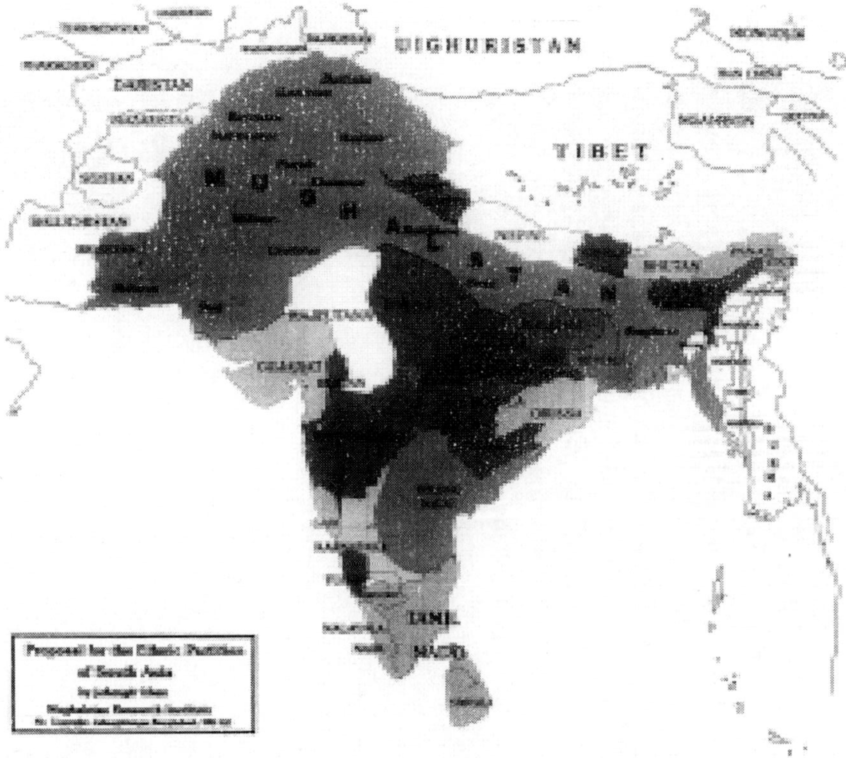
UIGHURISTAN
TIBET
TAMIL NADU
Proposal for the Ethnic Partition
of South Asia

Khagendra Mohan De, an eye witness of Noakhali riot, lived in a tiny village in the bank of Dakatia river under Faridgunge P.S. Chandpur Sub-Division, Tipperah District of undivided Bangal. In 1946, after Noakhali riot the disturbances spread over to Tipperah District. Just after Lakshmi puja day their village was attacked and torched along the surrounding villages. They fled away leaving everything and after staying two days at Faridgunge Dak Bungalow they were escorted by police to Chandpur where they took shelter in the Kali Bari. From there they came over to Sealdah Railway Station empty handed with one clothe on.

1
The Partition

The Viceroy Lord Mountbatten while broadcasting on 3rd June 1947 in the evening over All-India Radio, said that it had always been his firm opinion that, with a reasonable measure of goodwill between the communities, a united India would be by far the best solution; but it had been impossible to obtain agreement on the Cabinet Mission plan or on any other plan that would preserve the unity of India. "The Muslim League had demanded the partition of India, and the Congress had used the same argument for demanding, in that event, the partition of certain provinces. The argument seemed unassailable, though he was as much opposed to the partition of provinces as he was to the partition of India. Hence it was left to the people of India themselves to decide the question of partition."[1]

The Viceroy concluded : 'I have faith in the future of India and I am proud to be with you all at this momentous time. May your decision be wisely guided and may they be carried out in the peaceful and friendly spirit of the Gandhi-Jinnah appeal.'[2]

There followed broadcasts by the Indian leaders. Nehru said that "the announcement envisaged on the one hand the possibility of certain areas seceding from India and, on the other the promise of a big advance towards complete independence. It was with no joy in his heart that he commended these proposals, though he had no doubt in his mind that it was the right course. ... ... He referred to the violence in the country as 'shameful, degrading and revolting' and stressed that political ends were not to be achieved by methods of violence….."[3]

Jinnah appealed to every community, particularly to Muslim India, to maintain peace and order. The plan, he said, "did not in some important respects meet the Muslim League point of view and it was for the League to consider whether it should be accepted as a compromise or a settlement. (Ibid.). Collins and Lappiere stated that Mohammed Ali Jinnah was incapable of announcing to his followers in a language that they could understand the news that he had won them a state. He had to tell India's Moslems of the 'momentous decision' to create an Islamic state on the sub-continent in English, concluding with the words *'Pakistan Zindabad'.*[4] An announcer then read his words in Urdu.

Baldev Singh said that the plan steered a course which was obviously above the conflicting claims. It was not a compromise; he preferred to call it a settlement. 'It does not please everybody, not the Sikh community anyway, but it is certainly something worth while. Let us take it at that.'[5]

Gandhiji received the news of the decision while he was having a footbath after his evening stroll. One of his female disciples massaged his feet with a stone, another burst into tears. Sorrow seemed to spread like a stain over his pinched features as she talked. 'May God protect them and grant them all wisdom,'[6] he sighed when she'd finished.[6]

Mountbatten received an urgent communication shortly afternoon on 4th June : 'Gandhi was preparing to break with the Congress leadership and denounce the plan at his evening prayer meeting.' Mountbatten immediately sent an emissary to Gandhi inviting him to come to see him.

Gandhi walked into Mountbatten's study at 6 pm. His prayer meeting was at seven. That left Mountbatten less than an hour in which to ward off a potential disaster. His first glance at the Mahatma told Mountbatten how deeply upset he was. Crumpled up in his armchair 'like a bird with a broken wing', Gandhi kept raising and dropping one hand, lamenting in an almost inaudible voice, 'It's so awful, it's so awful.'[7]

Lionel Carter also mentioned in the words of Lord Mountbatten – "On the afternoon of 4th June I received an urgent message from Mr. Krishna Menon warning me that Mahatma Gandhi was in a very unhappy and emotional mood, and that some of the Congress leaders feared that he might denounce the Plan and its acceptance at his prayer meeting that evening. I immediately sent a message inviting Mahatma Gandhi to come round as soon as he could, and he arrived an hour before his prayer meeting was due to take place."[8]

He was indeed in a very upset mood and began by saying how unhappy he was. I replied immediately that, whilst I could quite understand and indeed shared his upset feelings at seeing the united India he had worked for all his life apparently destroyed by the new plan. He hoped that time would convince him 'this plan was the only course that was possible under the existing conditions.'

Lord Mountbatten told Gandhiji that although many newspapers had christened it the "Mountbatten Plan", they should really have christened it the "Gandhi Plan",[9] since all the salient ingredients – such as leaving the choice of their future to the Indian people themselves, avoiding coercion, and transferring power as soon as possible – were suggested by him.[9]

Mountbatten reminded him that in his earlier days he had not been averse to Dominion Status. Mahatma Gandhi admitted that this was so and that, even during the war, although no longer in favour of it, he had expressed himself as not being irretrievably against it. He later sent me an extract from *Harijan* dated 16th December 1939, in which appeared the words : "Similarly, I have said to a friend that, if Dominion Status were offered, I should take it, and expect to carry India with me."[10]

H. S. L. Polak was a journalist and a closest collegue of Gandhiji went both to India and England as Gandhi's spokesman in the cause of Satyagraha and eventually became a lawyer in partnership with Gandhiji. While he was to leave India after a business visit of some month's duration, in the course of which he had taken the opportunity of meeting a number of old friends with whom he had talked about political, social and economic developments in this country. He met Gandhiji with whom the personal tie had always been too close. He had seen him at Sheogan, when he discussed a number of matters with him in order to learn his point of view or his personal information.[11]

In the course of one of such talks, Mr. Polak asked Mahatma Gandhi, if he would tell him exactly what he meant by the phrase 'Complete Independence', as it was one that lent itself to a number of interpretations. The definition that he gave him appeared to be of such importance that he asked him if he would let him to have it in writing in precise language, with a view to publication. Gandhiji unhesitatingly agreed and sent the following letter :-

My dear Henry,

Owing to the pilgrimage to Travancore, it has not been possible for me to write to you earlier. Your question is whether I retain the same opinion, I did as at the R.T.C. of 1931. I said then and repeat now that so far as I am concerned, if Dominion Status were offered in terms of the Statute of Westminister, i.e. the right to secede at will, I would unhesitatingly accept it. – Yours sincerely BHAI.

The Pioneer of 14th February, 1937, published a news – Congress Socialist Party's Disapproval of Gandhiji's willingness to accept Dominion Status.

"A meeting of the Council of Action of the Bihar Congress Socialist Party held at Hajipur passed, among others, the following resolution :

The Council notes with grave concern the remarks made by Mahatma Gandhi regarding Dominion Status in his letter to Mr. Polak. In the opinion of the Council the goal of complete independence is in no manner compatable with the framework of the Empire nor Dominion Status in any shape or form can mean complete independence.

The Council considered it a matter of great regret that the solemn pledge which the Congress took at Lahore and which it renews yearly on January 26, should be traduced by such an eminent leader as Mahatma Gandhi.

The Council feels that such action cannot but weaken our struggle ... ... therefore the Council considers it its painful duty to record strong disapproval of this action of Mahatma Gandhi. – A.P.[12]

However, Mountbatten was informed next day that the line he had taken had been remarkably successful and that Mahatma Gandhi honestly felt that he had tried to follow his advice, and that he had thus taken a far greater part in shaping the future of India than had appeared to him at first sight from the way the plan was worded. Mountbatten stated, "Pandit Nehru and Sardar Patel also did their best to console Mahatma Gandhi and between the three of us we successfully prevented the frightful chaos and confusion which a public denouncement of the plan by India's greatest leader would have entailed, for no one had any workable alternative to suggest."[13]

Taking Vallabhbhai Patel in the chair Lord Mountbatten addressed a press conference on 4th June 1947. In his introductory speech Lord Mountbatten told about the background of how the Juine 3rd plan had been evolved. He pointed out that "at every stage and at every step he had worked hand in hand with the leaders and that the plan had come as no shock or surprise to them." All the leaders had wanted early expedition of transfer of power, but power could not be transferred to one or two separate Governments unless those Governments had a constitution. One of the governments was not even in being, nor was it certain that it was coming into being. The other government would presumably taken some time in framing its constitution. "The Government of India Act of 1935, suitably modified, provided the obvious answer to this difficulty. He stressed that independence through Dominion Status was complete and that the different administrations were at liberty to opt out of the Commonwealth whenever they pleased. He meant it most sincerely when he said that power would be transferred completely by the end of the year."[14]

The Viceroy had to face varied and numerous questions. Many questions were of a trivial character, but to every one the Viceroy gave a crisp and apt reply. In reply to one question as to why the voters had not been given the alternative to opt for independence, the Viceroy said that "it was a question of politics; if they could get the Congress and the Muslim League to agree, he too, would of course agree."[15]

In reply to a further question which concerned with the immediate devolution of power on the basis of Dominion Status, the Viceroy explained that the British Commonwealth of Nations was a completely free association of people. "Each State was completely independent, and, as far as he knew, they decided their own future. There was no power that he knew of to force them to stay in if they wanted to go out."[16]

Finally, Lord Mountbatten made it clear that the transfer would be in 1947 and not in June 1948. He said, 'I think the transfer could be about the 15th of August.'[17]

"It was the second time in the history of Britain's Indian Empire that a Viceroy gave a press conference. It was also the last. Three hundred journalists, correspondents of the USSR, US, China and Europe, mixed with the representatives of India's press, a regional, religious and linguistic mosaic of journals, all following with extra-ordinary intentness the monologue of the Viceroy."[18]

The Viceroy also had a meeting with Gandhiji. Some time later, Gandhiji during his usual prayer meeting said : 'The British Government is not responsible for partition. The Viceroy has no hand in it. In fact he is as opposed to division as Congress itself. But if both of us, Hindus and Muslims, cannot agree on anything else, then the Viceroy is left with no choice.'[19]It was, he added, on the basis of the plan that agreement could be reached.

Gandhi was still vehemently opposed to partition, yet he was shaken by the Viceroy's vigorous plea. Approaching 78, for the first time in 30 years Gandhi was uncertain of his grip on India's masses, at odds with the leaders of his party. In his despair and uncertainy, "he was still searching in his soul for an answer, still waiting for an illuminating whisper of the Inner Voice that had guided him in so many of the grave crises of his career. That June evening, however, the voice was silent and Gandhi remained assailed by doubt. Should he remain faithful to his instincts, denounce partition, even at the price of plunging India into violence and chaos? Or should he listen to the Viceroy's desperate plea?"[20] Gandhi was never late for a prayer meeting. Though Mountbatten had not finished presenting his case Gandhi left for prayer meeting.

Collins and Lapiere write – Less than an hour later, cross-legged on a raised platform in a dirt square in the midst of his Untouchables, Gandhi delivered his verdict. Many in the crowd before him had come, not to pray, but to hear from the lips of the prophet of non-violence a call to arms, a fiery assault on Mountabatten's plan. No such cry would come this evening from the mouth of the man who had so often promised to offer his own body for vivisection rather than accept his country's division.

Mahatma Gandhi said that "It was no use blaming the Viceroy for partition". He said - "Look to yourselves and in your own hearts for an explanation of what has happened." Louis Mountbatten's persuasiveness had won him the ultimate and most difficult triumph of his Viceroyalty.

As for Gandhi, many an Indian would never forgive him his silence, and the frail old man whose heart still ached for India's coming division would one day pay the price of their rancour.[21]

However, there was a general improvement in the political situation immediately after the announcement of the plan. The Muslim League mass movements in Assam and the North-West Frontier Province were abandoned and it was only in parts of the Punjab and in Calcutta that there were sporadic disturbances.

The plan had its opponents as well. The Working Committee of the Hindu Mahasabha met in Delhi and passed a resolution which stressed : 'India is one and indivisible and there will never be peace unless and until the separated areas are brought back into the Indian Union and made integral parts thereof.' The Mahasabha even called for all-India 'Anti-Pakistan Day'.[22] Earlier on 14th May, 1942 from Dadar, Bombay, Dr. V. D. Savarkar forwarded a copy of the resolution passed by hundreds of meetings held at Bombay, Poona, Calcutta, Nagpur, Lucknow, Amritsar, Peshwar, Patna, and hundreds of other cities and towns all over India to appraise Marquess of Linlithgow the intensity of the determination of Hindudom to oppose any scheme to break up the unity and integrity of Hindusthan.[23] (Full text of the resolution is enclosed in Annexure–1).

The extremists on the Muslim side were also dissatisfied; and the Khaksars, a group of militant Muslims (who demanded a Pakistan stretching from Karachi to Calcutta), staged demonstrations when the All-India Muslim League Council met in Delhi. Strangely enough, the Communists, who had been backing Jhinnah's demand for Pakistan, now changed their tune. They said that the partition and the Dominion Status together would enable Britain to maintain her control over India, but they did not explain how this would be possible.[24]

The Council of the All-India Muslim League met in New Delhi on 10th June and passed a resolution noting with satisfaction that the Cabinet Mission Plan had been abandoned. The only course open was the partition of India as proposed in His Majesty's Government's Statement on 3 June. "The Council was of the opinion that, although it could not agree to the partition of Bengal and the Punjab, or give its consent to such partition, it had to consider His Majesty's Government's Plan for the transfer of power as a whole. The resolution gave full authority to Jinnah to accept the fundamental principles of the plan as a compromise and empowered him to take all steps and decision in that connexion."[25]

Linlithgo remained fully convinced that Jinnah was playing a role in Indian politics which ideally suited British interests at that prticular juncture in the context of the worsening war situation and the growing pressure from the Congress side. The League's refusal to join hands with the Congress in exerting such pressure except on its own terms – quite unacceptable to the Congress – gave the British authorities a most effective argument in support of their policy of sticking on to their empire in India as long as possible.[26]

Lionel Carter stated - On the 9th June the All-India Muslim League Council held their meeting to consider the 3rd June Plan. This meeting was held in Camera under strict security precautions. This seemed a wise step; but it did not prevent Sardar Patel from sending me the transcript of shorthand notes of the whole proceedings. It was mentioned in the note that "the meeting took place on the first floor of the Imperial Hotel, New Delhi. An attempt was made by members of the Khaksars, the extremist Muslim organisation, to break in on it. Some of them got as far as the staircase before being turned back by members of the Muslim League National Guard, and considerable damage was done in the scuffle which ensued. Mr. Jinnah afterwards described the Khaksars' intervention as an attempt on his life."[27]

The resolution of the Muslim League provoked Nehru into writing a letter to the Viceroy in which he pointed out that, though the Cabinet Mission Plan had been modified to a large extent, they were still functioning in many ways in accordance with the plan. Thus the Indian Constituent Assembly had been meeting and would continue to meet under that plan. It was, therefore, incorrect to say that the Cabinet Mission Plan had been abandoned. By objecting to the partition of Bengal and the Punjab, the Council of the Muslim League had definitely rejected one of the basic provisions in the scheme. He went on to say that the Council had accepted the fundamental principles of the plan as a compromise, but it was clear what they considered those fundamental principles to be. The point was whether the plan was accepted as a settlement or not.

The report of the speeches that had been delivered to the conclusion that it was looked upon as a step to be utilized for the enforcement of further claims. The Council had given full authority to Jinnah to take all steps and decisions which might be necessary in connection with the plan, which meant that the Council itself had not accepted the plan as a settlement, but had given authority to Jinnah to do so if he choses. The least that could be done now was for Jinnah to accept the plan in its entiriety as a settlement on behalf of the Muslim League. Unless this was done clearly in writing, there was every likelihood that difficulties would arise in the near future.

The situation was very much embarrassing to the Viceroy. "In the light of past experience, the Congress was anxious to pin down the League, while Jinnah as usual was reluctant to commit himself to anything. In the end, Lord Mountbatten persuaded Nehru not to take the League Council's resolution at its face value."[28]

Meanwhile, a joint conference of various Sikh organisations was held in Lahore. Though welcoming the division of the Punjab, it was placed in the Conference on record its considered view that no partition of the province which did not preserve the solidarity and integrity of the Sikh community would be acceptable to the Sikhs.

On 14th June, the All-India Congress Committee met in Delhi and passed a resolution accepting the June 3rd plan. This resolution included an eloquent exposition of the essential unity of India :

"Geography and mountains and the seas fashioned India as she is, and no human agency can change that shape or come in the way of her final destiny. Economic circumstances and the insistent demands of international affairs make the unity of India still more necessary. The picture of India we have learnt to cherish will remain in our minds and our hearts. The A.I.C.C. earnestly trusts that when the present passions have subsided, India's problem will be viewed in their proper perspective and the false doctrine of two nations in India will be discredited and discarded by all."[29]

The resolution was moved by Govind Ballabh Pant, who

said that acceptance of the June 3rd plan was the only way to achieve freedom and liberty for the country. It would assure an Indian Union with a strong Centre which could ensure progress. "The Congress had worked and sacrificed everything for the sake of unity. The choice today was 'between accepting the June 3rd plan or committing suicide.' He argued that the present plan was better than the Cabinet Mission Plan with its groupings and sections and its weak Centre."[30]

Abul Kalam Azad while seconding the resolution disagreed with Govinda Ballabh Pant. He had all along held the view that the Statement of 16th May was the best solution of the problem; to that view he continued to adhere. But the choice before the Congress was not which plan to accept and which to reject, but whether the present state of indecision and drift should continue. Taking into consideration all the factors, the Working Committee had come to the decision that an immediate settlement was urgently required. Referring to the provinces which sought to cut themselves away; from India, Azad said : 'The division is only of the map of the country and not in the hearts of the people, and I am sure it is going to be a short-lived partition.'[31]

The Nationalist Muslims, members of the Hindu minorities in the proposed Pakistan provinces, and Purshottamdas Tandon opposed the resolution vehemently. In an impassioned speech, Tandon said that the decision of the Working Committee was an admission of weakness and that it arose out of a sense of despair. Accepting the June 3rd plan would benefit neither the Hindus nor the Muslims. The Hindus in Pakistan would live in fear and the Muslims in India would do the same.

Nehru asserted by intervening the debate, that there was no question of any surrender to the Muslim League. The Congress had all along been against coercing any unit to remain under the Indian Union. It was wrong to suggest that the Congress Working Committee had taken fright and therefore surrendered, though it was correct to say that they were very much disturbed at the prevailing madness.

Vallabhbhai Patel said that, looking at the Cabinet Mission's proposals in the light of his experience in the Interim Government during the past nine months, he was not at all sorry that the Statement of 16th May had gone. "Had they accepted it, the whole of India would have gone the Pakistan way."[32]

The issue was clinched when Gandhiji supported the resolution. He said that he was not pleading on behalf of the Working Committee, but the All-India Congress Committee must weigh the pros and cons of its rejection. He said that his view on the plan were well known. "The acceptance of the plan did not only involve the Congress Working Committee. There were two other parties to it, the British Government and the Muslim League.[33] If at this stage the All-India Congress Committee rejected the Working Committee's decision, what would the world think of it? *The consequences of rejection would be the finding of a new set of leaders, who would not only be capable of constituting the Congrerss Working Committee but of taking charge of the Government.*[34] They should not forget that peace in the country was very essential at this juncture. The Congress was opposed to Pakistan and he was one of those who had steadfastly opposed the division of India. Yet he had come before the All-India Congress Committee to urge the acceptance of the resolution on India's division. Sometimes certain decisions, however unpalatable they might be, had to be taken."[35]. The resolution was carried by 157 votes to twentynine, thirty-two members remaining neutral.

The Congress President Acharya J. B. Kripalani made the most forceful and a memorable speech, in the course of which he answered the charge that the Working Committee had taken the decision out of fear. He said : "I must admit the truth of this charge, but not in the sense in which it is made. The fear is not for the lives lost, or of the widows' wail, or the orphans' cry, or of the many houses burned. The fear is that if we go on like this, retaliating and heaping indignities on each other, we shall progressively reduce ourselves to a stage of cannibalism and worse. In every fresh communal fight the most brutal and degraded acts of the previous fight become the norm."[36]

And finally India was divided into two "free independent Dominions of British Commonwealth of Nations" [37] on 15th August, 1947.

NOTES AND REFERENCES

1. Menon, V.P., *The Transfer of Power in India*, p.378-79.
2. Ibid.
3. Ibid. p-380.
4. Collins Larry and Lapierre Dominique, *Freeedom at Midnight*, p-162.
5. Menon, V.P., *The Transfer of Power*, p.380.
6. Collins Larry and Lappierre Dominique, *Freedom at Midnight*, p.161-62.
7. Ibid.
8. Carter, Lionel, Mountbatten's Report on the Last Viceroylty, p.162.
9. Ibid.
10. Ibid.
11. *Towards Freedom 1937-47*, Vol. I, p-136. Ed. Dr. P. N. Chopra, Indian Council of Historical Research, New Delhi, 1985.

    When H.S.L.Polak, one of the Mahatma's oldest English associates who had worked with him in South Africa during his last visit to India, Frank Moraes asked him how much of Gandhi's teaching he thought survived in India. "Ostensibly a great deal but in reality, very little." "Gandhi's greatest contribution to India was not the achievement of freedom, for without him the country would have attained independence, possibly even earlier than it did. ... ... In the narrow technical sense the Mahatma was really not a politician. The movement for India's freedom preceded him by many years, the Indian National Congress being founded in 1885 when Gandhi was a lad of 16. Although the terms swadeshi and swaraj are commonly associated with his name they were used long before the Mahatma appeared on the political scene, the swadeshi movement being first launched in Calcutta in 1905 and swaraj being preached by Dadabhai Naoroji in 1906. Gandhi was in fact, as he himself confesses, "a loyal servant of the British Empire" until 1921 when he launched his first civil disobedience movement and returned the Kaiser-I-Hind medal he had received from the British Government." (Frank Moraes, *Sunlight and Shadow*, p-2&3).
12. Ibid.
13. Carter, Lionel, Mountbatten's Report on the Last Viceroyalty, p.163.
14. Menon, V.P., *The Transfer of Power in India*, p.381.
15. Ibid.
16. Ibid.
17. Ibid.

18. Collins, Larry and Lapierre, Dominique, *Freedom At Midnight*, p-164.
19. Menon, V.P., *The Transfer of Power in India*, p-382.
20. Collins, Larry and Lapierre, Dominique, *Freedom At Midnight*, p-163.
21. Ibid. p-164.
22. Menon, V.P., *The Transfer of Power in India*, p-382.
23. *Transfer of Power*, Vol.II, p.86-87.
24. Menon, V. P., *The Transfer of Power in India*, p.382-383.
25. Ibid.
26. Bimal Prasad, Maulana Azad Memorial Lecture 2005, *India's Partition in Historical Perspective*, p.49-50.
27. Carter,Lionel, Mountbatten's Report on the Last Viceroyalty, p.169 & 207.
28. Menon, V. P., *The Transfer of Power In India*, p-384
29. Ibid.
30. Ibid. p-385.
31. Ibid.
32. Ibid.
33. Ibid.
34. Ibid.
35. Ibid, p-386.
36. Ibid.
37. Carter, Lionel, Mountbatten's Report on the Last Viceroyalty, p-390.

2

AFTER-EFFECT OF THE PARTITION

INDEPENDENCE GIFT TO NEHRU AND PATEL

"India's joyful Independence Day was indeed a day of horror for the Punjab. ... ... Amritsar's red-brick railway station had become a kind of refugee camp, a clearing house for thousands of Hindus who'd fled from Pakistan's half of the Punjab. They swarmed around its waiting room, its ticket office, its platforms, ready to scrutinize each arriving train for missing relatives and friends."[1]

"Late in the afternoon of 15 August, the Station Master, Chani Singh, pushed his way through their near-hysterical, weeping ranks with all the authority his little blue cap and the red flag he clutched in his hands conferred on him. Singh was prepared for the scene that would follow the arrival of the incoming *Number Ten Down Express*. It was the windows and doors of the dust-yellow third-class *bogies,* carriages calling for a missing relative, looking for someone from their village who might bring them news. There would be the abandoned children weeping softly on a stack of luggage, the babies born in flight being nursed by their mothers in the midst of that milling mob.

"At the head of the platform Singh took his place and officiously waved the incoming locomotive to a halt. As its great steel frame rolled to a stop above his head. Singh glimpsed a strange sight. Four armed soldiers were standing guard over the sullen engine driver. When the hiss of escaping steam and the shriek of the brakes had died, Singh suddenly realized something was terribly wrong.

"The babbling multitudes packing the platform were petrified, frozen into an eerie silence by the sight before them. Singh stared down the line of eight carriages. All the windows of the compartments were wide open but there was not a single human being standing at any of them. Not a single door had opened. Not a single person was setting off the train. They had brought him a trainful of phantoms.

"The Station Master strode to the first carriage, snatched open the door and stepped inside. In one horrible instant he understood why no one was getting off the *Ten Down Express* in Amritsar that night. It was not a trainful of phantoms they'd brought him, it was a trainful of cropses. The floor of the compartment before him was a tangled jumble of human bodies, throats cut, skulls smashed, bowels eviscerated. Arms, legs, trunks of bodies were strewn along the corridors of compartments. From somewhere in that ghastly human junk-heap at his feet. Singh heard a sound of strangled gargling. Realizing that there might be a few survivors, Singh called out : 'You are in Amritsar. We are Hindus and Sikhs here. The police are present. Do not be afraid.'

"At his words a few of the dead began to stir. The stark horror of the scenes that followed would be forever a nightmare engraved upon the station master's mind. One woman packed her husband's severed head from the coagulating pool of blood by her side. She clutched it in her arms shrieking her grief. He saw weeping children clinging to the bodies of their slaughtered mothers, men in shock as they pulled the body of a mutiliated child from a pile of corpses. As the crowd along the platform realized what had happened, hysteria swept their ranks.

"Numb, the station master made his way down the line of bodies. In every compartment of every carriage the sight was the same. By the time he reached the last one he was ill. Reeling back on to the platform, his nostrils impregnated with the stench of death, Singh thought, 'How could God permit such a thing?'

He turned to look back at the train. As he did, he saw in great white-washed letters on the flank of the last car the assassins' calling card. 'This train is our Independent gift to Nehru and Patel, it read.[2]

Ganda Singh (1900-87) who was considered a doyen of the authors on the Sikh history wrote a diary during the most eventful days seen from the Punjab. The upheaval that the country saw immediately before and after its division in 1947 was unparalleled in the history. From what he heard from several first-hand secret sources in 1946 and 1947 of the activities of the Muslim Leaguers of Amritsar and Lahore, he felt that something extraordinary was about to happen. He mentioned that some indications of coming events came from the speeches of the League leaders. As early as the beginning of April 1946, Malik Sir Firoz Khan Noon said that 'the havoc which the Muslims will play will put to shame what Halaku did' (*Tribune,* Lahore, 11th April, 1946). And Halaku (Hulagu) Khan is known to the history of the world as one of the most cruel and remorseless destroyers of life and property. Sardar Abdur Rab Nishtar said in August 1946, seven months before the blood thirsty dagger was actually unsheathed, that 'Pakistan can only be achieved .... if need be, and opportunity arose, by shedding the blood of others. Mussalmans are no believers in the creed of *ahimsa.* We will do just as the situation demands' (*Tribune,* Lahore, 18 August 1946). And according to Raja Ghazanfar Ali's statement (31 August 1946), they were to wait 'until the fire order comes from Quaid-i-Azam Jinnah'. On 4 September, Khan Iftikhar Husain Khan of Mamdot, President of the Punjab Provincial Muslim League, appealed to the Muslim lawyers 'in the name of Islam and Pakistan ... to cast aside all thoughts of personal occupation, business and profit, and as shock troops of the Muslim League spread out all over the province, in every village, *qasha,* town and city, to do preliminary spade work of propaganda without which no revolutionary upsurge and determined struggle is possible'

(*Dawn,* 5 September 1946). Even the Quaid-i-Azam, Mr. Mohammad Ali Jinnah, thought of a civil war as an effective method of coercing his adversaries to agree to the demands of his Muslim League.

Preparations and training for a bloodbath, therefore, continued in full swing in the autumn and winter months of 1946 and the fire order was given in December, as a trial to begin with, in the north-western district of Haripur Hazara. This was predominantly a Muslim area and a stronghold of the Muslim Leaguers. There could, therefore, be no doubt about the success of the fire and sword operations there against the negligible minorities of Hindus and Sikhs who were taken unawares. Encouraged by their successes in the north-west, the Leaguers opened their offensive in the central Punjab in the cities of Amritsar and Lahore in March 1947. Considerable parts of these cities were burnt down in a few days. "The contagion soon spread to other places as well, and by the time the division of the country was declared in August, sword and fire had done incalculable harm to life and property in the urban as well as rural areas. As the Muslim Leaguers were found not to understand any language other than that of sharp steel, the Hindus and Sikhs of Punjab were left with no alternative. And this had the desired effect, although a little too late. ... .."[3]

V. P. Menon writes "soon after the announcement of the Radcliffe Award on 17th August, a determined campaign to drive out the Hindus and Sikhs was evident all over West Punjab and the North-West Frontier Province. There were serious disturbances in the Lahore, Sheikhpura, Sialkot and Gujranwala districts. A massacre on an unprecedented scale took place in Sheikhupura in West Punjab. This was followed by a violent anti-Muslim reaction in Amritsar. Thereafter communal frenzy gripped the people on both sides of the border, taking a heavy toll of lives and creating an exodus of population between the two Dominions, the like of which has never before been known in history."[4] The Hindus and Sikhs in West Pakistan made their way for the Indian border by the shortest possible routes – from Narowal to Dera Baba Nanak, from Lahore to Amritsar, from Kasaur to Ferozepur, from Montogomery to Fazilka, from the Muslim State of Bahawalpur to Bikaner, from Mirpur Khas to Jodhpur. This they did by air, by train, by car, by bus – by almost every conceivable means of transport, as well as in foot convoys. The exodus soon developed into a flood which, sweeping through East Punjab, engulfed the city and province of Delhi and overflowed into the western districts of the United Provinces.

"The uprooted millions were in a terrible mental state. They had been driven from their homes under conditions of indescribable horror and misery. Not many had the time to plan their evacuation; most had to move out at the shortest possible notice. They had been subjected to terrible indignities. They had witnessed their near and dear ones hacked to pieces before their eyes and their houses ransacked, looted and set on fire by their own neighbours. They had no choice but to seek safety in flight, filled with wrath at what they had seen, and full of anguish for numberless missing kinsmen who were still stranded in Pakistan and for their womenfolk who had been abducted."[5]

The destitute refugees comprised all classes of people joined the stream of panic-stricken people. There were the rich, who had been reduced overnight to poverty and penury; there were petty tradesmen and office-workers for whom the future was bleak and uncertain, and there were the Sikhs who had borne the main brunt of the communal fury.

"The holocaust in Western Pakistan had its repercussions in East Punjab. The streams of fleeing refugees with their tales of woe and suffering made a profound impression on the people."[6] All appeals were in vain and retaliation was no remedy. The trouble spread to Patiala and the East Punjab States and to the western districts of the United Provinces, especially Meerut and Saharanpur, the States of Bharatpur and Alwar, and ultimately to Delhi. There was a mass exodus of the Muslims to the Pakistan border.

The panic-stricken refugees poured into the city of Delhi,

the Capital buzzed with rumours of a deep-laid, long-prepared Muslim conspiracy to overthrow the new Government of Free India and to seize the Capital. Such rumours may now seem, if not baseless, at least extremely improbable, but so credulous has the people then become that they were very widely believed. Had not Delhi, before the advent of the British, been the seat of Muslim empires for centuries? Had not the Capital been the cradle of Muslim culture? The Muslim League High Command functioned from Delhi and it was from Delhi that the campaign of 'Direct Action' had been organized and conducted through the length and breadth of the country. "The militant National Guards had a well-knit organisation in the city. The Khaksars (who had made their appearance in Delhi early in the year) also boasted of a number of adherents. It was the general belief that plans had been made before the announcement of the June 3rd plan to organise and equip the Muslim community for communal violence. The majority of the ammunition dealers in the city were Muslims and it was easy for them to help their co-religionists in obtaining a wide variety of weapons and ammunition. There were also Muslim blacksmiths and arms-repairers who were alleged to have given a hand in the fabrication of bombs, mortars and other ammunition."[7]

The first recorded communal incident in Delhi took place in a predominantly Muslim locality. On 21 August there was an explosion in a house belonging to a Muslim science student. "It is believed that he had been trying to prepare a bomb. A few days later the first stabbing was reported from the vicinity of the Diwan Hall and the Wavell Canteen, the two places where arrangements had been made for the reception of incoming refugees. On 25th August, an altercation ensued, between a Hindu worker and a Muslim worker in the Birla Mills, which led to a free fight; but the police were able to control it and to restore order very quickly."[8]

The local administration was at a fix to face the situation far beyond its capacity. ... About fifty per cent of the civil and almost seventy-five per cent of the armed police force had been drawn from amongst the Muslims and all of them had their heart in, and were keen to opt for, Pakistan. They obviously could not be relied upon....... Many of the Hindu policemen had been drawn from the Punjab and they had heard of what had happened to their friends and relations in the western part of the province. The gaps in the officer cadre had hastily filled by optees from West Pakistan who had themselves witnessed or experienced the worst features of communal fury in West Punjab and the North-West Frontier Province.......... In an effort to preserve order with the help of the limited manpower at his disposal, the District Magistrate of Delhi imposed an extended curfew from the afternoon of 28 August to the early hours of September 1... On the morning of 4th September, the explosion of a bomb in a Hindu locality in Karolbagh was the signal for a serious outbreak of rioting and there occurred numerous isolated cases of arson and of looting and stabbing in different parts of the city. Muslim and Hindu localities were so intermingled that each locality feared an attack from its neighbour. An atmosphere of nervousness and apprehension pervaded the entire Capital.[9]

On 7 September some Muslims shot and killed a few Hindus... Trouble broke out afresh on a large scale and firearms were freely used. Some of the houses in certain Muslim localities were converted into powerful bastions where firearms were collected and stored for use. One of these houses was later found to contain considerable subterranean stores of arms and ammunition and even wireless sets. Firearms and ammunition were actually dug up from graveyards. In a situation such as this, the small police force was completely helpless and troops had to be called upon to give assistance. These comprised a small body of Gurkhas, the Rajputana Rifles, and the 4th Battalion, the Madras Regiment. The last-mentioned were rushed to Delhi from Poona. They were disposed in the areas of Sadar Bazar, Subzimundi, Paharganj and Karolbagh. Even with the help of the troops it was not easy to restore order... Both sides seemed well provided with firearms, were equally well organised and determined and were employing guerrilla tactics. ...[10]

"Organised rioting apart, sporadic and isolated incidents of looting, stabbing and arson were frequent in many parts of the city... Stabbing was developed into an art. The tragedy was that for the most part it was women, children and the aged who were the victims. Stabbing did not take place only in the alleys. Groups of bloodthirsty ruffians would even rush into houses and drag people out of them to be stabbed. For days together, no effective protection could be given against treacherous, sneaking and silent killing by individuals impelled by an uncontrollable urge to settle the score; an eye for an eye, a tooth for a tooth.[11]

The conditions in New Delhi had never before deteriorated to so serious an extent. In Connaught Place a number of shops were looted and there were also cases of stabbing. There was sufficient apprehension and uncertainty to induce almost the entire Muslim population of New Delhi to move out to the shelter of refugee camps. Nor was there a sense of security among the Hindus. The concentration of Muslims, particularly the turbulent Meos from the neighbouring villagers round about the Lodi Road area, was a potential source of trouble. "The lurid glow of fires in the horizon, the all-night shooting and the screaming and shrieking of victims, were enough to unnerve anyone. Food and milk were scarce and the majority of the staff absented themselves from the Central Government offices. Telephones worked fitfully and for two days the mail was not delivered at all. Even the airports were not spared by the rioters and air services were badly interrupted."[12]

While the trouble spread to the areas surrounding Delhi, to the villages of the neighbouring States of Alwar and Bharatpur and the adjoing districts of the United Provinces and East Punjab, large numbers of people – mostly Muslims – trekked into Delhi and greatly added to the already complex problem of protecting the local Muslim population.

The disturbances in Delhi is but a reflection of how the situation had developed in East Punjab, the western districts of the United Provinces and some of the Punjab and Rajasthan States. . The new province of East Punjab had not yet had time to reorganize its administration; even its Capital had not been settled, when there came this unforeseen challenge to law and order, which resulted in a complete – though short-lived – breakdown of the administration. Under the pressure of refugees fleeing from terror it was with the greatest difficulty that some semblance of order could be maintained even in the western districts of the United Provinces.

"The task that confronted the Government of India was threefold. Firstly, they had to retrieve the law and order position and to stop the communal frenzy; secondly, they had to bring about a sense of security among the Muslim minority and, if that was not possible, at least to afford those who wanted to go away to Pakistan safe transit across the frontier; and thirdly they had a moral duty by their brethren across the borders, to ensure the peaceable transfer of Hindus and Sikhs to India and provide for their resettlement."[13]

V. P. Menon stated that "It was particularly essential that Delhi should be saved from the impending chaos at whatever cost. Danger to the Capital meant a threat to the very existence of the nascent Dominion. It was clear that some extraordinary and forceful action was necessary to retrieve the position. I felt that it was only Lord Mountbatten's presence in the Capital that would save the situation. Because of criticisms on both sides, the Punjab Boundary Force had been dissolved, and the authority of the Joint Defence Council over it having come to an end, Lord Mountbatten felt that there was no necessity for his immediate presence in Delhi. He had therefore gone to Simla for ten days for a well-earned rest. He could scarcely have foreseen a situation that might develop so seriously as to affect his return to Delhi. I mentioned to Vallabhbhai Patel my idea of ringing up Lord Mountbatten to tell him how serious the situation was and to request him to return immediately. He readily felt in with my suggestion and assured me that the Prime Minister would also agree. On my telephonic request, Lord Mountbatten returned at once to Delhi and on his arrival I met him and explained the situation. Immediately afterwards he had a discussion with Nehru and Patel. That very evening an Emergency Committee of fifteen was set up. It consisted of Cabinet Ministers, the Commander-in-Chief, representatives of the Supreme

Command, the Chief Commissioner of Delhi, the Inspector-General of Police, the Director-General of Civil Aviation and representatives of the Medical Department and Railways. The Cabinet Ministers were Nehru, Vallabhbhai Patel, Baldev Singh (Defence), John Matthai (Railways) and K. C. Neogy (who was nominated as minister in charge of refugees). Others were co-opted as and when required. C. M. Trivedi, Governor of East Punjab, together with his Premier and Home Minister, also attended the meetings when called upon. The energetic and indefatigable Vernon Erskine Crum was appointed Secretary of the Committee.

Nehru and Patel insisted that Lord Mountbatten should be the Chairman. The Emergency Committee promptly plunged into an earnest examination of ways and means of dealing with the situation...."[14]

However, within less than two weeks normal conditions had been restored in the city. The movement of refugees from and to Pakistan was one of the most difficult problems which the Central Emergency Committee had to tackle. "It has been estimated that upto the middle of 1948 about 5.5 million non-Muslims were brought across the border from West Punjab and other provinces of western Pakistan. About the same number of Muslims moved into Pakistan from East Punjab (including the East Punjab States), Delhi, the United Provinces, Ajmer-Merwara, Alwar, Bharatpur, Gwalior and Indore. During the same period about 1.25 million non-Muslims crossed the border from Eastern Pakistan into West Bengal. These figures do not of course take into account about 400,000 non-Muslims who later migrated to India from Sind. There is today hardly a Hindu or a Sikh to be found in Western Pakistan."[15]

It may be noted that "the Sikhs had been driven out of their homes, contrary to all their hopes and expectations; that they had been deprived of their lands and property, their shrines and holy places; that their losses in men and property had been comparatively greater than those of any other community affected by the community upheaval; that nearly forty per cent of the entire Sikh community had been reduced to penury and had become refugees, with the necessity of having to start life afresh."[16]

The administration in the East Punjab had virtually broken down. C. M. Trivedi, the Governor, decided to make his Government's headquarters – at least temporarily – at Jullundur. He set to work with a small nucleus staff, and the rest of the Government secretariat was located in various places in East Punjab, wherever accommodation was available.

The situation of the Eastern Pakistan was no less horrible than Punjab. Moreso, there were suppression of news because of retaliation.

Prof. Bimal Prasad mentioned during his deliverance of Maulana Azad Memorial Lecture that "communal tension in almost all parts of northern India was reaching the boiling point. Ferocious riots soon followed in quick succession in such far-flung areas as Noakhali and Tiperrah districts of Eastern Bengal, Central and Northern Bihar, including the Patna district, and UP, particularly Garh Mukteshwar, a place of Hindu pilgrimage in the Meerut district."[17]

Our leaders thought that peace will prevail after the Partition of the country and this was the only solution to the festering communal problems but their hopes were soon proved futile. The influx of minorities from East Pakistan drew attention of the Indian Commission of Jurists, a non-Governmental organisation of the Lawyers, who took note of the situation arising out of the recurrent migration of non-Muslims from East Pakistan. The Jurist Commission comprised M. C. Setalvad, President, N. C. Chatterjee, Vice-President, Purshottam Trikamdas, General Secretary, Justice S. M. Sikri, Justice S. K. Dey, G. S. Pathak etc. were the Members. The representatives of the Commission visited West Bengal and the places from where the refugees were crossing over into India in large numbers. Thus they visited Hasnabad and Petrapol border areas and submitted a preliminary survey report to the Commission in 1965. In their observations, they noticed that in Hasnabad the refugees were walking across the frontier with little excepting the clothes they were wearing. Some of them took a dangerous, long and strenuous journey before they could cross over. At this centre alone, about 2000 persons were crossing over every day. "Many of them, including children, had raw and gaping wounds on their persons. At Petrapol, most of the refugees were coming over by train."[18]

The representatives visited the Howrah station where refugees were brought from different receiving centres to be sent along to the various camps.

Having received the preliminary report and after giving a careful consideration, the Executive Council of the Commission decided to institute a Committee of Enquiry consisting of Purshottam Trikamdas as Chairman and I. N. Shroff as Member.

The Commission resolved to enquire into the causes of the recurrent large-scale migrations into India from East Pakistan citizens of Hindu, Christians and Buddhist persuasions, to report what extent and in what manner such migrations were occasioned by violation of human rights and fundamental freedom enshrined in the Universal Declaration of Human Rights 1948 and by the practice of genocide as defined in Article 11 of the Genocide Convention of 1948.

In the first part of the report it was stated that in 1946, in undivided Bengal the Muslim League formed the Government. The policy and programme of the ruling party were largely based on "suspicion of the Hindus". H. S. Suhrawardy, the premier of Bengal declared the "Direct Action Day" on the 16th August, 1946 a public holiday in Bengal for the achievement of Pakistan. Nobody could guess in what form it was going to be observed. People thought it would be confined to holding mass meeting and processons. But early in the morning of August 16, "attacks on Hindus by organised and well armed gangs of Muslims, led by Muslim League volunteers, began and went on unabated for 4 or 5 days." The Premier, it is well-known, was sitting in the Control Room of the

Police Headquarter where reports were conveyed to him every minute by the Police. The Police, however, had been completely immobilised under his direct orders not to interfere. This resulted in what came to be known as the 'Great Calcutta Killings', in which thousands of Hindus were massacred and Muslim League volunteers who carried plenty of Petrol, set fire to Hindu Houses.

Stanley Wolpert writes that the Great Calcutta killings started in Manicktolla on Friday, August 16, 1946. The Muslim League's Chief Minister, H. S. Suhrawardy, proclaimed the day a public 'holiday'; hence there were no police or other officials on the street of India's most populous city when the bloodletting began. Mobs of murdering Muslims ran wild in every Hindu neighbourhood, killing or maiming any person they could find. Soon the retaliatory mobs of frenzied Hindus lashed out in opposite directions, and with the brutal murders came panic, with thousands fleeing Kipling's "City of dreadful nights", whose stench of blood would never leave its Bengali palaces or darkest slums. "It was unbridled savagery and homicidal maniacs let loose to kill and kill and to maim and burn." [19]In the next few days some ten thousand people were murdered in Bengal alone.

Soon after the Calcutta riots disturbances broke out in Noakhali.[20] By the end of 1947, about 4,25,000 Hindus had migrated from East Pakistan. In East Pakistan there were 13 million non-muslims and it was not easy to eliminate them by means of violence and atrocities."

It is alleged that right from the beginning discrimination against the non-Muslims became the rule. "The Muslim League Government in East Pakistan let loose a reign of terror on Hindus. Police and goondas were utilised for this purpose". The oppression of non-Muslims and periodical massacres had been a regular feature to frighten the minorities and to force them to leave the country.

In April 19, 1948 the Neogy-Ghulam Mohammed Agreement was signed to ease the situation of minorities by putting up Minority Boards in each country. While this was strictly implemented in

India what happened in Pakistan was described in the Memorandum of Congress Legislative party in East Bengal which was submitted to the Premier Mr. Nurul Amin in December, 1949.

In Dacca alone three thousand Hindu houses had been requisitioned. The licences to Hindu houses had been requisitioned. The licences of Hindus holding fire arms were cancelled and arms seized. Large number of houses and lands throughout Pakistan were forcibly occupied by Muslims. Temples were desecrated. Large number of reports of crimes against Hindu women were brought to the notice of the authorities but were ignored. Forced conversion and forced marriages after abduction were also mentioned. Large number of dacoities during which attacks on women had taken place had become a feature of rural life in East Bengal. Muslim mobs on the pretext of keeping an eye over disloyal Non-Muslims, raided Hindu houses. In the rural areas forcible removal of crops, plucking of fruits from trees, cutting of bamboos and catching fish from the tanks belonging to Hindus had become most common. The attitude of Government officials and police towards the complaints from Hindus was completely indifferent and some district Magistrates openly preached against the Hindus. The Minority Boards agreed upon by the Neogy Ghulam Mohammed Pact were either not brought into existence or were not allowed to function. Local Boards and Municipalities where the Hindus held the majority of seats were arbitrarily suspended.

In 1949 the Roman Catholic Missionary Father Thomas Cattaneo in his report on the district of Rajshahi described that entire Santhal villages were assaulted, their women in large numbers were raped and mass arrest were made.

In February 1950, there was a repetition of the pattern of Calcutta killing in East Pakistan, but this was more widespread. The atrocities which began in August 1949 all over East Pakistan continued almost for a period of three months. These incidents led to a fresh wave of migration and thousands of Hindus poured into West Bengal, Assam and Tripura.

On February 8th 1950, a small incident of a communal nature took place in Calcutta which was brought down by prompt action within two days. But the Dacca press published reports of sufferings of Muslims in India. The propaganda was against the Hindus and described them as Fifth Columnists. The Bengali and Urdu leaflets calling for "revenge of atrocities committed in Calcutta" were distributed all over Dacca and incited the people over megaphones. The Pakistan Radio and Press added fuel to the fire by announcing the killing of ten thousand Muslims in Calcutta. Another newspaper stated that the number of Muslims killed in Calcutta as high as one lakh. More so, there was a false rumour spread about the murder in Calcutta of Fazlul Haq, a prominent leader in East Pakistan. This led to a large scale killing of Hindus in Barisal. Actually the most honourable Fazlul Haq came to India to dispose up his property after Partition. Sooner he heard the rumour and atrocities on Hindus he immediately returned to Barisal and told the Muslims that he is alive.

During the disturbances, the officials including the police were completely indifferent and the Ansars took an active and leading part in loot, arson and murder, some high officials were also reported to have speeches of inflammatory nature. Bhupendra Kumar Dutta who was a prominent minority leader of East Pakistan raised the issue in the Constituent Assembly of Pakistan on March 16, 1950 wherein he stated "Sir, so far as we on this side of the House are concerned, we meet under the shadow of a great calamity that threatens our very existence as a community".

Liaquat Ali Khan, the First Premier of Pakistan who visited East Pakistan in March 1950, was presented with a long memorandum signed by the leading Opposition Members (Basanta Kumar Das, Ganendra Nath Bhattacharjee, Munindra Nath Bhattacharjee, Haran Chandra Ghosh Choudhury and Manoranjan Dhar) of the East Bengal Assembly wherein it was mentioned "Here in this Province took place only one sided diabolical killing and persecution of Hindus by Muslims". The Minority community stands here broken in pride and honour, shamed and bleeding. Their lives and properties seem virtually forfeited here. Hindu passengers, who arrived at Dacca by steamers and trains were killed at the stations. Hindus travelling by buses were stabbed, murdered and thrown out. By the evening of the 10th February, 1950 about 90% of Hindu shops in the Dacca city were looted and many burnt and about fifty thousand Hindus were displaced by more than seven hours' loot, arson and murders. The hoodlum continued unchecked for a few days. Even on the 12th afternoon about 60 Air passengers were attacked at the Kurmitola Airport.

It was observed that after 1950 killings Hindu holdings of properties fell to 12.7% and nearly 90% of the citizens of Dacca had migrated to India. Similarly, the Hindu student population before partition which was 2900 boys in schools only 2000 remained before February 1950 killings and at the end of December 1950 the number was reduced to 140 only. The population of Hindu College students fell from 65% at partition to 7% in January 1950 and at the end of the year only 12 remained. Similar was the case with the Lawyers. While there were 1500 Hindu shops at the time of partition but at the end of 1950 only 157 remained.

Jogen Mondal who was a leader of the schedule caste and accepted the cabinet appointment as Minister of Law and Labour in the Government of Pakistan, submitted his resignation letter and fled from Pakistan in September 1951. In his letter of resignation he mentioned with a heavy heart and a sense of utter frustration the first incident that occurred at a village called Digharkul near Gopalganj where on false pretext brutal atrocities were committed on local Namasudras. He complained that in Habibgunj (Sylhet) where there was a military camp the unfortunate Hindus were forced among other things to send the women at night to the military camps for satisfying the soldiers. At Nachole in the District of Rajshahi where in the name of suppression of communists not only the police but the local Muslims oppressed the Hindus and looted their properties. There was an instance of callous and cold blooded brutality which took place on December 20, 1949 in Kalshira under P.S. Mallahat in the District of Khulna. There he found the place desolate and in ruins. He was told in presence of the Superintendent of Police that there were 350 homesteads in this village, of these only three had been spared and the rest had been demolished. Country boats and cattles belonging to the Namasudras had all been taken away.

Jogen Mondal reached Dacca on February 10th 1950 at 5 O'clock. The riot broke out at 1 P.M. Arson, looting of Hindu shops and houses, and killing of Hindus wherever they were found commenced in full swing in parts of the city. He got evidence that arson and looting were committed in the presence of high police officials. Jewellery shops belonging to Hindus were looted in the presence of police officers. They did not attempt to stop the loot, but helped the looters.

He also mentioned in his resignation letter that "on February 10th, 1950 at about 10 O'clock in the morning a woman was painted with red to show that her breast was cut-off in Calcutta riot and was taken round the East Bengal Secretariat at Dacca. Immediately the Government servants of the Secretariat struck work and came out in procession raising slogans of revenge against the Hindus. The procession began to swell as it passed over a distance of more than a mile. It ended in a meeting at Victoria Park in the noon where violent speeches against the Hindus were delivered by several speakers, including officials".

By the time the employees of the Secretariat went out in procession, the Chief Secretary of the East Bengal Government was holding a conference with his West Bengal opposite number in the same building, to find out ways and means to stop communal disturbances in the two Bengals.

While narrating the incidents of sufferings of the people he stated that during his nine days' stay at Dacca he visited most of the riot-affected areas of the city and suburbs. The news of the killing of hundreds of innocent Hindus in trains, on railway lines between Dacca and Narayanganj and Dacca and Chittagong gave him the rudest shock. On the second day of disturbances he saw the Chief Minister of East Bengal and requested him to issue immediate instructions to the District authorities to take all precautionary measures to prevent spreading of the riot in district towns and rural areas. On the 20th February, 1950 he went to Barisal town and was astounded to know of the happenings in Barisal. At the Madhabpasha Zamindar's house about 200 people were killed and 40 injured. A place, called Muladi, witnessed a dreadful hell. At Muladi Bandar alone the number killed were more than three hundred. He visited Muladi village where he found skeletons of dead bodies at some places. He found dogs and vultures eating corpses on the riverside. He got the information there that "after the wholesale killing of all adult males, all the young girls were distributed among the ring leaders of the miscreants." All Hindu shops of Babuganj Bazar were looted and then burnt and a large number of Hindus were killed. In his estimation the casualties were 2,500 killed in the district of Barisal alone and the total casualties of Dacca and East Bengal riots were to be about 10,000 killed.

He was overwhelmed with grief. The lamentation of women and children who had lost their all including near and dear ones melted his heart. With great regret he recollected those days when thirty-two crores of Hindus of the Indo-Pakistan Subcontinent turned their back against him and dubbed him as the enemy of Hindu and Hinduism, but he remained undaunted and unswerved in his loyalty to Pakistan. He was then asked himself "what was coming to Pakistan in the name of Islam". [21]He took shelter in West Bengal.

In early 1950, how humanity was attacked under the Liaquat-Nurul Amin Regime can be cited by a statement of Ila Mitra, Communist leader who disclosed before the Court at Rajshahi with regard to inhuman treatment meted out to her only because she held a political opinion other than that of Liaquat-Nurul Amin Feudal class. Ila Mitra said in her statement before the court at Rajshahi – "On 7. 1. 1950 last I was arrested in Rohanpur and taken to Nachole the next day. The Police guards assaulted me on the way and thereafter I was taken inside a cell.... ..... all my garments were taken away and I was imprisoned inside the cell in stark naked condition. No food was given to me, not even a drop of water.... .... My legs were pressed between bamboo sticks and the people around the cell was being administered a 'Pakistani' injection." When the torture was going on they tied my mouth with a napkin. They also pulled my hairs, but as they could not force me to say anything, I was taken back to the cell carried by the sepoys, as after the torture it was not possible for me to walk. "Inside the cell again the S.I. ordered the sepoys to bring four hot eggs, and said, now she will talk. Thereafter four or five sepoys forced me to lie down on my back, and pushed a hot egg through my private parts. I was feeling like being burnt with fire, and became unconscious."[22] (Annexure-2)

Dhirendra Nath Dutta, spoke in the Constitutent Assembly at Dacca on March 29, 1952 that there was a great deal of mistrust. If any Hindu was put on loongi he was said to be disguising himself. If anybody puts on Dhoti then he was said to have come from West Bengal. Such a sense of mistrust had been created by the Government of Pakistan.

When the news of the disturbances trickled out, Jawaharlal Nehru, the Prime Minister of India suggested that Liaquat Ali Khan and himself signed an agreement to stop the recurrent massacres and large scale migrants. This agreement was signed on April 8, 1950 which was known as the Nehru-Liaquat Agreement. The agreement stated to ensure to the minorities throughout its territories, complete equality of citizenship, irrespective of religion, full sense of security in respect of life, culture, property and personal honour, freedom of movement within each country and freedom of occupation, speech and worship. While in India the agreement was followed strictly but the pact become practically a dead letter in East Pakistan. More so, on the 3rd Anniversary of Pakistan Independence Day on 14th August, 1950, Liaquat Ali Khan issued a message to people of Pakistan as follows :-

"If we are loyal to the memory of our Great Qaid-e-Azam let us remember the national watchwords he gave us – Unity, Faith and Discipline. Let us so live and act that hundreds of years hence when history recalls our times it will say : These people lived, struggled and suffered like true sons of Islam so that their children may live in honour and glory".[23]

Thus the Nehru-Liaquat Pact was ignored by East Pakistan and instead a 14-page circular was issued to all District Magistrates wherein instructions were given by no means to return the lands and properties to the returning migrants. There were another instruction which stated "to talk sweetly to minorities and their representatives, even with smile on your lips."

The Government sent a circular to the Chiefs of Commercial firms instructing them to obtain prior approval of the District Magistrate before appointing a non-Muslim. Cries of an Islamic State appeared to condone the policy of harsh discrimination practised against them by the Government. After all, non-Muslms must not aspire to have a comfortable living in the homeland of Muslims. Hindus engaged in trade and industry had no alternative but to wind up their business and leave. Even after Partition, at a time when the Muslims of East Bengal did not have the means to start many industries in their province and the Central Government was not interested in industrialising that province, some Hindus invested crores of rupees in industry. But the bureaucracy deliberately placed so many hindrances in their way, what the bureaucracy can always do very easily, that they had to consider migration to India and then, oddly enough, they had to face the accusation that they were Indian agents and they never tried to look upon Pakistan as their homeland. A more glaring example of an official policy, at once oppressive and hypocritical, could rarely be found. "It was a habitual trick on the part of the Government to get out of any inconvenient situation by blaming it on the Hindus. Even the assassination of Liaquat was initially sought to be attributed to a Hindu. If Pakistan's relations with India worsened at any time, the Hindus of East Bengal had to pay a penalty."[24] It would be surprising to note that one Central Minister of Pakistan made a curious announcement in a public meeting that Pakistan was not a nation-state but an Islamic State. Such utterances merely strengthened the belief, popular and advantageous to the majority community, that Muslims were entitled to play havoc with the rights of minorities, especially when the Government encouraged this foul play. "Muslims continued to occupy the houses of Hindus forcibly, to steal paddy or fish from the premises belonging to non-Muslims who became too demoralised even to lodge complaints with the police because of familiar police brutalities on these complainants."[25]

NOTES AND REFERENCES

1. Collins, Larry and Lapierre, Dominique. *Freedom At Midnight*, p-270.
2. Ibid. p-271-72.
3. Ganda Singh, A Diary of Partition Days, *India Partitioned : The other Face of Freedom*, Vol.II, p-28, Ed. Mushirul Hasan.
4. Menon, V.P., *The Transfer of Power In India*, p-418.
5. Ibid.
6. Ibid, p-419.
7. Ibid.
8. Ibid, p.419-420.
9. Ibid.
10. Ibid, p-421.
11. Ibid.
12. Ibid, p-422.
13. Ibid, p-423.
14. Ibid, p.423-24.
15. Ibid, p.431.
16. Ibid,p.432-33.
17. Bimal Prasad, Maulana Azad Memorial Lecture, 2005, *India's Partition in Historical Perspective*, p.70.
18. Recurrent Exodus of Minorities from East Pakistan and Disturbances in India : A Report to the Indian Commission of Jurists, New Delhi, by its Committee of Enquiry, 1965, p-1.
19. Wolpert, Stanley, *Nehru –Tryist with Distiny*, p.372-73.
20. Sukharanjan Sengupta, *Banga Sanhar Ebong*, p- 23-24.

    After the 'Great Calcutta Killings' in August 1946, the tension of communal feeling in Eastern Bengal districts rose very high and in the district of Noakhali it reached its climax. The great killing in Calcutta was attributed to by the League Leaders to the Hindus which naturally inflamed the Muslims on an 'Id' day on 29th August, the mischief-mongers spread throughout the district a false and flying report that Hindus brought Sikhs and arms and kept them concealed in some important houses though not one was ever found. The designing men took the opportunity of 'Id' congregations in many parts of the district and openly incited the illiterate masses to violence. The infuriated mobs armed with deadly weapons raided many Hindu houses and places of worship, killed some, assaulted and injured many more, looted some houses, shops, bazars in different areas of the district and subjected the Hindus to various forms of oppression and indignities. Idols and temples were to broken or desecrated. Cases of conversion and attempt of conversion were also reported. Extortion of many from the terror-stricken Hindus in the name of subscription for the Muslim League became a common practice. Journey by road or boat were very much insecured. All business collapsed. Hindus did not dare to report to the Police for fear of further oppression and harassment.

P.D.Martyn, Additional Secretary to the Government of Bengal, in his Top Secret note about Noakhali Situation wrote - "The third category is the most dangerous. To this class belong those Muslims who, for reasons of religious zeal, economic jealousy or personal enmity, hate the Hindu and want to see him wiped out. This class would not ordinarily be powerful, but circumstances have combined to make it so today and it has the advantage of having attracted to its side the goonda element of the District, which sees in disturbances the prospect of the easy acquisition of wealth and power. Many persons who fall in this category are able, if violent, speakers and can work up a mob into a state of frenzied anger. To this class belong Abul Kasem and Ali Akbar, the two most important absconders. ... All parties were agreed that the number of goondas had increased enormously since the war, and a further accession of strength has been lent to this class by the gradual return of disgruntled ex-servicemen in the last eighteen months; over 56,000 men of this District joined the services during the war."

21. Jogen Mandal's Letter of Resignation to Liaquat Ali Khan, the Prime Minister of Pakistan, Oct. 9, 1950.

22. Maleka Begum, *Ila Mitra*

23. Recurrent Exodus of Minorities from East Pakistan and Disturbances in India : A Report to the Indian Commission of Jurists, New Delhi to its Committee of Enquiry, 1965, p-11

24. Ray, Jayanta Kumar, *Democracy and Nationalism on Trial*, p-80.

25. Ibid, p-82.

3

THE GREATEST HOLOCAUST

The exodus of Hindu Minorities from East Bengal in the early stages after the partition was but a trickle. It assumed critical proportions much later, and then the Hindus from the East Bengal also had to undergo severe hardships and privations. In fact, it was when the West Pakistan officials had established themselves in the East Bengal, the exodus of the Hindus began in earnest.[1] V. P. Menon said - "It has always been my belief that the East Bengal Muslims, if left to themselves, would have been content to live with their Hindu brethren as one family, and that it was the policy of the West Pakistan officials that was responsible for the mass exodus of the Hindus from the East Bengal. The flood of refugees had already severely strained the resources of the West Bengal Government, while more and more continued to come across the border."[2]

Although after the Nehru-Liaquat Ali Pact acts of violence against the Hindus decreased to some extent, the migration continued because of lack of a sense of security. In 1950 alone 1.75 million refugees came to India and the figure for 1951 was six hundred thousand. This continued right upto 1956.

While appreciating the visit of the Prime Minister of Pakistan on 20th March, 1950, the representatives of the minorities submitted a Memorandum[3] and stated that the ill-fated minority community here is inexorably faced with a grim prospect of virtual extinction. The lingering shadow of an unprecedented and sweeping orgy of communal disturbances and carnage of recent occurrence, the dreadful enormity and experience of which far surpass those of the hectic days of the holocausts of 1946. Here in this province took place only one-sided diabolical killing and persecution of the Hindus by Muslims. Terrible things of unparalleled magnitude have happened. The way in which the occurrences took shape with unmistakable political manipulation and bearings and the manner in which the administrative authorities generally handled the situation have naturally given rise to an almost irremovable apprehension in the minds of the most miserably plighted minorities in general that something equally or more terrible may happen every moment. Their sense of security thus stands completely shattered. In the midst of this all-encompassing gloom and sufferings, they see no ray of hope as to the protection of their life, honour, religion and property. Tragedy is alround and seems almost complete. Today the minority community stands here broken in pride and honour, shamed and bleeding. Their lives and properties seem virtually forfeited here. We feel that this tragic state of things is but a culmination and cummulative effect of gradually but steadily generating forces of lawlessness and communalism in this province which in our opinion finds every nourishment from the existing non-secular political set-up and preaching. These forces of reaction and regress were rearing their heads in a sporadic manner throughout the province since the partition, to the dark forebodings whereof we draw the attention of the Provincial Government through written and verbal representations on various occasions with fervent requests for taking effective steps for arresting the growth thereof. For a long time a process of squeezing out all the Hindus from the East Bengal was being followed in the shape of indiscriminate house-requisition, forcible dispossession, non-payment of compensation, illegal exactions, arrests and detention without trial. We had also opportunities of drawing your personal attention to those developments with all their ominous possibilities in course of our joint interviews with you on two past occasions. During our first interview with you we had submitted a written memorandum embodying therein a fairly long list of typical isolated communal incidents and acts of oppression against the minorities. During our second interview with you too, we submitted before you a written representation, wherein we requested your intervention to check the worsening trends of the situation. We pointed out that on the one hand communal fanaticism was gathering force much to the detriment of the minority community and on the other the tone of the General administration was slackening and deteriorating and the machinery of law and order was not asserting itself against the growth of lawless elements. In December last, when the Assembly was in session our Assembly party as a whole met the Hon'ble Premier of the East Bengal and submitted to him a written representation about all these facts. But unfortunately the situation continued unrelieved. Fed and nurtured by persistent and reckless anti-Hindu propaganda of the local Press and rabid communal preachings by various elements of the majority community including some Muslim League stalwarts, undeterred by any authoritative interference though sought for by us, the force of lawlessness had been gathering strength quite demonstrably for the few months. ... ... The perverse spirits that actuated the isolated incidents so far and that lie behind the slow process of devitalising and demoralising the minority community in various ways now seem concealed into an organised plan for giving a final and fatal blow to the minority community as will be clearly evident particularly from the nature of the latest happenings with their flaming trails of sufferings for them yet. An irrecoverable atmosphere of prejudice and hatred against the minorities prevails here which is very likely to heighten more and more.

The representatives also said since your last visit, a few major incidents had taken place in more or less quick succession in the Province, in which Muslim mob violence with the direct connivance of and in collusion with the police and Ansars, with the knowledge of the District authorities even, broke out against the minorities on fairly large scales, letting aside the many minor ones. Let us briefly mention them.

In August 1949, some villages under Bianibazar and Barlekha

P.S. of Sylhet district were raided by a large band of Muslim villagers in company with the police and Ansars. Houses were looted, broken and burnt. Hindu villagers were murdered and assaulted in large number. Women were assaulted and raped even by policemen. The whole atrocity was committed in a visibly organised manner. We took up the matter with the Provincial Government. We discussed the same on the floor of the Assembly and earnestly demanded remedy, but to no avail. Nothing has been done to relieve the distress of the people nor to punish the wrongdoers. Then followed the incidents in Bhandaria in the District of Barisal, where similar persecution of the minorities was enacted in the whole village and the neighbouring localities apparently under the instruction of the district authorities. We approached the Provincial Government for redress but failed to impress upon them the need for taking any just action against the offenders. That seemingly studied indifference of the Government in tackling the growing lawlessness was bound to encourage the outbreak of lawlessness in the country. That happened actually. On the 10th December the Muslim mob attacked the Putia Rajbari in Rajshahi town and took forcible possession of the house and their treasures. The terrible atrocities of Bagerhat (Khulna) followed, involving mass looting, breaking and burning of houses, killing and assaulting persons, conversion, desecration of images and rape of women on a large scale affecting about a score of villages. Some troubles happened in Bagerhat town also. Similar troubles took place in Santal village in P.S. Nachole and Gomastipur in Rajshahi district. Apart from other accounts, the local Roman Catholic Missionary Father Thomas Cattaneo in his report on the district of Rajshahi described that entire Santal villages were looted and burnt by the police and the military, the Santal villagers were assaulted, their women in large number were raped and mass arrests were made. Generally everywhere police, Ansars and the Muslim mob directly and indirectly combined to wreak vengeance. Here also, our attempts at getting remedy failed significantly enough. On January 4th the Police raided and arrested about a hundred

Hindus in villages Kalaskati in Barisal district. Mass arrests of an assaults on the Hindus in Habibganj town in Sylhet District were made following an accidental fire in the criminal court buildings on January 22nd. An exciting meeting and a procession were held, whereafter Sri Suresh Chandra Biswas, M.L.A. was severely beaten and rendered unconscious. Later on he was admitted into hospital. A few days after he was arrested and Jailed. In Comilla town, Muslims raided the townhall on January 25th and the Hindu shops on January 26th and pulled down pictures of the Hindu deities and leaders. Then followed, a few weeks after, incidents on 2nd February in Feni (Noakhali) involving stabbing and murder, looting of the shops of the Hindu shopkeepers and merchants.

The representatives of the minorities sought to discuss the situation by means of adjournment motions in the Assembly on the 6th February over the incidents of Nachole and Bagerhat. They said that the motions were disallowed. Thanks to the adverse attitude of the majority party and the Government, that legitimate attempt of ours was thwarted. In reply to our rightful demand of discussion, the Hon'ble Premier made a statement thereby clearly making us feel that we are reduced to the intolerable position of hostages so far as our protection and security is concerned and making our fate clearly contingent upon the conditions of the minorities in the West Bengal. This statement was supplemented by highly provocative and offensive observations of some members of the majority party. We were thus prevented from exercising our just right and privileges as representatives of the people in the matter of giving voice to the grievances and sufferings of the minorities which were admitted to be true at least to some extent. Our voice was practically throttled. We cannot accept the position of hostages directly or indirectly. We have always demanded and still demand, as a matter of fundamentals, same rights and protections as are due to any loyal law-abiding and peaceful citizen of the state irrespective of what may happen elsewhere. We made our position in this respect clear in a statement made on the floor of the Assembly on 7.2.50 wherein inter alia we demanded an enquiry by a committee of the House headed by the Hon'ble Premier into the incidents at Nachole and Bagerhat. That statement was greeted by angry outbursts inside and outside the Assembly. A vitriolic press campaign was started against us. A distorted version as to our stand was catered to the people with a view to prejudice them against us, taking advantage of our forced silence. Generally speaking too, press campaign, through comments and presentation of news prejudicial to the minorities assumed a furious character which contributed most towards worsening the situation and inviting crisis and chaos. The local newspapers which have all along been exciting communal hatred by publishing highly inflammable news and articles came out on the following day with headlines characterising the opposition members in the Assembly as "Fifth Columnists". On the 7th February we walked out of the assembly in protest and absented ourselves for some long period having no other means of ventilating our grievances. The Muslim press and the Muslim leaders and even the Radio started a violent campaign to rouse communal passion to the highest pitch. And even one member of the Cabinet broadcast on the Radio condemning the action of the opposition and distorting their stand. Some incidents alleged to have taken place in West Bengal were exploited by them to the full. Inflammatory leaflets calling for blood were distributed in the city of Dacca and in other places in muffusil areas. Posters of similar nature were also pasted in different places in different districts. Radio Pakistan on the night of the 6th and the afternoon of the 7th February announced the following in between scheduled items of programme :

"Brother, you have heard about the inhuman atrocities being perpetrated on our brother Muslims in India and West Bengal. Will you not prepare yourselves? Will you not gather strength?"[4]

Thus a stage was being set for some grave developments. At last the presaged crisis came on the 10th February. On the morning of that day four women were shown round the Secretariat offices at Dacca with conchshell bangles on their wrists, vermillion on their forhead and blood-stain on their clothes. They alleged that they were forcibly converted into Hinduism in Calcutta and were victims of oppression by the Hindus. The Secretariat staff then left their office at about 11 a.m. during office hours and took out procession from the gate of the Secretariat building shouting exciting slogans. They held a public meeting at Victoria Park at about 12 noon. As soon as the meeting dispersed, there was a simultaneous flareup in all parts of the city resulting in arson and loot of the Hindu houses and shops and killings. Hindu passengers, who arrived at Dacca by steamer and trains, were killed at the Stations. The Hindus travelling by train and buses were stabbed, murdered and thrown out. Out of hundreds of the Hindu shops in the city of Dacca, about 90% were looted and many burnt. By the evening of the 10th February about fifty thousand Hindus in the city of Dacca were displaced from their houses and had to take shelter in refugee centres which sprang up in different parts of the city. Some Hindu officials and M.L.A. also had to do so. For more than seven hours loot, arson and murders continued unchecked. The military were then called out and placed in certain parts of the city and curfew was imposed. On the 11th and the 12th also the disturbances continued. On the 12th afternoon about sixty air-passengers who had assembled at Kurmitola Airport near the military headquarters at Dacca were attacked by a mob with deadly weapons resulting in a large number of deaths and injuries. So the city of Dacca witnessed one of the worst tragedy that history knows. A reign of terror prevailed. The whole region was under the sway of communal brigands. It seemed that the administration abdicated in favour of Goonda-Raj. All manner of crimes were being committed in the metropolis under the nose of the Provincial Government, before the eyes of the police, who were in some places found abetting the same. For all practical purposes, administration seemed to have collapsed. Murder, loot, arson, assaults and attacks on men and women were committed on an extensive scale in broad daylight. The Government must have had sufficient warning as to the coming events. From all indications the aforesaid procession and meeting were seemingly the signal for the disturbances to follow. The Government was still sleeping over the growing crisis. Thus a hell was let loose over the city and surrounding localities. During the following days the flare spread to the other districts and the killings and stabbings of passengers in trains and steamers almost throughout the Province continued for a week or so. The worst riot affected areas in the province were the Dacca city and its suburbs, parts of the Sadar and the Narayanganj sub-divisions, the Jamalpur and the Kishoreganj sub-divisions of the Mymensingh district, the town of Chittagong and its suburbs, parts of police stations Hathazari, Fatikchari and Sitakunda in the district of Chittagong, the town of Feni and its suburbs, the town of Sylhet and some rural areas of the Sadar and the Sunamganj sub-divisions of the Sylhet district, the town of Barisal and police stations Muladi Babuganj, Nalchiti, Jhalakati and Rajpur of the Sadar sub-division of the Bakerganj district, and the Talshar area of the Brahmanbaria sub-division of the Tippera district. Almost everywhere heinous offences against women were committed. In some places this most barbaric sort of crimes took place on a large scale. Mass conversions also took place in some places, apart from isolated cases here and there.

All outward indications and the manner in which the atrocities have been committed lead to the irresistible conclusion that the whole troubles took place and were allowed to take place according to a preconceived plan.

However, we are giving brief accounts of the incidents and casualties so far as we have been able to gather amidst so many difficulties of free movements and contact. .. …Confidence of the minorities in the ability and willingness of the Government to protect them is completely shaken. In such surcharged atmosphere exodus has started. (For a brief account of the incidents and casualties see Annexure - 3).

Pravash Chandra Lahiry, a freedom fighter and a member of terrorist Bengal who did not leave East Bengal after Partition said that one of his old friend Shri Atulananda Guha of Dacca who was also a freedom-fighter of the bye-gone days came to know from a

Muslim friend that a communal riot would start at Dacca on the 10th February after the Jumma prayer of the Muslims and this information proved correct. Shri Lahiry also said that during the period of uncertainty from the date of birth of Pakistan in 1947 to 1950, the communal disturbances of February 1950 in East Pakistan claimed all its previous records superseded in both intensity and extensity. "Hundreds and thousands of men, women and children of the minority communities were killed on the streets and in the houses of Dacca, Barisal and almost every other districts of East Pakistan. Even the passengers of the minority community running by trains were not spared. The moving trains were stopped on the Bhairab Bridge in the district of Mymensingh and near Shantahar in the district of Rajshahi and all Hindus were picked up and stabbed and thrown into the river or in the fields."[4] This riot was a pre-planned and pre-arranged affair – most of the Muslims knew about it previously. Thus the killing of men, women and children, burning and looting of houses and abduction of women and girls of the minority community seems to have been a wilful, purposeful and deliberate conspiracy of the Muslim community.

During 1953 to 1956 about one million six hundred and forty thousand refugees arrived in India. The flow still continued as indicated by the figures from 1957 to 1961 which amounted to about 40 thousand in West Bengal and Assam. In 1962 there were attacks on the non-Muslims and their properties and women in Rajshahi District. Thereafter by the end of December 1963 about 8,50,000 refugees arrived in India. The Committee of Enquiry examined all the witnesses who had stated the reason for their migrations was utter lack of security. The atrocities took place as a result of incitement after the Hazarat Bal incident on December 27, 1963. The population of minorities in East Pakistan had been reduced from 13 million at the end of 1947 to 8.25 million by the end of 1964.

Trailokya Nath Chakrabarti, popularly known as Maharaj, was born and bred in East Bengal. A great revolutionary who organised Dacca Anusilan Samity a leading revolutionary party of the undivided Bengal lamented at the age of 75 who was then suffering from Cardiac problem. He never thought of leaving East Bengal. He was then staying with Swadesh Nag at his house at Hemendra Das Road, Dacca. He was preparing for a minorities conference fixed for January 11 & 12, 1964. But he was forced to postpone the meeting under stress of the circumstances. On the 14th with a Khaddar coat and Dhoti on, he was on his way to Hatkhola when Swadesh accompanied him to get a statement published in various newspapers about the postponement of the Conference, a Muslim youth asked them not to proceed further as someone had been murdered.

He said, "From the afternoon of the 15th January, 1964, Hindus of the neighbouring area including women and children started sheltering at Swadesh's house and their number swelled to about 300. Though curfew had been imposed, a particular class of people were noisily loitering in the streets. We decided to stay on in the house. Swadesh was arranging for *dal-bhat* for everybody. As the night advanced the fear of danger mounted making every one restless. About midnight several Muslim friends advised Swadesh to leave the house."

Trailokya Maharaj in his letter dated 19th March 1964 stated that Government trucks were collecting the minorities from the disturbed areas and carrying them to the Court Compound of Dacca. It was a pitiable sight at the Court Compound, which was packed to capacity. "Some of those who came had either seen ghastly or themselves had suffered frightfully. Many did not know where the other members of their families were, or if they were alive at all. Some were wearing only a piece of cloth, others not bring any money with them. A pall of sorrow had fallen over the place. In that terrible Winter night those who had no bedding or clothing with them suffered most. Next day about ten O'clock we were removed to the Jagannath college refugee camp."

It may be recalled that Trailokya Maharaj spent a total of 30 years in Jail for the freedom of India-Pakistan and went underground for five years. Even after 17 years of Independence he had to be in a refugee camp. At the Jagannath College camp there were about 7000 refugees. The College authority never thought of having 7000 souls at a time and there was no arrangement for latrines. Hence this was the greatest inconvenience in the camp. Soon after the few latrines had become unusable and unapproachable and the large number of men, women and children, had, therefore, no other alternative than to ease themselves wherever they could around the camp. They used the verandahs at night for the purpose. There were no sweepers. He was in Room No.35 on the first floor of the Commerce building. As the floor of the room and the verandah was on the same level, at night their beds were soaked with urine rolling outside. For two days the Hindus of Tantibazar and Shankharibazar fed the refugees with *khitchuri* and the youngmen serving as volunteers.Trailokya Maharaj exclaimed "What an irony of Fate? We are citizen of this State, but cannot move about freely, are confined in a cage and friends of the other community come to see us in this cage." It may be noted that Ataur Rahaman Khan, Ex-Minister, Sheikh Mujibur Rahman, Mamud Ali, Zalur Hossain, Manik Mia of Ittefaq and others visited them. Even the Principal Sayeder Rahman and his wife served tea & snacks to some Professors at their house. "While members of the other Community can walk the streets freely, have opened stalls on the camp compound and are hawking goods there, I don't have that freedom. Why ? What crime have I committed?" he asked himself.

He also lamented "What has happened this time is not rioting which can occur only between two contending parties, but one-sided attack, looting and killing. One side attacks and the other flees in fear of life. Those who have been victims of looting or have been killed, ask what crime have we committed since we do not dabble in politics, do not meddle with the activities of the people of the other community, do not quarrel with our neighbours, are citizens of this country, share its prosperity, sorrow or happiness, pay Government rent regularly, are loyal subjects, then why should we be killed, why our houses should be looted and burnt, our children killed before our eyes, our womenfolk dishonoured ?"[5]

The Jurist Commission in their Enquiry report mentioned that the news of the happenings in Narayangunj and Dacca had been suppressed. In *Pakistan Times* dated January 16th, 1964, while there was no mention of the happenings in Narayangunj and Dacca, meetings and statements by various organisation and individuals were reported about the Calcutta disturbances.[6]

In a signed editorial of Mr. Abdul Hamid Ansari, Editor of an influential Urdu daily *Inquilab* published from Bombay on January 15th, 1964 stated : "There was not a single leader, newspaper or Radio Station in Pakistan which had not been continuously emitting venom against India and making a display of false sympathy for the Kashmir and Indian Muslims. Then on the basis of suppressed excesses on Indian Muslims, propaganda was unleashed and foolish and beastly attempt made to wreak vengeance on the Hindu minority in Khulna and Jessore."[7] Half of Dacca, the old part, was completely cut off from the new city because of the imposition of curfew from the first night of disturbance.

The sacred relic of Hazrat Bal was recovered on January 4, 1964 and the miscreants were arrested. But the incident proved to be a further cause for more inflammatory statements. On January 5, 1964 the Pakistan Radio described it as a fraud. On January 6, 1964 the *Sangbad*, a Bengali daily published from Dacca, criticised 'reactionary circles' for inciting communal passions over the Hazrat Bal incident, resulting in the Khulna riots.

The worst had happened in the Dacca-Narayangunj area. The atrocities which started in Khulna and in Mangla Port had been spread over to different parts of the East Pakistan.

The incidents in Dacca and the surrounding areas had been described in a despatch from Dacca and published in the *Globe* and *Mail* (Canada) on March 2, 1964 which states – "Here in Dacca where thousand of frightened Hindus await permission to leave, there is an air of impending crises, of mob violence. Calls for '*Jehad*' or holy war against infidels are shouted in sections of Pakistan. In rural areas outside Dacca are burned out houses and untilled fields of Hindus whose Muslim neighbours suddenly descended on them in night-time raids. The owners those who lived - fled with what they could carry."

On both sides of river Sitalakha in P.S. Fatulla there were number of Cotton Mills. In one side were Adamji Mills Nos.1 to 4, next to it was Dhakeswari Mill No.2, next to that was Chittaranjan Mill and then Lakshmi Narayan Mill. On the other side of the river Dhakeswari Cotton Mill No.1 and Adarsha Mills, some of these were owned by Hindus and a large number of Hindu workers were employed. A large number of workers were living outside the Mills' compounds, some quite close to the Mills and some in the surrounding villages.

In a pre-planned manner the Adamji Mills were closed on January 13, 1964 and that it was learnt that arms were being manufactured in the Mills. At late night arms were distributed among the Muslim workers of all the Adamji Mills. To incite the workers Karim the Manager of the Adamji group spread rumours that his brother was killed in Calcutta and had asked his workers to take revenge.

Accordingly, from the night of January 13th, 1964, a few thousand workers from the Adamji Mills went on a rampage of loot, arson, murder and rape. Late at night, the attacks started on the surrounding villages largely inhabited by Hindu workers. Later early in the morning of January 14, the attacks on Hindu owned Mills on both sides of the river commenced.[7]

In the Dhakeswari Cotton Mill No.2 the attack began at 6 AM and went on till 9 AM. Again at 4-30 PM there was a further attack. At about 7 AM about 2 to 3 thousand Hindu men, women and children rushed in to the Mill premises. The gate was manned by Noakhali Muslims who opened the gates and about 2000 Muslims rushed in. They were armed with lathis and iron rods and started assaulting. There was extensive looting of the staff quarters. In this Mill alone about 800 were killed and by the evening 25,000 injured. One gentleman who arrived from Dacca said that when the Mail trains from Chittagong and Sirajgunj came to Tongi and Tejgaon Railway Stations, the Hindus were asked to get down. All those who so got down were slaughtered.

The Police warned the persons who had taken shelter in the Lakshminaryan Cotton Mills not to go outside and instead requested some outside Muslims to fetch milk and food for the children. They took the money but did not return. These people had no food for 4 days from 16th to 20th January, 1964.

Even the Buddhists and the Christians were not spared. So far as the Chittagong Hill Tracts were concerned, they were largely inhabited by the Chakmas, a hill people, who are Buddhists. In this area there was very little killing and arson, but the stories of lack of security of property as well as molestation of women were rampant. The Committee members interviewed a large number of those in a camp near Silchar in Assam, where about 6000 of them were housed, one of the main reasons for their migration was the denial of religious freedom. Their festivals which they used to celebrate near their temples had been prohibited in the months prior to their migration into India. They found it very difficult to find seats in the Schools for their children. In colleges there was the same difficulty and in the hostels attached to the colleges it was almost impossible for a chakma to get a place. Even an educated Chakma got no chance of a job in Govt. institutions or otherwise. About 21,000 of the Chakmas have arrived in India in 1964.

In Sylhet, so far as the border areas are concerned, there were organised and determined efforts to drive out the minority communities. Those communities were largely Christians.

The organised efforts took shape of "creating a climate of omplete insecurity for the minorities and finally of large scale attacks on villages where looting and burning of houses took place, the unfortunate occupants of those houses were driven out in the bitter cold of January 1964 and were told that there was no room for them in Pakistan as Pakistan belonged only to the Muslims."

The Indian Commission of Jurists by its Committee of Enquiry reported - We have a few thousand statements from all areas of East Pakistan. In these areas and particularly in Khulna and Dacca districts, killings, arson, rape and plunder on a large scale have been reported. It will be relevant here to refer to the memorandum of 21 minority leaders of East Pakistan presented to the Governor of East Pakistan on June 2, 1964. The extract is reproduced. below :-

"The January, 1964 disturbance throughout the province showed clearly that Civil Administration failed to protect the life and property of the minority community and completely shook the sense of security and confidence of minorities. Heavy exodus started again. Disappointment, despair and uncertainty, confusion, fear and feeling of helplessness seized the mind of the minority community. The unhappy relation between the two States also remarkably contributed to the deterioration of the communal situation. Hundreds of people are leaving their hearths and homes for unknown destination.

There is complete lack of sense of security in the minds of the minority community. Theft, looting accompanied by murder, rape of women, robbery, abduction, forcible cutting away of standing crops catching of fish, taking away of trees and other articles, dispossessing from land has spread in epidemic form, threat, intimidation, coercion, insecurity of movements, insecurity of travels in trains, steamers, buses and in rural areas where they are subjected to extortion of money and tortures are rampant and are nearly normal features of their life. The Union Councils and Committees have publicly announced that sale of movables and immovables including huts and trees have been prohibited by the Government. As a matter of fact, sale of immovable properties even for unavoidable and pressing needs have come to a standstill. The minorities are permitted to sell moveables on payment of heavy ransom to the anti-social elements. The Police and basic democrats barring a few are indifferent and in some cases hostile to the minorities."[8]....

Mr. Abdus Sabur Khan, the Communications Minister of Pakistan hails from Khulna and has a house over there in the suburbs of Khulna town. When the Hazarat Bal incident took place he was in Khulna and he became very active in organising protest meetings in many places in the district. It was reported by some witnesses that he made speeches in those meetings were not only anti-Indian but also anti-Hindu. The last meeting that he addressed was at Daulatpur, an industrial area close to Khulna town on January 3, 1964. Immediately after the meeting ended, thousands of workers who attended the meeting spread out in various directions and started indiscriminate assaults, some of them murderous, on the Hindus. They also went on an orgy of looting and burning of the Hindu properties. For about 4 days this went on unchecked and even when the army was called out they had orders only to patrol but no orders to shoot. The police was all the time completely inactive and the atrocities went on in their presence. The attacks were not confined to the Khulna town. All over the district similar attacks were made from the next morning suggesting a certain amount of pre-planning. In these attacks hundreds of Hindu men, women and children were killed, Hindu temples were desecrated. It is impossible to give even an approximate estimate of the loss of the Hindu property as a result of plunder and arson. The abduction and attacks on women also were numerous. Thus Khulna being contiguous to India, this started a wave of migration towards India which is still going on.

The part played by Sabur Khan can be evident from the witnesses as reported below :-

Ajit Kumar Ghorami, (Witness No.K 475), Baijo stated - "Before the riot, district council election was going on. Mr. Sabur Khan, the Minister came to our village and appealed to us to vote for his nominee Majid Mia. But the election result was quite reverse. Mr. Sabur Khan became furious and came to our village and threatened us that no place for Hindus will be possible in Pakistan. After a few days riot broke out ....”

Manoranjan Sarkar (Witness No.K 476), Gorkhali stated – “The nominee of Mr. Sabur Khan, the Pakistan Minister lost in our area in an election. Being furious Sabur Khan threatened us with the worst consequences. The riot broke out after a few days.”

Prafulla Kumar Gil (Witness No.K 468), Chamkuri stated – “Chairman, Union Board, said that Hindu population of Dakup P.S. will be treated like rats because they did not vote for Sabur Khan, the Minister of Communications.”

The witnesses have also referred to the forcible occupation of large plots of land belonging to one Rup Chand Biswas by Sabur Khan and the litigation which resulted from this. It is stated that when Sabur Khan lost in the courts the immediate result was the burning down of the house of Rup Chand Biswas, who was his next door neighbour.

Ajit Kumar Ghorami (Witness No.K 475), Baijo stated – “Mr. Sabur Khan some years back forcibly occupied the land of Shri Rup Chand Bniswas, a Hindu land owner of Matekhali village. The land was about 30 bighas. During the last 4 years, he erected 3 storied building and furnished it. Case was instituted against him. The Court decided against him. Thereafter one morning the house of Rup Chand Biswas was burnt to ashes. The nearby houses of other Hindus were also burnt. The riot began thereafter throughout Khulna District.”

Arabinda Kumar Roy (Witness No.K 852), Bilpabla stated- “Sabur Khan had forcibly occupied the land of Rup Chand Biswas 4 years ago and erected palatial building on that plot of land. Case was instituted against him. The court decided against Sabur Khan and decreed Rs.1,35,000. Sabur Khan approached Rup Chand for settlement but nothing came out of it. Sabur Khan organised meetings regarding theft of Hazarat Bal. Thereafter the attacks on Hindus began.”

Ganesh Chandra Roy (Witness No.K 1035), Santipur stated

– "I learnt about the case instituted by Rup Chand Biswas. Sabur Khan lost the case. So people were instigated to start assaults on the ground of the lost relic of Hzarat Bal. The whole of the locality of my village and nearby was burnt. I hid in Khulna for 3 days."

Some of the witnesses who were present at the meetings which were addressed by Sabur Khan and others, said - in the name of protest against the theft of Hazrat Bal, incited the mob.

Rabindra Nath Saraswati (Witness No.K 334), Buridanga stated – "he attended 3 meetings held by Sabur Khan in Rampal where anti-Hindu feelings were fomented. Leaflets, in which Hindus were warned that there would be terrible riots in Pakistan and that all Hindus will be killed, were distributed. It was stated in these leaflets 'Leave Pakistan immediately. You have no right to stay here."

He also stated that the police also fomented such feelings by saying "Kill the Hindus and take their property. Don't burn property or what will you live on."

Jaya Bandhu Adhikari (Witness No.K 340), Simartola said – Hindus were told "Sabur Sahib will show you what is the pleasure of living in Pakistan."

Birendra Nath Das (Witness No.K 1067), from Khalishpur, an industrial area in Khulna Town, said that on the day of the strike a few thousand workers from different mills in his area assembled in a meeting where speeches against the 'Hindu conspiracy', regarding the theft of Hazarat Bal, were made. The men were well armed. When they dispersed, they spread around the neighbouring localities and during the next few hours Hindu houses and properties in Senhati, Maheshwarpasha, Pabla, Daulatpur, Chandani Mal and other areas were looted and burnt, and many persons were brutally assaulted and killed. The witness says that next day when he passed through Maheshwarpasha, he found not a single house undestroyed. He added that a week later many houses in Khalispur were set on fire.

Manindra Kumar Kirtania (Witness No.K 1274), Tilok said

– "At a meeting in Loppur Bazar, Sabur Sahib said he would make shoes with the Hindu skins torn from their back, incited full communal fury against the Hindus and did everything to excite the gang of Muslims who plundered and murdered covering a vast area inhabited by thousands of Hindus."

"I saw guns in the hands of miscreants supplied by Soleman Sahib, Chairman of Loppur who came to our village after ravaging Khulna Sadar (town)."

A week after the large scale atrocities had begun, Mr. Sabur Khan addressed a meeting at a place in P.S. Baitgata. Raj Kumar Mandal (Witness No.K 746), said – "On the night of January 3, 1964, a large mob attacked and set fire to Hindu houses in the village. People started running and they were chased.

Quite a lot of persons got killed, others burnt to death. The mob was shouting with glee and also shouting the slogan of '*Jehad*'. Many women were abducted, ravished and killed. Among many, who were found dead from burns, were old people and children.

This continued for 3 days without intervention from the authorities though our place was only two miles away from Khulna town. Next day Sabur Khan, under whose connivance riot occurred was informed. He was entreated for police and military help but nothing happened.

We came back to the village after a week. Some of the houses were still smouldering. We were chased by the Muslim goondas so we ran away again and did not return for the whole month. Later on I heard Sabur Khan speaking. He said nothing about the suffering and loss of the Hindus but said that he would see to it that even the leaves of the trees of the land said '*Allah*'. He also said that he would see to it that Hindus did likewise."

Ananda Mandal (Witness No.K 396), Burbia (Kathakali) stated that the whole of Khulna was flooded by anti-Hindu activities of Muslims incited by Sabur Khan. Several other witnesses refer to similar statements made by Mr. Sabur Khan. A similar meeting was held and addressed by Mr. Sabur Khan at Daulatpur on January

3, 1964. The meeting was attended by a large number of workers.

The Millhands of Daulatpur about 20,000 strong took out a procession after a meeting. They obstructed rail and road traffic and went on beating up and killing the Hindus on their way to Khulna town shouting slogans. They seemed to have reached the town about sunset and indulged in an unchecked orgy of arson and loot of the Hindu homes and killing any Hindu who came in their way. Cases were also reported of abduction and rape of women fleeing from their homes along with their men folk.

The workers from Daulatpur also spread out in different directions working similar havoc wherever they went.

Prafulla Kumar Biswas (Witness No.K 1270), Laban Chora said that "On the day prior to the breaking out of communal riot in Khulna town, Hindus were not allowed to wear shoes, use umbrellas or ride in a rickshaw. This had to be observed as a mark of mourning for the loss of Hazarat Bal in Kashmir. I got the news of the planned riot in Khulna from a Muslim friend and left for Mangala port to stay with my uncle. I had actually jumped from the frying pan into the fire. Mr. Sabur Khan, we believe was at the root of all troubles. He was in Khulna during the riots for the marriage of his niece. What happened in Khulna was a savagery let loose. He bitterly says, "What was a game to them (Muslims) was death to the minority community. Massacre of Hindus was a part of the marriage ceremony in Khulna."

Ajit Kumar Nandi (Witness No.K 1047), Daulatpur said that "One day I went to office and heard that we will have to take off our shoes or observing the strike for the lost Sacred relic of Hazarat Bal. I went back home and after sometime saw a procession going about the town shouting a slogan 'Kill the Hindus'."

Although the disturbances started on January 3, 1964, in Khulna town and nearby areas and from Mangala port and neighbouring areas on January 4, 1964, before the large scale attacks subsided, the whole of Khulna district was affected.

Aswani Kar (Witness No.K 1310), Laban Chora stated that at the time of the attack in his area by the employees of the ship yard, Dada Company, Ispahany Company, Kata Company, etc. Sabur was present in the area.

Aravinda Kumar Roy (Witness No.K 852), said that "Our village was just near the Khulna Town. We heard that Mr. Sabur Khan organised a meeting and the people, who attended the meeting , dispersed in two ways. After their dispersal the mob went to the different Hindu villages and set fire there. Mr. Sabur Khan engaged himself in a marriage ceremony in his house. Sri Arabinda Bhattacharya, a reputed pleader of Khulna, repeatedly rang Mr. Khan for necessary action, but he regretted his inability as he was engaged."

Several other witnesses have referred to the presence of Mr. Sabur Khan in his house in Khulna (Witnesses No.K 1047, K 1312, K 1315, K 1316, K 1317). It is significant that the havoc went on all round the place while the Communication Minister of Pakistan was busy celebrating the marriage of his niece. The Governor of East Pakistan, Mr. Abdul Moneim Khan, also attended the marriage and so did the Provincial Minister. Mr. Kazi Abdul Kadar, Member National Assembly and several members of Provincial Assembly and local officials and the elite of the town as reported by Morning News, January 6,1964. These various high officials were busy celebrating the marriage in Khulna while large scale attacks on the minority community were going on.

In Khulna Sadar area there was extensive terror and the stories told by the refugees are of large scale looting of the Hindu houses and destruction by fire. There are also the same stories of wanton killing, raping of unfortunate women and destruction of the Hindu temples.

Dhiren Biswas (Witness No.K 1255), Harintala, stated that "In the first week of January, local Muslims with the help of workers of a match factory, attacked at about 8 p.m. At first they looted our houses and then set fire to them. We fled to another village, 4 miles away. When we returned after four days, we found that every thing was burnt." The witness has given the names of some of the miscreants and also the names of the persons among others whose houses were destroyed. He said that the whole village was burnt and gives names of 12 persons who lived near him, whose property was looted and houses were destroyed. He also refers to the kidnapping and rape and gives the name of the unfortunate woman. He states that she was taken away and returned after one day. The same incident has been referred to in by Witnesses K 1256 and K 1289. These two statements also corroborate the looting and the burning of the area.

Rabindra Dhali (Witness No.K 1229), Shop keeper at Khulna, said that "It was 2nd January, 1964, just at 4 P.M. the Muslims started their actions against the Hindus. I was then at another shop and met the hooligans on the way. I was made bare-footed. I returned to my shop and took shelter in the house of the L.L. By that time the mob reached that house. I again started for a safer place. The house I took shelter in was attacked at 6 P.M. L.L. and Dhiren Ghosh were stabbed and his daughter – Lila (18) unmarried – abducted. She was still untraced. I ran and ran and took refuge under the hyacinths in a pond, with a hyacinth in my hand. Darkness came down by that time. The Muslims could not follow me. Curfew was imposed at about 8 P.M. I got up. Then I went home. My three brothers were at work at Mangla Port. I came back to Khulna after 3 days and found that all my belongings in my shop were looted and destroyed. While coming to Khulna, two Goondas threatened me. Some Muslims at Khulna advised me to go away."

Snehalata Chandra (Witness No.K 1262), said that "My son was working in M/S Dada Co. at Matikhali. On January 3, 1964 at 3 P.M. he came back to the house and informed us that a procession was coming shouting anti-Hindu slogans from Dada Co. On that evening the Muslim mob attacked our area and we took shelter in timber depot (Swami Singh Co.) at Matia Khali. The mob looted our house and burnt other houses. I saw Natabar, my next door neighbour was cut down with a sharp knife. His dead body was found on the main road."

Sanyasi Mandal (Witness No.K 1200), said that "about 250 men devastated the area and also looted. I know two men Natabar Biswas and his brother Netai Biswas were murdered."

Phani Bhushan Roy (Witness No.K 277) had a shop in Khulna, said that "I was returning from my shop when 3 miscreants attacked me and robbed me. When I reached my house I found it empty. Hearing that Hindus were taking shelter in Paddy fields, I searched for them and came back home and found that lot of Hindu houses were burnt. We took refuge in a village 5 miles away and returned to Khulna after a week."

The atrocities which started in Dacca and the surrounding areas have been described by the witnesses which are reproduced below:-

There were a number of mills on both sides of the river Sitalakha. On one side there were the Adamji Mills No.1 to 4, next to it was the Dhakeswari Mills No.2, next to that is the Chittaranjan Mill and next to that is the Laxmi Narayan Mill. On the opposite site of the river were the Dhakeswari Mill No.1 and the Adarsha Mills, some of these were owned by the Hindus and a large number of the Hindu workers were employed there. Out of these workers a large number of workers were living outside the Mills' compounds, some quite close to the Mills and some in the surrounding villages.

The Adamji Mills were closed on January 13, 1964 and it is said that arms were being manufactured in the mills and that late at night they were distributed among the Muslim workers of all the Adamji Mills. The attack which started early morning of January 14th, appeared to have been preplanned because the attack was not confined to the nearby Mills but also took place in the adjoining areas where there were large number of villages in which the Hindu workers of all the Mills were living. Some of these Mills had got quarters also in which some of the officers and a number of workers lived. Some quarters were not only inside the compounds but also outside the Mills. The attack seems to have been simultaneous in different areas.

Bhupen Roy (Witness No.1338), Narayangunj, said that "I was Secretary of Laxminarayan Cotton Mills' Staff Union. M.A. Motleb was General Secretary of Workers Union. I was a weaving clerk. I had been staying in the room allotted to the Staff Union Mess inside the Mills compound. This was about a mile from the house of Motleb. My Mills were working on 14th. The other Mills were Adamji Adm. 1-4 Jute Mills, Dhakeswari Mill No.2 were at a distance of about 5 minutes walk.

On 14th I got up at 6 a.m. I saw Dhakeswari Mill No.2 was burning and heard lot of hubbub. I went to telephone the firebrigade in Narayangunj and Dacca but the fire engines did not arrive. Police did not reach till 10 a.m. I telephoned also to Sunil Bose, Managing Director of Dhakeswari in Dacca. He said that his Mill Manager had phoned him at 3 a.m. and he had asked for police and military. He had spoken to some Ministers, Inspector General of Police and Superintendent of Police. The name of manager and weaving master was Satyen Roy. I heard the account of what had happened. At about 7 a.m. about 2 to 3 thousand Hindu men, women and children rushed into the Mills and collected in our Mills. My mill was running but it was stopped and the workers went into the outer compound. Gate was closed but because of the insistence of large number of Hindus who had collected outside, the gate was opened and by 9 a.m. there were 10,000 persons in the compound. At 9 a.m. the Noakhali Muslims who were Darwans opened the gates. On this about 2,000 Muslims rushed in. Many were armed with lathis and iron rods and started assaulting. Everyone tried to rush into the mill but all could not and many were badly injured. Thereafter the Darwans closed the factory gate. Thereafter the Muslims left. No police came but Ansars came and assured us that there would be no attack. Three persons died and about 10 or 12 were injured. Many went out of the factory and went to the quarters.

I telephoned the Superintendent of Police, Officer-in-Charge of the Police Station and Deputy Inspector General of Police and many others at Dacca. At 4 p.m. 20 armed police along with an Officer came to our mill from Dhakeswari. The Officer instructed them to fire at the feet if there was an attack.

At 4-30 p.m. there was a further attack. Large numbers rushed in and attacked those in the outer compound. The police fired only in the air. On that the mob rushed out. One of the workers was killed.

In Dhakeswari Cotton Mill No.2 the attack began at 6 a.m. and went on till about 9 a.m. About 800 were killed. By the evening about 25,000 people had gathered in our compound. The police asked them to do so because the police said that they could not give protection to all the mills as the police strength was limited. Three of the staff sleeping in the Mess which was outside the main compound wall were stabbed on the previous afternoon. We came to know about this next day. They were - Pabitra Chakravarty (died later), Manoranjan Pal and Kalyan Bhowmick.

The telephone inside the Mills was controlled by the Police and they did not allow us to telephone, nor was permission granted to use the motor launch of the mills. The police said that they would take the injured for treatment. They actually took them the next day. One died, two recovered. The manager's house which was outside, was attacked in the morning (9 O'clock) on the 14th. The manager with his family rushed into the mill but his house was wholly looted. The name of the manager was Kshetra Nath Ghose. On the 15th at about 11 a.m. Motleb sent his brother and two others with whom I went to the house of Motleb which is about a mile away. I stayed with him for about 12 days. On the 15th and 16th night Mohalla Nagarkhanpur, where quite a number of well to do Hindus were staying, was attacked and looted. This I learnt from Motleb. On 16th one Harsimal's father-in-law who lives in Dacca came. He said that when the mail trains from Chittagong and Sirajgunj came to Tongi and Tejgaon Railway Stations, the Hindus were asked to get down. All those who so got down were slaughtered. The people who had taken shelter in the Lakhminarayan Mills were not allowed to go out by the police and some outside Muslims were asked to fetch milk and food for the children. They took the money but did not come back. These people had no food for 4 days from 16th to 20th.

I learnt from Sukumar Pal who had gone with the D.S.P. to visit the affected area, that at Langalbandha, where about 20,000 people had colleted from neighbouring villages, were attacked and all round the road he saw corpses lying. Five thousand to Six thousand persons had been killed. After about a few days I went to Dacca and met Dr. S. K. Sen. He said that at Golakandail (90 miles away from Dacca) there was Poush Sankranti Mela on Tuesday 14th January. This *Mela* (Fair) goes on for 7 days. About 70,000 people had collected. These people were attacked by a large mob of Muslims. There was some resistance and even some local Muslims joined in the resistance but 5,000 to 6,000 people were massacred. Quite a number of persons were treated by Dr. Sen who got information from these people. I learnt from people from Sonargaon who had come to Dacca for their migration certificates, that while I was in Dacca, the Ashram of Ramkrishn Mission was burnt and some persons killed. At Lohia Sewagram, 5 to 6 miles from Dacca, the F.M.E. School, Public Library, Vivekananda Physical Club and Hiralal Lohia Charitable Dispensary were burnt down. This was on the 16th. I was one of the founders of some of the institutions and I learnt about it at Dacca when I had gone to obtain the migration certificate."

The witness said that "Karim, the General Manager of the Adamji Group on 15th or 16th spread a rumour on the January 12, that his brother had been killed in Calcutta and declared the mills closed on January 13th and 14th." There were a few thousand workers in this group and they were supplied with weapons of various types. It was these people who started the large scale attacks. They were later joined by workers of the Demra and the Bawamy Jute Mills, the Karim Jute Mills and the Shermin Textile Mills. The workers broke up into different groups and after creating havoc in Madhavdi Bazar, they reached Golakandail.

Sumati Barman (Witness No.DF-93), a woman employee of the Laxmi Narayan Cotton Mills said – "On January 13th, 1964 the trouble began at night. The villages near the Adamji Mills were set on fire. My village was a short distance away and I could see the glow of the fire in the sky. In the morning myself and my husband with the children ran towards the L. N. Mills. The gate was closed. The gatemen was a Muslim whom I knew and I implored him to let us get inside. The gate was slightly opened and along with my two daughters and son I got into the Mills' compound but the gate was closed and no entreaty of mine would induce the gateman to let my husband in. We took shelter in the big hall. There were already about 500 or 600 persons in the hall. The mob thereafter broke open the main gate and rushed inside. They were armed with iron rods, knives and daggers and they were also carrying empty bottles of soda water and bottles containing petrol. A man caught hold of me and gave me a deep cut on my right elbow and I ran forgetting even my children and entered into a vacant room in the staff quarter. I waited there with five or six others. Then there was hammering on the door and the door gave way and a Hindu was attacked. He was stabbed twice. The man fell down unconscious. Some one among the attackers wanted to catch hold of me but the other miscreants said "Kill all the males, including male children but leave the women alone as the women will be ours." The mob attacked the mills four times. Later some military came but they did nothing and it was only much later when a large contingent of military men with rifles came that the attacks ceased after night. If the military had acted earlier lot of lives would have been saved. We remained inside the mills for 6 days and for 3 days were without food, not even enough water.

When after a week the riots subsided, we were taken with the help of military to our villages. I found that my house was completely burnt.

With the help of Kshetra Ghose, the Manager of the mills, I searched for my husband and I came to know that he had been killed on the very first day. While searching for my husband I went to the river and I looked for his body among the large number of dismembered heads and other bodies which were lying there. I could not find him among the dead.

The water of the river had turned red and remained unfit for use for a number of .days. "Dead bodies were seen floating in the river, and being carried away for some days. I saw several villages where not a single house had been left unburnt."

Santi Bhushan Datta (Witness No.DF 157), who was serving in the Chittaranjan Mills but on the day when the trouble started he was in the Dhakeswari Mill No.2. He said that "early in the morning when the first shift began about 20,000 mostly non-Bengali Muslim workers from the Adamji Jute Mills entered the Mill compound by scaling the walls, breaking open the gates as well as breaking down some portion of the wall. They rushed in swarms and turned the entire area into a vast slaughter house. Loot, arson and murder went unchecked from Sun-rise to Sun-set."

Properties both of the Mill and of the Hindu workers and their quarters were looted and burnt. At least 700 Hindus including women and children were massacred during the day. Several women were also abducted. Police came late, only with tear-gas and they used the tear-gas half-heartedly. We were taken in the evening to the Laxmi Narayan Mills. When we left, the entire mill area had a terrifying appearance. Very large number of dead bodies were scattered all around and the mill machinery was found badly damaged. Lot of cotton and cotton textiles were burnt as also doors and windows. He mentioned "names of 3 of his relatives who died inside the mills. They were his maternal grand-father, maternal-uncle and his wife. He also mentioned the names of three girls who were abducted from the mills."

Haladhar Chandra Day (Witness No.DF 130), who was serving as a Mechanic in the Dhakeswari Mill No.2 and living in the mill quarters, said that "At about 5.10 a.m. on January 14th, 1964 about 25,000 Muslims attacked the Mills. They were armed with various weapons including guns. As soon as they had broken into the Mills they started killing the Hindus indiscriminately not even sparing women and children. They set fire to the temple, cloth godowns and the quarters of the Hindus. Plundering and arson continued till noon. About 12 to 13 hundred were killed and 2,000 injured. I saw a large number of dead bodies. All this happened while the S.D.O. was there. He came at about 7 a.m. and seized the guns belonging to the Mills making it impossible to offer any resistance.

I saw large number of dead bodies floating into the river and the water was completely polluted." The witness also mentioned the names of three girls whom he knew, were missing from the Mills.

Atindra Chandra Routh (Witness No.DN 252), who was a worker in the Dhakeswari Mill No.2, living in the Mill quarters outside the Mill, where about a thousand families were also living, said that "they saw fire in Simalpur at about 1 a.m. and they apprehended something ominous. He, however, heard from some body that it was a faction fight among the members of the two Unions of the Adamji Mills.

Early in the morning thousands of these Muslims encircled the quarters. They tried to get to the gate but the gate was closed. He said that the helpless Hindus were killed mercilessly. He also mentioned that the Nepalese Darwan had opened fire to disperse the hooligans. But the S.D.O. seized the guns and thereafter savagery was let loose. He mentioned that the names of 20 persons, some of them his near relatives, who were killed in the quarters. He, his wife and his mother were all injured. He saw a number of Hindu girls being abducted. He gave the name of one who was abducted, raped and killed thereafter. He also gave the names of seven of the attackers whom he recognised. Three of them were Sardar and Mistries in the Chittaranjan Mills. The names were – Saijudin Mia, Jamal-ud-din Mistry and Razak Mistry. One of the attackers was Wazuddin Mia, an Ansar Commander. Wadur-Rahaman an Administrative Officer, Chan-Mia, Sardar of the same Mills and one Nur Islam of Narayangunj."

The holocaust which began on the night of January 13th, 1964 continued unabated for at least 5 days, although Narayangunj is only about 9 miles away from Dacca, the capital of East Pakistan. The widespread atrocities which began almost simultaneously led to the only conclusion that this was a preplanned and preconceived tactics of which the Government was quite aware. The incitement which had started after the Hazarat Bal incident was still going on. It immediately led to wide spread trouble in Khulna which had not yet abated and which should have made the Government wary. But instead of this Pakistan leaders, their news papers and the radio kept on blaring the same voice of *Jehad* and revenge against the Hindus with the inevitable result in the destruction of Hindu lives and properties difficult even to estimate. As in Khulna district, here also the exodus which began soon after the atrocities in Khulna, has not yet been halted. The reason for the exodus was the total lack of securities of the minorities. The unfortunate victims of the mob fury were of the villages namely, Bariakhali, Bhagwangunj, Chiraipara, Tejpur, Govindkul, Dassargaon, Tinggaon Jaharpur, Saharup Bazar, Bongaan Lamba Bardi, Dhamgarh, Barpara, Cochimara, Kalinagar, Kalibari, Panchamighat, Nandipara, Ananda Nagar, Kashipur, Ramgali, Nabigunj, Kumarpara, Banipar, Masaba, Nagar Khanpur etc.

Nirmal Chandra Day (Witness No.DTN-1), Nathartai Bazar, Dacca Town said – "On January 13, 1964, a meeting regarding Hazarat Bal was held in the stadium at Dacca. Witness, feeling the tension, took his family to Munshigunj. He returned later on and found his house had been looted and set on fire. This had happened on January 14th, 1964."

Sabitri Boral (Witness No.DC 1), who was a third year student of nursing and midwifery in Dacca Medical College Hospital and resident in the nurses' quarters. She said that "a large number of Hindus with stab and other wounds were brought to the hospital in heavy trucks and admitted into the hospital. Many of the indoor patients were discharged in order to make room for the injured. Some of these discharged patients were admitted in the Mitford Hospital.

No other hospital excepting the Medical College Hospital admitted victims of the assaults. About noon on January 14th, a large number of injured began to arrive in the hospital. Among them was one J.C. Ghosh, a well-known business man. He died in the hospital. We got the information that the large number of wounded and dying persons were lying on the roadside on the way to Narayangunj. The hospital authorities sent a truck to bring them to the hospital. The capacity of this hospital was about 1,100 but many more than that were already in the hospital and other injured persons had to wait for admission. There were 26 wards in this hospital. Rush of injured persons was so heavy that every available inch of space had to be utilised. The patients from the city, Narayangunj and surrounding areas were being brought all the time. The death rate in each ward was about 20 to 30 per day.

On the night of January 14th, there were three Hindu and one Muslim patients in one small room. The Muslim had accidentally received a gun-shot wound. He unfortunately died and a rumour was spread that the Hindu nurses were injecting poison into the Muslim patients. As a result of this rumour the jamadars (sweepers), ward-boys along with some miscreants collected at the back of the nurses hostel. The matron separated the Hindu from the Muslim nurses' charging the Hindu nurses with poisoning. The Hindu nurses were not allowed to go into the hospital and were locked in the hostel. Luckily Dr. Alam, a professor in the College, who performed the post mortem on the next day, declared that death was not due to any poison and he asked the Hindu nurses to rejoin duty. This did not satisfy the Jamadars, ward-boys and others who tried to attack the hostel. Then the police came and fired a few shots and the rioters dispersed.

For about 3 days there was complete chaos in Dacca. On 14th and 15th about 1,000 patients died. On the 16th Governor and the Health Minister were coming to the hospital. Before they came quite a number of patients were discharged. The Superintendent of the hospital Shamsuddin Ahamad showed only 508 injured persons as admitted owing to the disturbances when the Governor and the Health Minister visited the hospital. No Hindu dead body was handed over to the relatives but was removed to some place for disposal."

Prithi Rani Saha, who was a teacher of Vidyarthi Bhavan and also Superintendent of minority Girls hostel at Ramkrishna Road, largely a Muslim area stated that "When we heard the attacks, on January 13th, 1964, we became panicky. One Miss Sofia Khatun, a Professor in Eden Girls College, and her brother who was a C.I.D. Inspector got some constables posted there on January 13th and 14th. On January 15th, the general situation in Dacca had deteriorated and Mrs. Rokeya Kabir, a professor of Eden College came to our hostel along with the editor of *Sangbad* and tried to get more help from the police but no such help came. Therefore, they took the 40 girls from the hostel, put them in cars and took them to University Womens Hall when an attempt was made to attack them near the Ittefaq Office but the editor and women Professors managed to prevent it. The provost of the hall did not allow the girls to stay more than that night because that hostel was being threatened. Therefore, Mrs. Kabir sought assistance from the Deputy Commissioner, Dacca and the Director of Public Instruction who were on the board of the minority hostel but no help could be obtained and the girls were taken to the houses of her various relations in Ramna area where they remained for 15 days before they left for Calcutta by air, thanks to the arrangements made by Mrs. Kabir.

In Ramkrishna Mission, Tikatuli, two Hindus were stabbed to death on January15. Bani Bhaban, a minority boys' hostel at Iswar Das lane was broken into and completely looted. The boys ran away and took shelter in a camp.

There was an attack on Nari Shiksha Mandir Girls High School where at noon the miscreants broke into the School and killed Abani Guha Roy, a head clerk, and a senior teacher was stabbed on the back. While the attack was going on a young man

Hamid Ali jumped into the school compound and started shooting at miscreants with his revolver. The name of the stabbed teacher was Jagajiban Bose."

Jagajiban Bose, (Witness No.DC 3), who was a senior teacher of the Nari Shiksha Mandir Girls' School said that "During the second week of January 1964, excited, rather restless atmosphere was observed all over the city of Dacca, and movement of a particular class of people seemed suspicious – Communal tension became high and alarming – Radio and personal propaganda announcing false rumours, such as so called Greater Calcutta killing of peaceful Muslim citizens. Just after the Khulna riot where we learnt, more than 20 to 25 thousand ruffians and Mill-hands were allowed to enter the town of Khulna at a time with deadly weapons and in excited mood one evening. They were already being excited by constant propaganda of top rank authorities, such as Mr. Sabur, Minister and others. The police were inactive. Labour class people were constantly excited and induced to attack and kill a minority Hindus whose number was tolerably high in Khulna area. There were also the Christians and the Buddhists in large number in Mangala Port. They killed and destroyed property from Khulna to Bagerhat Road side, as stated and published even in local newspapers of Dacca. Thus, we the minority Hindus and the Christians, particularly the educated section, naturally became anxious and apprehended serious danger in the city of Dacca, because the Muslim migrants and common people coming from West Bengal and Calcutta area were spreading all such rumours, which caused the outbreak of serious communal disturbance organised and planned by government and a class of Muslim Mill owners. The riot-mongers began to spread more false rumours that in West Bengal working class people, mostly Hindus were determined to destroy the Muslim Bustees (slum areas) and other properties. Colourful rumours of havoc and massacre and exciting propaganda created the back-ground for unprecedented and inhuman atrocities in Dacca area that cannot be compared with any parallel incident anywhere in the World. The January communal disturbances in Pakistan surpassed all previous records and it seemed that there was no police or government organisation for some days to come.

We also noticed that in areas of Dacca like Wari, Ticatuly and in every prominent place, road-side walls were covered with slogans in bold type, "KILL HINDUS" – "HINDU, MARWARI MARO" (Kill Hindus and Marwaris) – slogans of this nature were also heard here and there; and whenever they got opportunity, the little boys rose against stray Hindus individually and pelted stones at them here and there.

Some little boys also shouted in the streets – "Ekta duita Hindu Dhar, Sakal Bikal Nasta Kar" [9](Attack one or two Hindus and kill them for breakfast and lunch).

Some prominent minority Hindu leaders approached Mr. Abdul Moneim Khan, Governor of East Pakistan, Dacca requesting him, in a joint representation, whether he would protect the Hindus, their life and property and whether the Governor wished Hindus to stay or leave Pakistan? At this, the Governor avoided them with the evasive reply that he was leaving Dacca for West Pakistan to meet the High Command at Rawalpindi.

Jagajiban Bose said that leaving aside those digressions, I just get down to my personal affairs. I am aged 58, and a graduate from the Dacca University. I was a senior teacher in the Nari Siksha Mandir Girls High School, Dacca-3, East Pakistan – for a period of 6 years. As to my identification I possess an operation mark on my forehead, which may please be noted here. While in Pakistan school service, I had been living at 20,HatkholaRoad, Dacca-3; and that my permanent home address is "Kuthi Bari", P.O. Rajanagar. The village stands on the river Ichhamati. Population of the village being about 5,000 – Hindus and Muslims – in half and half proportion – But after partition most of the Hindu population, especially caste Hindus, left their hearths and homes. Our landed properties, dwelling houses were mostly occupied by the local influential Musalmans, enjoying them free without any embarrassment. Hindu population is now 20%.

Personally, I have left about 3 acres of high lands, pucca building with 6 rooms, pucca yard, fruit garden, tanks and agricultural plot of lands - valuation approximately Rs.23,000/-.

I used to live in Dacca city, occasionally visiting the village home, which was under a caretaker – a Muslim, whom recently the Chairman of the Union has driven out and my home and building is being allotted to a refugee family.

The school was going to be closed on that day for the Ramzan holidays and the distribution of the progress reports and the filling up of forms and payment of salaries were to be made. Myself and the head-clerk reached the school at 10 a.m. Abani Guha Roy's house in Bonogram had been attacked the previous night and he had taken shelter at the camp at Wari Street from where he had come to the school. Thirty Muslim girls alone were there for the results and no Hindu girl had come, as looting, arson, stabbing and killing had occurred the previous night at Nababpur, Dacca, Narayangunj and Bonogram. All the girls except 3 left the school at 11 a.m. These three wanted to fill up their forms. At about noon we heard the sound of breaking open the main gate. The attackers had surrounded the school. The teachers and the girls were in a room and the others were elsewhere on the premises. The Muslim attackers were armed with daggers and iron rods. We tried to hold the door but it was broken open and Abani Roy was stabbed to death.

"I was stabbed on the back thrice. One Hamid Ali jumped inside the school premises with his revolver and started firing and the attackers fled. I was removed to the hospital where I remained for 17 days."

He has related that he was told by Hiralal Chatterjee, residing at Bonogram Road, that that locality was attacked at about midnight when the attackers started looting, setting fire to houses and stabbing. In his house four families consisting of 11 members were residing. All these 11 persons were stabbed. Four of whom died immediately. Hiralal along with his son went from the roof to inform the police. He came back with the police but during his absence his two daughters and his wife were seriously injured. Her arms were badly fractured and they were brought to the Medical College Hospital.

A relation of his, Geeta Ghosh, was going to Barisal from Calcutta via Khulna. At Khulna Station the miscreants started attacking the Hindus inside the compartments. Luckily in their compartment there was a Muslim family and she was given a 'Burkha' to cover herself.

The witness has related another incident of a young Hindu who was taken out of a bus near Tongi bus line and stabbed in his abdomen and left for dead. When he regained consciousness he tried to bandage himself after tearing some of his clothes. This was noticed and the miscreants put lot of hay on him and set it on fire.

The witness said that when he was in the hospital he had seen many patients with stab, gun-shot and other injuries. He mentioned the case of a young girl from Simlapara area who was brought to the hospital. Her house was broken into and looted. The miscreants thurst an iron rod through her vagina. The doctors said that she might survive this attack.

While in the hospital the witness heard from the staff that 2 morgue rooms were full of dead bodies.

The witness relates another case. One Gokul Chandra Paul was residing at Bonogram Road. He also had his tailoring shop there. The house was attacked and this man, his brother, son, and wife were killed. They spared the daughter who was a student of Eden College, but put her under a Burkha and started marching her along with themselves. On the way she saw a Muslim friend of her father and shouted to him and she was saved."

Mrs. Sujata Ghosh (Witness No.DC 4), who was the Head Mistress in Nari Sikha Mandir, Girls High School, Dacca said that "a number of miscreants, non-Bengali Muslim goondas with deadly weapons attacked the school premises, breaking open the main gate and stabbed two of her school staffs – one teacher and other the head clerk – the later case became fatal and died in a short time – the other was removed to the hospital and came round in 17 days and left Pakistan for good and arrived in Calcutta on March 1st, 1964.

In a nearby village, about 4 miles from Dacca, the miscreants killed the old mother and sister-in-law of late Abani Guha, head clerk, Nari Sikha School and the goondas also murdered the old mother of Profulla Guha, on the office staff of the Dhakeswari Cotton Mills.

In Damra village, near Dacca town the cousin sister of Sunil Bose, Director, the Dhakeswari Cotton Mills along with her children, numbering 5, were murdered on the spot – only the lady was removed to hospital where she succumbed.

The witness adds that in Lal Mohan Saha Street, Dakshin Maishandi, Dacca, the house and building of Dr. C. M. Banik, along with all furniture, huge stock of medicines, household goods and the 3 storeyed building all were burnt to ashes. Dr. C. M. Banik was the Secretary of the Nari Siksha Mandir. In the same street, their lady teacher Miss Krishna Mukherjee lost all her belongings, as the said house was also burnt to ashes with petrol and other inflammable material.

Dr. C.M. Banik lost stock of goods, furniture, building, cash amounting to about Rs.2 lacs. The incident happened in the night of January 14th, 1964. About 3 to 4 hundred miscreants forcibly entered the house of Dr. C.M. Banik and set fire to the house and next the day in the presence of armed police the goondas broke open the iron chest. The Police were absolutely inactive.

Four shops of the famous Sadhana Oushadhalaya were looted and the shop of Dass & Co. Photographers, was burnt and the shop of the O. K. Photographers and a cycle shop at Nawabpur were looted. One sweetmeat shop was looted. Approximate loss was more than one lac in all.

Nihar Ranjan Chatterji (Witness No.DC 5), who was living in staff quarters in the East Regional Laboratories, Pakistan Council of Scientific and Industrial Research, Dacca, said that "A little before Ramzan, attacks on the Hindus started in the older parts of Dacca. In the beginning houses, shops restaurants and hotels belonging to Hindus were looted. Later on arson and murder began and violence spread from the city to Narayangunj and other adjoining suburbs and areas. For the first 2 or 3 days the Government did nothing. Most of the houses and shops in Nawabpur, Thatari Bazar, Paulpara and other areas were looted and burnt. One of his relatives, also working in the laboratory, was killed and another relative, also working in the same place, was injured.

During the trouble the police refused to give any assistance on the ground that no police was available. He adds "We passed the following day and nights helplessly amidst looting, arson and killing." He says that when the trouble began he was told by some policeman that they had no orders to fire and that they were afraid of taking any action. Although some police officers were sympathetic, they were helpless.

Many Bengali Muslims in Dacca did not like what was going on but they were not bold enough to say anything. The majority of the miscreants were the non-Bengali Muslims who were creating this havoc. The educated Bengali Muslims became very frightened and asked their neighbouring Hindus to take shelter in camps. A few, however, gave shelter. Three respectable Muslims were killed while trying to protect the Hindus. Thus the number of Hindus killed was very large but the number was difficult to estimate.

An M.Sc. student (Witness No.DC 6), who resided at the Jagannath Hall in Dacca said that "the trouble started on January 14th, 1964. January 15th was the worst day. About 400 Hindu men, women and children took refuge in the Assembly hall and remained there for ten days. Then the Government compelled them to leave.

One of the refugee was a carpenter from Rayer Bazar. Mostly carpenters, potters and daily labourers lived there. The carpenter said that about 10 a.m. a large group of miscreants surrounded the area, looted it and set it on fire. Those who came out of burning houses were killed.

Three or four days later a group of about 13 or 14 women and children came to the camp. They had been injured and discharged from the hospital. The witness saw the injuries and says that even children and babies had many injuries. One of the babies had an injury on its neck. They were treated by doctors who had sought refuge in the camp. These women and children were, from the Chittaranjan Mills, Narayangunj and Tongi. The Tongi group said that their houses had been looted and burnt and there was no trace of the men. They had been taken to the hospital.

The witness refers to the attack on the Physical Training College hostel near Tejgaon. The hostel was surrounded. The Superitendent said that there were no minority person. Later on a servant boy was able to get out and with the aid of the police the Hindu students were removed. He says that in his area a girl was abducted by some Muslims but the Hindu boys rescued her. The complaint to the police proved useless.

He said that there was discrimination in Universities and hardly any jobs were available to Hindus." Hari Saran Chaudhari (Witness No.DTN 3) of 125 Nawabpur Road, said that "On January 13th, 1964, some parts of Dacca, Nawabpur, Mirpur, Rayer Bazar, Dakinmossundi, Uttermossundi, Banagram trouble had already started. On the next day the trouble started in Narayangunj, Chashara, Fatulia, Jatrabary etc. Almost all houses in his area were burnt and properties were looted. Lots of persons were killed. He went and took shelter in the Jagannath College. His neighbour Dr. Satish Chandra Deb, 126 Nawabpur Road was injured. He also says that from that house a girl of 17 was abducted on January 14th, 1964."

Bhopal Sarkar (Witness No.DSP 15) of Bonogram said that "this was a riot for which the Government was responsible and the riot was created to drive the Hindus out of East Pakistan. On January 13th, 1964, the Mill area and the adjacent areas were attacked and a large number of people were killed. Also large scale looting and arson went on. This continued for days together. Military took charge of Dacca on the 5th day and it took the army about 14 days to reach the worst affected areas.

"I saw goondas being carried in buses. Buses seemed to have been arranged to take the attackers, who were armed with deadly weapons, to carry them to the Hindu localities. Government was indifferent even about giving relief to the Hindus who had lost everything. Relief fund was raised by the Hindus of Sakhari Bazar, who gave relief to thousands who have taken refuge in the various camps. The Governor pretended not to know anything and was in fact in Karachi. Large number of women were abducted and compelled to marry the Muslims. I saw a young woman being snatched away from her husband. Dead bodies were scattered on the streets, drains, here and there. Hindu corpses polluted the river Lakha."

The principal airport of Dacca is situated at Tejgaon which is quite close to Dacca. AB (Witness No.DT 1331), who was working as a telephone operator, Trunk Exchange, Dacca and living in Tejgaon said that "On January 14th, 1964, attacks on the Hindus began in the evening at Kawran Bazar in Tejgaon. Two Hindus were stabbed to death at about 4 p.m. At about 6 p.m. the house in which she lived was set on fire. The inmates would have been killed but for the intervention of the police. There was a police camp nearby and at night time with the help of the police, she with her sister, ran hurriedly to the house of Krishna Paul, where a large number of Hindus had collected. Her brother-in-law hid himself in the house.

Next morning the neighbouring house of Surya Paul where 50 women had taken shelter, was attacked. There were only two men inside who tried to keep the door from being forced. But it was forced open. Some armed police came and started firing at random and ruffians went away, but as a result of that firing a number of persons died inside that house. Then the ruffians proceeded towards the 'South Paul Para' setting fire to the Hindu houses. Then the witness, along with others, left that house, started going towards theNorth Paul Para and took refuge inside the large open area bounded by walls. In this compound about 600 Hindus had taken shelter. Witness said that she saw that the Chittagong-Dacca-Narayangunj train was stopped at Kawran Bazar and a large number of Hindu passengers were taken out of the train and butchered. After this incident the police told them that they were unable to help the unfortunate Hindus, and were not going to risk their lives. The police then left some time after this. One of the Hindus went to nearby saw-mill to telephone the Tejgaon Police Station. The police sent some assistance and at mid-night the police took them out to a safer place. When they got out, she said there were dead bodies lying on the road. In spite of the police escort the miscreants attacked the Hindus from behind. But the Police fired and the attackers retreated. Ultimately about 800 Hindus were approaching the Tejgaon police station but once more they were attacked near Tistari Bazar.

They remained at the Police Station for 5 days and then were shifted to the Jagannath Hall camp in Dacca and there they stayed for 7 days.

While in the camp, she used to go out passing herself off as a Muslim and visited several camps in the city as well as the Medical College Hospital. She said that she used to shudder at the dreadful horrors which she saw."

Rayer Bazar is a locality on the outskirts of Dacca city. This area was one of the worst affected areas. It must be noticed that the attacks went on unabated for several days as in other places.

Lal Behari Paul (Witness No.DT 128), said that "his area was attacked at about 3 p.m. All the houses were looted and about 250 houses were burnt. At the time of the attack the assailants entered his house by breaking open the doors. His father was hit with a rod. His right arm was fractured and he received other injuries too. His elder brother was stabbed to death. His sister's husband was stabbed to death in the street. He said that more than 150 Hindus, men, women and children were killed while they were running to find safety. He, along with his mother and sister, took shelter in the house of Kalipada Paul, which was set on fire afterwards. He mentioned the names of a mother and daughter who tried to seek shelter in the house of Chairman Unus but they were driven away. They were caught hold of by the ruffians and raped on the street. The husband and father tried to intervene but he was stabbed. The women were kept in the house of some Muslims from where they were later rescued.

In this area there were numerous cases of rape but we do not propose to deal in detail with these cases. It is, however, necessary to mention that the several women of a Paul family were the unfortunate victims. This had been mentioned by numerous witnesses. Some of them are the relatives of the unfortunate girls. There were several other cases whereas witness DT 30, said her pregnant daughter-in-law was raped at the point of a dagger. And when she was recovered, she had to be taken to the hospital."

Bidesh Chandra Paul (Witness No.DT 129), an old and blind man, says that he was in his house with his son and other members of his family, when he heard that Muslims were attacking the Hindu houses and looting and burning them. Excepting his eldest son, the rest of the family left the house. Soon thereafter the assailants rushed into his house. He heard his son's entreaties but his son was killed. Thereafter he himself was hit on the head with a rod and fell down unconscious.

Saradhani Dasi (Witness No.DR 93), said that "On January 16th, 1964, in the morning a Muslim mob came to the village in 11 buses. They ran away and took shelter in a bamboo thicket. "During the attack", she said – "My sister who was struck with an iron rod by a Muslim and her belly was knifed open, then the unborn child was pulled out from the womb and killed with a dagger. They placed the dead body under the dead mother's head. A two years old son of my sister was killed with the dagger."

Ramananda Mitra (Witness No.DR 22), of village Masaba, who was a boy of 13 years old said that "they heard in the middle of January that the attacks on the Hindus in various villages had started few hours earlier. Large number of Hindus from nearby villages being panicky came to this village which was largely a Hindu village. The loot and arson were continuing in the nearby villages and they were apprehending an attack. They sent the chowkidar to Rupgunj P.S. The officer came and he later sent two armed policemen. They asked the police when they saw a mob at some distance, to fire in the air but the police refused and they went away. His father had started shifting their belongings to the house of one Islam Bhuia of Chandpara, a friend of his father, where the family also shifted. Accompanied by Islam Bhuia he and his father went back to the village to get some more of their belongings. This was during the day. While they were in the house the attack came and he saw that it was led by Abdul Hamid and Zomma, policemen of Perabo. He saw Abdul Hamid taking money from two rich fleeing Hindus on the threat of killing them. He then slipped out of the house and went to the house of a Hindu neighbour. The house was empty and he saw Shahajuddin of village Parabo struggling to lift a heavy load of booty. He threatened witness with a dagger unless he helped to lift on his head which the witness did. He again saw Hamid taking away everything from a Hindu who was trying to flee.

Next morning his uncle went in search of shelter in a Hindu house in the nearby locality and the witness went to Golakandyl. While he was there he saw in the morning a large number of armed Muslims shouting 'Jehad going along the road when soon thereafter a part of this mob attacked this village. He ran and hid himself in a bush. He says that from his hiding place he saw this mob killing the Hindu men, women and children. The witness was dressed as a Muslim and therefore he luckily escaped the fury. He said he saw all around fields strewn with innumerable mutilated bodies. Among these assailants he saw his Muslim teacher armed with a big dagger who recognised him and told him to run towards the southern direction if he wanted to save himself.

The witness started running but all around he saw the same scene. Among the dead and injured he saw his neighbour Chandra

Sarkar, an old man, lying badly injured. A Muslim who knew the witness came and demanded money from him. He had only four annas which he offered to give to the Muslim. But this was contemptuously refused. He then returned to the house of Bhuia and was told that his family had been shifted to another place, otherwise they would have been murdered as the assailants were searching the Muslim houses.

While he was resting there Bhuia's brother Alam asked him if he would become a Muslim and on his keeping silent, threatened to kill him but he was saved by Bhuia. During the night he slipped out of that house and proceeded towards his own village and saw on both sides of the fields innumerable dead bodies and some injured who were groaning in pain. He came near a pond and decided to hide himself there behind the bushes, but seeing a floating head he got scared and spent the night in the field in the bitter cold.

Next morning a group of Muslim fishermen met him and one of them taking pity on him offered to adopt him. The witness, however, refused and he proceeded towards his village thinking by that time trouble might have subsided. There was not a soul to be seen and the houses had been completely ravaged and were still smouldering. He ran from there towards the village Bhulta. There a large number of Hindus who had taken shelter in the house of Gol Box Bhuia, had been murdered and the nearby pond was full of swelling decomposed bodies.

Then he ran again and returned to the house of Bhuia. Alam met him but by now he had softened. Later Alam told him to go with him to collect loot from Golakandyl. When they reached there the Muslims were taking away everything they could. He helped Alam to collect the booty and on their way back they saw a very badly injured woman lying in a ditch. Alam wanted to kill her but the witness managed to persuade him not to do. They went back. Next morning he learnt that his parents were staying in a refugee camp in the village Diraba. Later they returned to their own village and Islam Bhuia helped them in every possible manner to resettle and returned to them all that they had taken to his house for safe keeping. The whole family, however, decided to leave Pakistan because of complete insecurity."

Jagat Chandra Malik (Witness No.DR 126) of the village Ariaba, was a Chowkidar in charge of 5 villages. When he saw that the nearby villages, among them were Nandipur, Kalibari, Bhekur, Diabari, Singlaba, Kachpur and other villages under police station Baidur Bazar, were burning he sought help from the police station and two armed police were sent. Similarly he says that the chowkidar of Masaba which is a neighbouring village had also asked for help. Later on in the evening when he reached with the police the village of Masaba, they saw fire in another neighbouring village Sutalara and he asked the police to fire in the air but they refused and ran away. He has described the scenes of slaughter of fleeing Hindus in the nearby fields and fires all round. In this attack he and many of his family members were badly injured. He fell down unconscious. His elder brother was killed. He says that although he was in his Chowkidar's uniform, he was not spared. When he became conscious he did not know what had happened but he heard the voice of his wife. A boy who went in search of water was caught hold of. A gang of Muslims put his head under the mud. But thereafter the assailants left and the boy was saved. While they were lying in the field a gang came at noon and stabbed to death number of injured Hindus. Same thing happened later on in the evening. "He and his wife finally managed to reach the village of his mother-in-law. He has shown the injuries to the questioner."

It is evident from many other villages in P.S. Rupganj witnesses have given accounts of attacks on the villages similar in nature and names of their relatives who were killed and names of some of the women who were raped. The affected villages were thus known as – Naora, Kaotola, Nayamati, Gaptali, Ichapur Saughat, Basulla, Bailpara Titabo, Gurgaon, Boruna, Taipkia, Bahila Bainadi, Soni, Harigaon, Rupshi, Saunaurapara, Golpara, Bania, Dighia Pur, Chani Narsingaon, Bansinagar, Meshrabaz (Dighirpar), Bolabo, Atlarpur Damra, Shewgaon, Murari, Hatipara

Khadone, Kiravo, Tetlabhog etc.

Santiprabha Rai (Witness No.DJ 3), of Jaydebpur, P.S. Jaydebpur, Dacca, said that "On the night of January 13th, disturbances began. In terror, we fled to nearby jungles. Next day there was arson, looting and stabbing in full swing. Miscreants, dagger in one hand and bottle of wine in the other, danced devilishly putting ghungur (dancing bells) on their feet and thus stabbing people. We saw dead bodies in pools of blood on roadside. When we were in jungles our house was looted. After staying for eight days in jungles we went to Rajhari camp. After staying there for six days we came back to our own house. But at night we did not dare to sleep in our own house, went to a neighbouring Hindu rich man's house. Habejuddin Miya gave us shelter for the whole day but at night drove us out.

Similar are the accounts given by witnesses from Channa, Rudrapur, Kamarjuri, Kaddanandan, Majlispur, Titargati, Palasona, Padmapara, Bisiakuri bari, Babupara, Deora, Kudaba, Pagar, Chikalia, Mudipara Andharal, Dhippur, Mashertek, Gacha, etc.

Both in the Khulna and the Dacca districts practically all the witnesses have said that there was no security of life or property or honour of women and they were living in constant fear of Muslims who took from them whatever they wanted, reaped away their harvest, lifted their cattle, bamboos, paddy, hay, vegetables, utensils, fishing nets, boats and any other valuables they may have. They also say that in many places they were told by the local Muslims that there was no place for Hindus in Pakistan. All the people, who have come away, have left behind their lands and properties, in some cases substantial. Many had flourishing business but because of this utter insecurity they came away with the clothes they were wearing. There were also numerous cases of forced conversions or threats of such conversions and forced marriages. Large number of people who have come away are humble folk like cultivators, weavers, shop keepers, fishermen and industrial workers.

Mrityunjoy Saha (Witness No.BMS 3), Jhautala Road, Barisal town said that "when riot broke out, Mr. S. Nur Mohammed, a Bengali District Magistrate took swift action and arrested 50 notorious Muslim goondas from Chamarpati, imposed section 144 and kept the situation under control.

The local influential Muslims, including lawyers, organised a secret meeting and sent a joint petition to Dacca High Command, demanding S. Nur Mohammed's immediate removal, for they said, he was siding with the Hindus and oppressed good Muslims. Witness said that Mr. Mohammed got his transfer order within 2 days as demanded by the local influential persons. The new Magistrate withdrew Section 144 and released all the arrested goondas. He said that the attacks began in a renewed fury. Quite a large number of Hindu shops were looted and burnt. Several were murdered. Chaos and confusion took hold of the town and the Hindus were the defenceless victims. Witness said that he and his family moved out of the town and left Pakistan for India.

Monoranjan Roy (Witness No.BMS 43) of Kumarkhali village said that in the month of January riot broke out in Barisal town where he had his furniture shop. It was burnt by the Muslim miscreants with petrol. He was hit by a spear on the right leg. He left for his village home Kumarkhali and left Barisal for the following reasons :-

1) Life was insecure.
2) Cows taken away.
3) The daughter of Sri Aswini Kumar Datta (age 16) was forcibly taken away. The daughter and wife of Sri Kamini Kumar Paik, were also taken away. They were traced out with police help after a month from the Muslim's Houses.
4) Economic boycott. Had no employment there. Could not start my business anew.

There were many other witnesses who were also the victims and expressed the similar atrocities on them. The similar incidents of atrocities occurred in Comilla District, Rajshahi District,

Mymensingh and Sylhet districts. Rev. N. A. Kirkwood, Liaison Officer for Church World Service in his report of a survey of Garo Hills Refugee Camps, made in March, 1964 said that "A book could be written on the atrocities, shooting, bayoneting, baton attacks and raping inflicted by the East Pakistan Rifles and Ansar personnel of the East Pakistan border forces upon the fleeing refugees. Stories of looting and of the abduction of tribal maidens by the Muslim men of the area are common. More could be written concerning reasons for the fear and insecurity which caused this mass exodus of these minority groups into the Garo Hills from this border strip of East Pakistan."

There are similar reports in the World Press ranging from Argentina to West Germany which mention the mass migration from Mymensingh District into the Garo Hills of Assam. The southern border of Assam (India) coincides with the northern border of Mymensingh District. The northern part of Mymensingh District which is also hilly is inhabited by various tribes like Marak, Sangma and Momin, who are largely Christians. There are also the Hajongs who contain a mixture of Christians and non-Christians. There were also the Hindu tribes of Rajbansis, Kochs and Kacharis. These tribals live mostly in the hills but there are some who inhabit the plains, south of the hills.

In this area also the general insecurity had been existing for a considerable time but the large scale atrocities which began in early January in Khulna and the other southern districts and in Dacca District from January 13, 1964, resulting in large scale attacks on these unfortunate tribals largely composed of Christians.

The first wave of migrants entered the Garo Hills of Assam on January 18th, 1964, most of these being Christians. Soon the attention of the world became focussed on this migration. The World Press reported it widely, because by the end of February 80,000 refugees had crossed into Assam. It may be mentioned here that the exodus of Christians in large numbers led some foreign correspondents to go to Tura, where the fleeing refugees were being received and housed in an improvised camp.

On February 6th, 1964, a large group of about 3,000 refugees started for India. These were from the villages close to the border. They were ambushed on the way and fired upon, and only 1500 managed to cross the border. Many of these injured were treated for gun-shot wounds in Tura hospital. How many of the 1500 were killed is not possible for us to determine but the witnesses who managed to cross the border on that fateful day described a large scale shooting by the Pakistani police or the East Pakistan Rifles in which many people were killed and many more injured.

Seeing that these unfortunate people were driven out of their homes and told to leave Pakistan, it is difficult to understand why the shooting took place. It is possible, as the large scale exodus of Christians had aroused a tremendous interest in the Christian World, as reflected by the World Press, that the authorities in Pakistan wanted to stop a further exodus. And if that was the intention, it could only be achieved by stopping the harassment and the attacks on the villagers. However, that was not done and the exodus continued unabated. It may be mentioned that the attacks which began in January 1964, were led by members of the E.P.R., the police, the Ansars and the Chairmen and Members of the Union Councils.

On February 7, the Chief Secretary of Pakistan was informed about the firing by a telegram by the Assam Government. The Ministry of External Affairs of India presented a formal note to the Deputy High Commissioner of Pakistan on February 13th, 1964, in which the shooting was referred to as "cold blooded murder".[10]

The World Press took notice of the atrocities and reported the reason for this exodus. *The Observer* (U.K.), February 23, 1964, published a despatch by James Mitchell date lined, Tura, February 22, 1964. In this despatch reference had been made to James Wood, Baptist from Lincoln, Nebraska and Julius Downs from New York City, both missionaries who had lived in Garo Hills for more than 10 years. These two confirmed the stories of the refugees mentioned in the despatch. The despatch also mentions Father Antoni Buccieri, a Sicilian priest heading the Roman Catholic Mission in Tura (in

Garo Hills, Assam), since 1939. All these missionaries agreed that the refugees had been driven out of Pakistan.[11]

The Sunday Telegraphs (U.K.), February 23, 1964, published the following abstract from its New Delhi correspondent : "About 35,000 Pakistani Christians including children from border areas between Mymensingh in East Pakistan and the Garo Hills District of Assam have been fleeing from alleged religious intolerance for the past month."[12]

The Globe and *Mail* (Canada), March 2, 1964, refers to the despatch from Dacca which said – "Calls for 'Jehad' or holy war against infidels are being shouted."[13]

The Nepali, March 3, 1964, in its leading article stated : "As a result of '*Jehad*' against the minorities in East Pakistan for the last two months or so, news has been coming about the flight of the afflicted people in large numbers as refugees."[14] (The evidence of the victims are enclosed in Annexure – 3).

The Committee of Enquiry reported that "it is now a matter of history that there were no communal disturbances in any part of India prior to January 10, 1964. From about January 5, 1964 started pouring into India an influx of several thousand people per day from East Pakistan. People who had lost their near and dear ones in unprovoked and merciless attacks and people who had been looted of all their possessions and belongings and people who had left the land and houses where they had been born and brought up and which they had at one time loved and cherished."

It was also reported that the authorities in India and particularly the Government of India and West Bengal could hardly have anticipated such mass migrations of men, women and children who had fled for their lives leaving their next-of-kin butchered or dying and their properties and belongings pilfered or reduced to ashes. Though completely taken unwares and overwhelmed by the problem of receiving daily, thousands of migrants and providing to them medical-aid, food and shelter, the Government of India and the Government of West Bengal took all possible steps to ameliorate the sufferings of the grief-stricken migrants. Among the refugees, there were parents who had lost their sons and daughters and grandchildren, women whose husbands had been butchered before their very eyes, husbands or brothers who had seen their wives and sisters being raped or abducted, children who had lost their parents or whose father had been killed and mother abducted. There were men, women and children who had been injured and still bleeding or whose wounds had not been healed. There were women who had not only been deprived of what little ornaments or jewellery they had but of some of the clothes which they were wearing and who entered this country either wholly nude or semi-nude. There were men, women and children who had walked miles after mile, without food or water and who had blisters on their feet rendering them incapable of walking any further. The only reason, they could think of, for these atrocities and suffering was that they had the misfortune of being members of the unwanted minority community, who were being eliminated and driven out and that the government and the authorities in East Pakistan did not care whether they lived or died or left East Pakistan.

The harrowing tales told by these migrants infuriated a certain section of the people in West Bengal and the goondas and hooligans seized upon this or indulging in what came to be known as communal incidents in Calcutta city and in the suburbs.

Later, in March 1964, there were similar incidents in industrial townships of Jamalpur and Rourkela and a few other places. Since communal incidents have taken place in Calcutta, Jamshedpur and Rourkela and a few other places in India and there has been loss of life and property, it was considered necessary to investigate into these incidents as well. It may be observed that the Government of Pakistan, the President of Pakistan, Cabinet Ministers and politicians and the press in Pakistan did their very best between December 28, 1963 and January 3rd, 1964 to arouse a mass hysteria against the minority community in East Pakistan and that the large-scale murders, rape, abduction, looting and arson were the direct results of such mass hysteria which, when fanned and at its zenith, the Pakistan authorities did nothing or little to put down. They burnt the effigie of Jawaharlal Nehru, the Prime Minister.[15] On the contrary, even after the find of the Holy Relic the responsible members in the Pakistan Government made fiery speeches doubting the genuineness of the Relic and thereby aggravating a situation which had already taken a vicious turn resulting in the loss of a few thousand precious and innocent lives and rendering more thousands insecure, homeless and destitute.

The Pakistan authorities flatly denied the happenings in Khulna, Mangla Port and other places and adopted the role of advising the Government of India to maintain law and order in India and to protect the minorities when communal incidents took place in Calcutta and its suburbs on January 10th, 1964 and on the subsequent days.

NOTES AND REFERENCES

1. Jayanta Kumar Ray, *Democracy and Nationalism on Trial*, p-25.

   "Immediately after Partition, the Punjabi bureaucrats, with their Muslim League collaborators, set assiduously to the task of tyrannizing the minorities and those Muslims who abhorred communal violence. They drafted hooligans into the National Guards (also called 'Ansars'), and patronized the 'Kuttis' in order to accomplish this task. The Kuttis were the descendants of riffraffs imported from Bihar by the Nawab of Dacca who employed them to provoke or mastermind communal riots, clearly set apart from the general body of East Bengalee Muslims and Hindus, spoke a dialect that was a mix-up Dacca Bengali, Hindi and Urdu. After Partition, they became the unofficial army of the Muslim League and began to carry out the mission of oppressing the minorities systematically and to create an atmosphere of horror from which the Hindus could only seek an escape into West Bengal."
2. Menon, V. P., *The Transfer of Power In India*, p-435.
3. Memorandum submitted before the Hon'ble Prime Minister of Pakistan by Members of the Opposition Party (Assembly), East Bengal on 20. 3. 1950.
4. Pravash Chandra Lahiry, *India Partitioned and Minorities in Pakistan*, p.26.
5. Letter of Trailokya Nath Chakrabarti, published in the Hindustan Standard on March 19,1964.

6. A Report to the Indian Commission of Jurists by its Committee of Enquiry, Recurrent Exodus of Minorities from East Pakistan and Disturbances in India, p-51.
7. Ibid.
8. Ibid, p.56-57.
9. Taslim Nasareen, *Dwikhandita*, p-252.
10. Lok Sabha Debates, Ref. Column 2578, Wednesday February 26, 1964.
11. *The Observer*, UK (dt.Feb. 23 1964), James Mitchell date lined, Tura, February 22, 1964.
12. *The Sunday Telegraph* (UK), February 23, 1964.
13. *The Globe* and *Mail* (Canada), March 2, 1964.
14. *The Nepali*, dt. March 3, 1964.
15. *Pakistan Times*, January 3, 1964.

    The Pakistan Times reports on January 4, 1964, that on the previous day hartal (protest stoppage of work) were observed and at the meeting, among other things, a call for 'Jeehad' was made. Effigies of Mr. Nehru, the Indian Prime Minister, as a symbol of communal hatred, were burnt

4

THE CONTRAST

In glaring contrast to the roles played by the Pakistan authorities and the press of giving provocation for and abatement of the atrocities committed in East Pakistan on helpless minority community, the attitude adopted and the steps taken by the Indian leaders and the press and the right-thinking citizens speak eloquently of the position of the minority community in India.

COMMUNAL VIOLENCE IN CALCUTTA AND WEST BENGAL[1]

On the morning and late night of Friday January 10th, 1964, communal incidents occurred in Taltola, Beniapukur, Entally and Beliaghata police station areas of Calcutta where stray cases of assaults, arson and looting were reported. The police opened fire on five occasions and used 36 rounds of tear-gas.

On the afternoon of January 11th, 1964, to aid the civil authorities, the military took positions in different parts of Calcutta. On the same day, an order under section 144 Criminal Procedure Code 1898 was issued banning all processions throughout the city. On the same day, (10 p.m. to 5 p.m.) curfew was also clamped down, in the four above mentioned police station areas as also in Amherst Street police station area and in Nadia and Howrah districts.

The Chief Minister Mr. P. C. Sen, who was in constant touch

with the Indian Home Minister Mr. Gulzarilal Nanda in New Delhi, toured the disturbed areas for over two hours. Members of both communities had to be evacuated from certain trouble spots.

The Muslim leaders of West Bengal viz. Mr. Kazim Ali Meerza, M.L.A., Mr. Jehangir Kabir, M.L.A., Mr. Ziaul Haque, M.L.A., Mr. Mohamed Syed Mian, M.L.C., Mr. Karim Hossain, M.L.A . and Mr. T. M. Zarif issued a statement condemning the oppression on the minority community in East Pakistan and expressing hope that the people and the government of East Pakistan would immediately arrange to stop the communal orgy. They also mentioned that "We, who belong to the Muslim minority community in India have been living peacefully with equal opportunities and privileges .. .."

On January 11, 1964, Mr. Gulzarilal Nanda, Indian Home Minister, who was constantly in touch with the Chief Minister of West Bengal issued statement for safeguarding the rights, and life and property of all our citizens regardless of any provocations from elsewhere which may stirred them.

The West Bengal Government has taken prompt and firm measures and will continue to take all actions necessary to put an end to the activities of the hooligans and lawless elements.

In a statement, on the night of January12, 1964, Mr. Nanda said : "Every Muslim life is sacred to us. For the life of a single Muslim the whole force will be mobilised, if necessary."

By the night of January 12th, 1964, over 2000 persons had been arrested and detained by the police and by January 15,1964, 3473 persons had been arrested and detained in Calcutta city alone. The number in the districts totalled 4500. The relief department of the state of West Bengal took prompt steps for finding food and shelter for nearly 50,000 people, of both communities, who had been evacuated. The number of casualties in the disturbances in Calcutta and the Districts till midnight of January 14th, 1964 were 163 killed and 622 injured.

Miss Padmja Naidu, the Governor of West Bengal placed

eight rooms in the Raj Bhavan at the disposal of the State's Rehabilitation Minister Miss Abha Maiti for giving shelter to the homeless. She had also offered a portion of her kitchen at the Raj Bhavan to the Women's Branch of the West Bengal Citizen's Council for cooking food for 2000 displaced persons.

On January 14th, 1964, there was considerable improvement in the situation and the hours of curfew were reduced from 5 p.m. to 7 p.m. The District Magistrate of Nadia, on January 14, 1964, imposed heavy punitive taxes in the disturbed areas within the police stations of Tehatta, Kotwali, Santipur, Ranaghat, Chakdah and Haringhata. The Block Development Officers of the respective areas were asked to assess the damages after collecting petitions from individual victims. The total assessment of the punitive tax in a particular area being the total loss suffered by the victims.

In the early morning of January 15th, 1964, the Calcutta police raided the Chhoti Masjid in J. K. Ghosh Road (under Maniktolla police station) and recovered one six-chamber revolver, two pipe-guns, one country-made pistol, 62 rounds of live cartridges, about 300 grams of arsenic sulphur, about 150 grams of potassium chlorate and one chopper.

The Chief Minister of West Bengal stated on January 15th, 1964, that as a result of the incidents in Nadia and 24 Parganas, 5271 Indian Muslims had gone over to East Pakistan. As against this, Pakistan Radio claimed that the number was 1,05,000.

About 30,000 citizens of Calcutta joined a peacemarch organised by the Central Peace Committee on January 16, 1964. The Chief Minister Mr. P. C. Sen and the Mayor of Calcutta also took part in this peacemarch. The procession also included numbers of the State Legislature, trade unionists, politicians, educatioinists and writers.

Maulana Mohd. Umer Kamal Al-Madani, Pesh Imam (chief priest) of Nakhuda Mosque, Calcutta issued a statement on January 19, 1964 wherein he said that "All right-thinking men will deplore the recent tragic events in Khulna and Jessore in East Pakistan and their repercussions in Calcutta and its suburbs and also in other parts of West Bengal.

I am grateful to the Government of West Bengal and the military authorities for the prompt, firm and effective steps they have taken to bring the situation under control, as a result of which the situation has greatly improved.

But what about the future? I, in the name of humanity, earnestly appeal to the Governments of Pakistan and India to provide full protection to the minority communities in both countries and to ensure all possible measures to prevent recurrence of such tragic events in future.

I also appeal to the press in Pakistan and West Bengal to avoid the publication and comments of such news which cause tension, panic and repercussions; and thus to contribute effectively in promoting harmony and goodwill in both countries. I hope my appeal will not fall on deaf ears.

The Calcutta Corporation Councillor, S. M. Salauddin Khan and his brother were arrested on February 16th, 1964 in the Beniapukur area of Calcutta under the Defence of India Rules for indulging in anti-national activities. Another man Maulana Wasim Ahmed who was a resident of Badauni in the State of Uttar Pradesh and who was indulging in anti-national activity was externed from West Bengal on February 16th, 1964, in exercise of the powers under the Defence of India Rules.

The influx of refugees from East Pakistan kept mounting up day by day. During March 12th-14th, 1964 alone, the daily average of arrivals of refugees in West Bengal through Gede, Petrapole and Hasnabad was a little over 3,000 persons. On March 13th, 1964, about 1900 refugees left Calcutta for Dandakaranya. On March 14th, 1964, another batch of 1,650 left; besides, there were 1000 each still waiting for transport at Gede, Petrapole and Hasanabad.

On March 14th, 1964, about 1,100 migrants left Hasanabad for Howrah in the 'refugee special train.' But by afternoon, more than 1,200 men, women and children reached Hasanabad from beyond the border and nearly 400 had crossed into Hingalganj by crossing the river. Most of these migrants stated that they had been harassed and tortured by the Pakistani police and by the majority community.

Sixteen non-political Muslim organisations of West Bengal made an appeal on March 19th, 1964, to His Holiness the Sheikhul-Azhar of Cairo, H.H. Grand Mufti of Palestine and H.H. the Mufti of Saudi Arabia. In this appeal, they requested these Divines to issue a *fatawa* against Pakistan for stopping further atrocities on the minorities in Pakistan and for exposing the hollowness of the repeated cries of *Jehad* from Pakistan. According to them, *Jehad* was only reserved for the protection of 3 holy places in Arabia and not for Kashmir or for any other purposes which had nothing to do with Islam.

In justification of their appeal the signatories stated that "according to the fundamental principles of Islam the *Zimmis* (The non-Muslim citizens of an Islamic state) cannot be tortured or victimised either by the Government or by the people of an Islamic State and if a non-Muslim is killed by a Muslim the Government must hang the killer or a compensation of at least Rs.10,000 shall be paid to the heirs and successors of the non-Muslim victim with the consent of the heirs of the non-Muslim victim. But the so-called Muslim rulers of Pakistan have openly violated the orders of *Quran* and *Hadis* of our Prophet Hazrat Mohammad [Peace be upon Him (PBUH)] by committing atrocities on the unarmed and helpless minorities of East Pakistan.

The Pakistan rulers should bow down their heads and should pray to *Allah* with their folded hands to request him to forgive them for their inhuman atrocities committed on the non-Muslims of Pakistan, otherwise they are destined to go to hell after the doomsday."

As stated earlier the special refugee trains would pass through Tatanagar (Jamshedpur) in the state of Bihar, Rourkela, Jharsuguda and Brajrajnagar in the state of Orissa and Raigarh in the state of Madhya Pradesh. The distance from Howrah to Tatanagar being 250 Kilometers, to Rourkela being 415 Kilometres and to Raigarh being 585 Kilometres the refugee trains used to make short halts at Tatanagar, Rourkela and Raigarh Stations and very often local citizens of these places took food to these stations for feeding the Refugees.

INCIDENTS OF RAIGARH IN MADHYA PRADESH

In the early hours of January 19th, 1964 there was sudden outbreak of communal violence in Raigarh town. In this, nine members of the minority commuity lost their lives and several more got injured before the police came on the scene. There were a few cases of arson as well. On their arrival, the police evacuated the members of the minority community from the affected areas and accommodated them in the police station premises. The Deputy Inspector General of Police, Eastern Range and the Commissioner of Police, Bilaspur Division, rushed to Raigarh with a large armed police force. Curfew was clamped down and an order prohibiting assembly of more than 4 persons or carrying of weapons was issued. Home guards were also summoned to help prevent recurrence of troubles. The Madhya Pradesh State Government also issued, immediately, an appeal to the people to remain calm and to refrain from any action that might aggravate the situation. There were no further incidents in Raigarh.

INCIDENTS OF JAMSHEDPUR IN BIHAR

On the afternoon of March 19th, 1964 a crowd of about 400 persons was returning from the Tatanagar railway station, after seeing off several batches of East Pakistan refugees proceeding to Dandakaranya from Howrah through Tatanagar station. Some members of this crowd attempted to set fire to wayside shops but the police arrived on the scene in time and averted mischief. A section of the crowd then attacked the police party by hurling stones and brickbats resulting in injury to three persons including a sub-inspector of police. On the same day, a crowd of about 50 persons set fire to four wayside shops in Bermo Mines Bazar area. The police arrested about half a dozen miscreants on the spot. There was a lot of tension in the township but no case of assault had taken place.

On March 20th, 1964, there were some cases of assault on the minority community as a resultof which six persons died and several others were injured. The trouble spots were the suburb of Adityapur and Jugslai. There were also some stray cases of incendiarism and looting. Earlier a mob of about 1000 attempted to raid the Tata-Patna train at Tatanagar station. An eight hour curfew from 9 p.m. to 5 a.m. was imposed and continued till March 22, 1964. An order prohibiting, during the next fortnight, assembly of more than 4 persons or carrying of weapons was also issued.

The casualty list until 2 a.m. on March 21st, 1964 was 31 killed and 21 injured in stray incidents. By March 21st, 1964, the trouble had also spread to other localities of Jamshedpur town viz. Kasidih, Bhalubasra, Bagbera and Karnandih. One person died and some others were injured in police firings in Kasidih, Bhalubasra, Bagbera and Karnandih areas of Jamshedpur. The mob frenzy was at its peak on this day. The death-roll in Jamshedpur was 55 till 6 p.m. on March 21st, 1964. One among these was a result of police firing. Intensive Magesterial and police patrolling of street and armed pickets at strategic points helped to halt further casualties and damage. There were 261 miscreants arrested and detained.

The Chief Minister of Bihar Mr. Krishna Ballabh Sahay and the Education Minister Mr. Satyendra Narain Sinha camped in Jamshedpur from March 21 to 24, 1964 on which latter date they left for Patna. During their stay, they guided and supervised the arrangements for restoring law and order and for affording relief and resettling the minority community who had been evacuated to safe places.

Most of the members of the minority community numbering about 30000 to 36000 were evacuated and given shelter in two big camps in safer areas and in the premises of schools and cinema houses numbering about 15.

Mr. Gulzarilal Nanda, the Union Home Minister accompanied by Mr. S. P. Singh, Special Secretary in the Union Home Ministry came to Jamshedpur on March 25th, 1964 and stayed on for two days. Sarvodaya leader, Mr. Jayaprakash Narayan, visited Jamshedpur and addressed six largely attended meetings in different parts of Jamshedpur which helped in toning up the morale of the people and in creating an atmosphere congenial for restoration of confidence.

The Citizens' Committee collected and spent over Rs.3,67,406/- on food, clothing, utensils, medical relief, water supply, health and sanitation etc. The major industrial concerns in Jamshedpur paid to their 6500 to 7000 Muslim workmen, basic wages and dearness allowance amounting to over Rs.6,83,000/- for the entire period of their absence from work during the period of disturbances. The industrial concerns contributed a further sum of about Rs.34,000/- for reconstructing the bustee houses of their muslim employees. Similar assistance was given by the Government to the owners of houses in the bustees outside the areas of the industrial concerns. The industrial concerns also undertook to have their labour quarters, damaged during the disturbances, quickly repaired at their cost. Similar action was taken by Government in respect of Government quarters in Adityapur and Baghbera. The companies decided to advance interest free loans amounting to three months' salary recoverable in 36 istalments to the employees in distress. The companies had also taken a decision to generous compensation to the next-of-kin of their unfortunate employees, who were killed during the disturbances, on the same scale as if these employees had been killed while on duty.

The Muslim employees of various companies in Jamshedpur viz. TISCO, TINPLATE, INDIAN OXYGEN, TELCO, I.C.C., I.T.C., I.S.W.P. resumed work by 3rd April, 1964 to 10th April, 1964. All the camps were officially disbanded by the 27th April 1964 as most of the inmates had moved on, either to own houses or to their friends and relatives.

Mr. J.R.D. Tata, while addressing a meeting of the

Jamshedpur Citizens' Peace Committee at Area Peace Committee at the United Club Hall, on April 8th, 1964, stated that he 'believed that the incidents in Jamshedpur, Rourkela and elsewhere at least the result of organised plot of loot, arson and murder and hoped for the holding of an independent enquiry. ..'

The Committee of Enquiry reported that – "Some of the witnesses, whom we examined, suggested that the incidents were provoked by Pakistan agents who had been going about these towns during the preceding few days. Some other witnesses also suggested that the incidents were inspired and brought about by members of a political party who were acting to the detriment of India and to assist the enemy of our country.....".

The Committee of Enquiry undertook a severe strain to explore the truth and causes of inhuman sufferings and torture inflicted to minority community of East Pakistan. They have visited the camps, verified the incidents with 12,000 heads of families consisting of 50,000 persons who were the real sufferers throughout East Pakistan and submitted a detailed 400-pages report to the President, Indian Commission of Jurists, New Delhi on 20th January, 1965.

Again during the Liberation Movement of Bangladesh there were great influx of refugees. It would be surprising that during this holocaust in East Pakistan both Non-Muslims and Muslims took refuge in India. Mrs. Indira Gandhi spoke at the German Society for Foreign Policy, Bonn 11 November 1971, "With regard to the number of refugees, our officials say there are 9,700,000. It may be that they are 200,000 or 300,000 fewer. ... ... According to us, there are nearly 3 million Muslim refugees; they are leaving the Hindus, Christians and Buddhists. ... when we drew the attention of the UN, we were given the answer : 'It is an internal problem of Pakistan. We cannot interfere in it'. There are nearly 10 million people and the UN says 'we are very sorry, we do not mind if million people have been killed in Pakistan; it is an internal matter of Pakistan."[2]

U.S. Senator Edward Kennedy in his report gives the following details about the refugees from Bangladesh in 1971. As of October 25th, 1971, 9.54 million refugees from East Pakistan had crossed over to India. The average influx as of October 1971 was 10,645 refugees a day. Hence the total refugee populaton at the start of Bangladesh war on December 3, 1971 was about 10 million[3]....

"In the 1971 war of liberation 200,000 women were raped ... Hundreds of thousands were victims of mass murders"[4]

NOTES AND REFERENCES

1. Recurrent Exodus of Minorities from East Pakistan and Disturbances in India. A Report to the Indian Commission of Jurists by its Committee of Enquiry, Disturbances in India, Part --IV.
2. Salam Azad, *Contribution of India in the War of Liberation of Bangladesh*, p-175.
3. Roy, Tathagata, *My People Uprooted*, p-239. Source : '*Bangladesh : The Birth of A Nation*', A handbook of Background information and Documentary Sources compiled by Univ. of Chicago Group of Scholars, by M. Nicholas, P. Oldumbarg, Ed. W. Morehouse, M. Seshachalam & Co., India, 1972, P. 7.
4. Ibid. Mrs. Sheikh Hasina Wajed, Prime Minister of Bangladesh, Addressing the U.N. Millenium Summit, 7th September, 2000, quoted in *The Times of India*, Mumbai Ed. 9th September 2000, P. 12.

5

THE GREAT BLUNDER

The Partition was the great blunder in the history of Independence struggle of India. Abul Kalam Azad said that the partition of India would be harmful not only to Muslims but to the whole country. He also warned Jawaharlal Nehru that "history would never forgive us if we agreed to partition." [1]It would be surprising to note that prior to Partition Pandit Jawaharlal Nehru who was going to take over power in 17 days' time as the Prime Minister designate of the Dominion Government, was denied to enter Kashmir to obtain the release of his friend, Sheikh Abdullah who was then arrested. The Maharaja of Kashmir Hari Singh begged Lord Mountbatten not to allow any leaders to visit his State, at all events before 15th August. He pointed out that "there had so far been no bloodshed in Kashmir despite the differences which had taken place across the border in the Punjab."[2]

Pandit Jawaharlal Nehru whose family had originally came from Kashmir naturally shocked him more than anything. Lord Mountbatten stated that 'It was only with the greatest of difficulty that Pandit Nehru was persuaded to acquiesce in this decision. I was privately informed that when Sardar Patel tried to reason with him the night before our meeting, Pandit Nehru had broken down and wept explaining that Kashmir meant more to him than anything else.'[3] It would also be embarrassing for Lord Mountbatten when the world press took the news badly and the whole plan might be jeopardised.

Lord Mountbatten's hasty decision of transferring power within a limited period made him more strained. In end of June he told Patricia – "Dear old V. P. Menon ... ... came to me a couple of days ago (I was looking rather worn out and haggard). He said he thought all the leaders had gone neurotic and that Nehru was heading for breakdown. He said, that 'the only man who can hold India now is your Excellency. If you break down too all will be lost, everyone on both sides hangs only on you.' Unfortunately that is true and I get so worn out by the scenes and squabbles about Partition, I really get harassed and depressed at times and dare not show it to anyone for its only by a tremendous show of optimistic confidence. I keep them all together."[4]

However, to get a relief from the verge of breakdown, Lord Mountbatten gave a Silver wedding dinner-party on 17th July 1947, for 95 guests. All the members of the Cabinet and many of the Princes as well as Jinnah and Nehru were present. "There was Indian dancing and music; the Viceroy was totally at ease, obviously enjoying himself, without an apparent care in the world." An American diplomat, George Merrill, and the Governor of the United Provinces Sir Francis Wylie, 'decided one evening when we were watching Lord Louis and his consort in action that in all history no revolution had perhaps ever been put through with so much grace.'[5] Cambell-Johnson who always maintained an extreme left-wing view, but he shook hands with the Press attaché and exclaimed : At last, after two hundred years, Britain has conquered India.'[6] Ismay wrote "It is the greatest *personal* triumph for you and Edwina of modern times – far more so than winning a great battle or even a great campaign. I confess that I had not much hope that you'd do the trick when I volunteered for the term, but I was absolutely positive that NO ONE ELSE IN THE WORLD could do it."[7] Walter Lippmann wrote in the *Washington Post* "Attlee and Mountbatten have done a service to all mankind by showing what Statesman can do not with force and money but with lucidity, resolution and sincerity."[8]

The ceremony for the Transfer of Power observed in New

Delhi on the 15th August 1947, was one of the great memory which stated - "would be the crowds, the multitudinous hordes inundating in a human sea the event that had been designed as the high point of the new nation's independence celebrations. It was the official raising of the Indian flag at five o'clock in the afternoon in an open space near New Delhi's India Gate, a sandstone arch dedicated to the 90,000 Indians who'd died for the British Empire in World War One." It was also mentioned "the roar of untrammelled happiness burst from half a million throats as the folds of the flag rose above the heads of the crowd. In the joy of that sublime second, India forgot the battle of Plassey, the vengeance of 1857, the massacre of Amritsar. Forgotten for an instant were the humiliations of martial law, the *lathi*-swinging police charges, the executions of her independence martyrs. The three difficult centuries were set aside to allow her to savour unfettered the delight of that moment."... .... Mountbatten thought "the whole thing was 'a kind of an enormous picnic of almost a million people all of them having more fun than they'd ever had in their lives. He immediately understood that this spontaneous, uncontrollable, but utterly happy outburst was far truer reflection of the meaning of this day than all the pomp and pageantry he'd planned for it."[9]

He also stated "the ceremony in the Council Chamber was extremely dignified and my speech was well received. ... ... As we were about to depart they said that it was doubtful whether the 400 men of the Guards of Honour could keep the way clear to the coach, so Nehru went on to the roof and waved to the crowd to go back; the door was then opened and surrounded by our staff we fought our way through to the coach."

It took us half an hour to go to the short distance back, for we had to go slowly through the crowds. Once we were held up for some five minutes by the pressure of the crowds. Apart from the usual cries of *Jai Hind* and "Mahtma Gandhi ki Jai" and "Pandit Nehru ki Jai", a surprising number shouted out "Moutbatten ki Jai", and "Lady Mountbatten ki Jai" and more than once "Pandit Mountbatten ki Jai".[10]

Alone at last in the private chamber of their palace, 'Louis and Edwina Mountbatten fell into each other's arms. Tears of sheer happiness poured down their faces. The wheel of their lives had come to a full circle.'[11]

Realising the inevitable consequences Louis Mountbatten had sent his former Secretary, George Abell, to caution Attlee against any excessive jubilation at such declarations. Abell told Attlee in the garden of his residence, the manner in which independence had been achieved, was a great triumph both for his Government and the man he had chosen as his last Viceroy. But he warned, don't celebrate the triumph too quickly or too publicly, because the inevitable consequences of partition was going to be 'the most appalling bloodshed and confusion.' "Attlee puffed at his pipe and sadly shook his head. There would be no boastful trumpetings, no self-satisfied proclamations coming from Downing Street, he agreed."[12] Abul Kalam Azad said "The joy was almost delirious but lasted hardly forty-eight hours. The very next day news of communal troubles began to cast deep gloom in the capital."[13]

Kushwant Singh, a Sikh lawyer from Lahore, was totally indifferent to the gay crowds around him in New Delh. 'I had nothing to rejoice about,' he would bitterly recall. 'For me and millions like me, this Independence Day was a tragedy. They'd mutilated the Punjab, and I had lost everything.'[14]

As apprehended the bloodiest phase of the revolution was then to begin. The Provincial Assemblies of Bengal and the Punjab by the end of June had voted for Partition. Mountbatten never suspected that this was a 'prescription for disaster', acceptable only because no alternative was conceivable. 'The more I look at the problem of India, he told the Secretary of State, the sheer madness .... No one would ever induce me to agree to it were it not for this fantastic communal madness that has seized everybody and leaves no other course open.'

On Bengal he said, 'I have no doubt myself that Unity is

necessary,' yet when he asked the Governor, Sir Fredrick Burrows, whether he was still sitting on a barrel of gunpowder, he got the reply: 'Good Lord, no, we got off that a long time ago and are now sitting on a complete magazine which is going to blow up at any time.'[15]

The Punjab was still worse, 'An agreed partition of the Punjab appears to me virtually impossible', [16]wrote Evan Jenkins, the experienced and prudent Governor. (*Transfer of Power*, Vol.X, p-506, Jenkins to Mountbatten, 30 April, 1947). In Bengal, for the most part, the problem was that of awarding tracts of land to one side or the other; in the Punjab the task was still more complex; every village, every house almost, seemed to provide grounds for argument.

There were already large numbers of murder and arson on a scale so menacing that both Nehru and Jinnah urged Mountbatten to take drastic steps to restore order. When Mountbatten refused to impose martial law – not out of squeamishness but because the Governor assured him that it would merely make things worse – he was abused in the Cabinet by representatives of Congress and the League alike. 'Nehru, as usual, completely lost control of himself and demanded the sacking of every 0fficial, from the Governor downwards, that same day. I had to reprimand him publicly for this irresponsible suggestion.'[17]

The Constituent Assembly, on the night of 14th August, 1947, where Pandit Jawaharlal Nehru called upon the members to take a pledge of dedication to the service of India: "Long years ago we made a tryist with destiny, and now the time comes when we shall redeem our pledge … .. At the stroke of the midnight hour, when the world sleeps, India will awake to life and freedom." … … The Constituent Assembly endorsed the request of the Congress leaders that Lord Mountbatten should become the first Governor-General.[18]

Lord Mountbatten having received a message from His Majesty the King conveyed the same to the India Constituent Assembly on 15th August 1947 : "On this historic day, when India takes her place as a free and independent Dominion in the British Commonwealth of Nations ...... From today I am your Constitutional Governor-General and I would ask you to regard me as one of yourselves ..." and handed over power to Pandit Jawaharlal Nehru as to the first Prime Minister of India.

There was the tumultuous joy on that day all over India. Lord and Lady Mountbatten were greeted by the enthusiastic crowds. But Lord Mountbatten recalled a contrast while he visited in 1921, the boycott of the Prince of Wales.[19] Similarly, we remember another contrast when on July 6, 1944, Subhas Chandra Bose made an impassioned and moving appeal to Gandhiji, in a broadcast from Radio Rangoon that the troops of Azad Hind Fauj were fighting the Allied forces on Indian soil. Netaji sought his blessings. He said that "the Provisional Government has, as its one objective, the liberation of India from the British yoke through an armed struggle. Once our enemies are expelled from India and peace and order is established, the mission of the Provisional Government will be over."[20] The Provisional Government of Azad Hind Fauj received international recognition by Japan and eight more countries of the World viz. Burma, Croatia, Germany, China, Manchukuo, Italy, Thailand and the Philippines. The flag of the INA was the Congress tri-colour with the emblem of the Leaping Tiger on it.

Meanwhile the great son of Bengal, the greatest Revolutionary of India reached Manipur. "On 18 March, 1944, Col. S. A. Malik, the INA Commander, hoisted the tricolour National Flag of India at the historic Moirang Kangla near Imphal in the liberated area of Manipur, on behalf of the Provisional Government of Free India. The valiant men of the Indian National Army were jubilant when they set their feet on the sacred soil of their Motherland. They prostrated on the ground and kissed the soil."[21]

They went on shouting with joy and sang their National Anthem. Col. S. A. Malik, the Commander of the Unit, received an enthusiastic welcome and support from the people of Manipur. A good number of British – Indian troops surrendered. Netaji conferred on Col. Malik the title of Sardar-e-Jung for the splendid job done in the area. There were innumerable sacrifices and heroic acts by the INA volunteers. Heroism was displayed by Captain Rao, Lt. Mansukh Lal and Lt. Ajaib Singh in successfully defending their Regimental Headquarters under Col. I. J. Kiani of the Gandhi Regiment.[22]

The Newspapers in abroad carried bold headlines that "*INA enters India. Netaji issues a proclamtion*"... Japanese prime minister Tojo declared :"*The Japanese government guarantees that the liberated areas inside India will be under the administration of the provisionsal government of Free India.*"[23] Accordingly, Netaji had appointed Lt. Col. Chatterji as the governor of the liberated areas and that the governor and his staff were getting ready to move into their area of operation.

Netaji also said that "I can assure you, Mahatmaji, that I and all those who are working with me regard themselves as the servants of the Indian people. The only reward that we desire for our efforts, for our suffering and for our sacrifice is the freedom of our motherland. There are many among us who would like to retire from the political field once India is free. "Nobody would be more happy than ourselves, if by any chance our countrymen at home should succeed ... or if by any chance the British Government accepts your 'Quit India' Resolution and gives effect to it ..." It may be noted that while Netaji's appeal to Gandhiji was being broadcast, a furious battle was raging in Manipur. The INA and the Japanese Army were fighting shoulder to shoulder against the Allied troops, having already made innumerable sacrifices.[24]

NOTES AND REFERENCES

1. Azad, Moulana Abul Kalam, *India Wins Freedom*, p-167.
2. Carter, Lionel, *Mountbatten's Report on the Last Viceroyalty*, p-249.
3. Ibid, p-250.
4. Zeigler, Philip, *Mountbatten*, p-399, Source : Lady Mountbatten's Papers, 29 June, 1947.
5. Ibid, p-400. Source : The Partition of India, Policies and Perspectives, ed. C. H. Philips and Marry Wain Wright, London, 1970, p-524.

6. Ibid, p-424. Source: Mission with Mountbatten, Op. Cit. p-168.
7. Ibid, p-426. Source : 25 August, 1947. BA E 83.
8. Ibid, p-428.
9. Collins, Larry and Lapierre, Dominique, *Freedom At Midnight*, p- 277-278.
10. Carter, Lionel, *Mountbatten's Report on the Last Viceroyalty*, p-425.
11. Collins, Larry and Lapierre, Dominique, *Freedom At Midnight*, p-279.
12. Ibid, p-280
13. Azad, Moulana Abul Kalam, *India Wins Freedom*, p-187.
14. Collins, Larry and Lapierre, Dominique, *Freedom At Midnight*, p-270.
15. *Transfer of Power*, Vol.X, p-539, Viceroy's Personal Report –5, May 1, 1947.
16. Ibid, p-566.
17. Ibid, Vol.XI, p-680.
18. Menon, V. P., *The Transfer of Power In India*, p-413.
19. Ibid, p-415.
20. Adiraju, V. R., *Netaji Subhas Bose: The Great Revolutionary*, p-328.
21. Ibid, p-323.
22. Ibid.
23. Ibid, p-325.
24. Ibid, P-329

6

TOWARDS ISLAMISATION

After Partition why Genocide took place in East Pakistan? Can Hindus be eliminated in this manner? Hitler tried to exterminate the Jews. But he could not, rather he brought his own ruin. Why innocent people were killed? Why members of the other communities merely looked on like silent-onlookers? Is not their inaction an indication of their tacit consent? These were the questions asked by Trailokya Maharaj and he was compelled to leave East Pakistan. He died at Delhi with a broken heart. The worst tragedy of Pakistan is that while Z. A. Bhutto wanted a thousand years' war with India, he was hanged not by any Hindu but by his own sect. Gen. Zia-ul-Haq was extinct (Bomb Blast) in the air along with his Generals.

Who gained ultimately by dividing the country? What was the position of the Muslim leaders who advocated and joined the orchestra of Pakistan along with the Muslim League leaders? The tragedy of Pakistan was that the Father of Pakistan M.A. Jinnah did not survive fourteen months after the partition and he died in a most pathetic way and in isolation. The Prime Minister Liaquat Ali Khan was assassinated. Mujibur Rahman and his family members were brutally murdered by the Military Junta. There was hardly anything of civil liberty left in East Pakistan. They treated East Pakistan as the Colony of Western Pakistan. A large number of erstwhile League leaders of the North-West and Eastern Pakistan were in detention without trial. H. S. Suhrawardy, the architect of the Great Calcutta Killings, was virtually a Pakistani prisoner who later on had "to move under permit and open his lips under orders." A. K. Fazlul Haq who was dearly loved by all as the grand old man of Bengal also supported the Lahore resolution, later on ploughed his "lonely furrow in the precincts of the Dacca High Court of Judicature."[1] East Pakistan contained larger population than all the Units of Pakistan put together and Sheikh Mujibur Rahman who commanded the vast majority of votes could not be blessed to hold the prize of Prime Ministership as Pakistan denied Democracy. Later Pakistan lost her Eastern-wing and five lacs Bihari Muslims were stranded immediately who were driven out from Bangladesh. Nawaz Shariff the Prime Minister was deported from Pakistan surrendering all his property worth Rupees Sixty crores and Benazir Bhutto is roving in exile.

Mahatma Gandhi, Indira Gandhi and Rajiv Gandhi were assassinated. Jawaharlal Nehru died in frustration. Dr. Shyama Prasad Mookherjee and Lal Bahadur Shastri died a mysterious death. Even the chief architect of the Partition who on the 15th August, 1947, graced by a surprising number shouted out "Mountbatten ki Jai", Lady Mountbatten ki Jai" and more than once "Pandit Mountbatten ki Jai" [2]met his destiny unprecedented in the history.

In a confidential conversation at Dacca on 25 May, 1950, with Mr. T.V.Venkatraman, Calcutta Correspondent, *The Hindu*, Jogen Mandal who was nominated as a member of the Viceroy's Executive Council in the Interim Government as a Hindu member of the Muslim League group and later a Minister of Labour in the Cabinet of Pakistan said that "the Hindus in East Bengal to a man are emphatic that they have no place in Pakistan and are determined to leave. I have advised them to wait for a few weeks more and that I too am prepared to accompany them to India. So long I have been claiming to be a representative only of the Scheduled Castes, but after what I have seen and heard, I feel I can speak for the entire Hindu community here.

"I have informed Delhi that it is only a question of time before the last Hindu reaches India from East Bengal. You must be prepared to receive us and rehabilitate us, and if necessary throw out enough Muslims to make room for us. If India is not prepared to do this, we shall appeal to the world, become Buddhists, Christians, but we will not submit to slow process of Islamisation.[3]

"My idea is that there should be no East Pakistan. There is a feeling in Pakistan that the Delhi Pact provides a breathing time for Pakistan; or to put it bluntly, to make Pakistan a permanent and lasting fact. Every Muslim feels that there should be no Hindus left inside Pakistan. India should not be foolish enough to believe that after driving out the Hindus, Pakistan will live in peace with India. West Pakistan is sufficiently armed and protected. They are now buying arms and ammunition openly in the world markets and it will not be long before East Bengal is also well armed. Orders have been issued to strengthen the defences of East Bengal. If in February there had been an armed intervention in East Bengal from India, it would have been all over with East Bengal, like Hyderabad, in the course of fifteen days. When East and West Pakistan are well armed, surely the Muslims are not going to rest content. They will launch a two-pronged attack on India. I caution India to be on the alert and not to be complacent and think that Pakistan will adhere to the Delhi Pact or any pact..." Jogen Mondal also said that East Bengal muslims in their enthusiasm wanted bread and they have received stone instead. Finally he warned the Pakistan Prime Minister Liaquat Ali Khan – "Hindus will never allow themselves whatever the threat or temptation, to be treated as Jimmies in the land of their birth." (For the full text of the conversation see Annexure - 5)

During Sheikh Hasina Wajed's Government in Bangladesh she took some positive steps in right direction which had enabled her to maintain to some extent a stable position in her Government. In an interview with the Senior Correspondent of *The Statesman*, Manas Ghose, presently the editor of the Dainik Statesman, Sheikh Hasina disclosed that during Id festival women could move well for shopping till past midnight. Dacca University was then free from students unrest and continued to prevail normalcy. The food production raised to over 25 million tons against 19 million tons during BNP rule. Rice sold at ten Taka a Kg and this had enabled the poor to have two meals a day. Due to bumper harvests the inflation rate had been lowered by 1.3 p.c.

Every month boys attending schools were given ten Kilograms of rice in the villages and the girls attending schools were given 50 per cent more. This had effected to a new phenomenon that more children attend the "job-oriented regular schools than to "Mulla Schools" whose products found it difficult to get jobs". Sheikh Hasina also sets an example that "after every general election its Parliament of 300 elects women to the House. The High Court of Bangladesh declared *fatwa* illegal. Prof. Kabir Chowdhury of Dhaka University said that "People of Bangladesh will no longer tolerate *fatwas* given by fundamentalists to achieve their ulterior motives. They are out to retard development and social justice". All these measures boost up the morale of women in Bangladesh. In addition, she introduced a host of beneficial schemes for the weaker sections of the rural community. The exports, industrial production and revenue collection enhanced by about 20%. The economic growth stood at 6%.

The Chakmas have returned to their home. Sheikh Hasina already took steps to allow the Hindus to worship in some temples and it was at the time of Awami League Government that both communities began to live together in harmony. It may be noted that still there are considerable number of Hindus living in East Bengal who command one-sixth of the peoples representative in the Bangladesh Parliament. The left-out properties of Hindus are estimated the worth Rs. 60,000 crores.

Salam Azad of AMITY FOR PEACE in Bangladesh wrote a book *Hindu Sampradaya Keno Bangladesh Tyag Kareche?* (Why Hindus left Bangladesh?). In his observations he has mentioned five main reasons for this debacle viz. Communal oppression, Communal atrocities, Declaration of Enemy Property Act, Forceful occupation of Religious property, Depriving Government services to Hindu Community etc. The modus operandi is the same as was done since the creation of Pakistan. The author has identified and specifically mentioned the incidents of torture of the victims. He has collected evidence, right from the University teachers, Jurists, Justices, Politicians, Intellectuals, Bankers, Government officials, NGO workers and different social workers who are all humane and helped him in writing his book. In the name of Enemy Property which has been amended as the Enemy Property Continuance Emergency Provision (Repeal) (Amendment) Ordnance number 93 of 1976, occupied the Hindu landed Property for which torture and repression on the Hindus were increased due to the harassment and land grabbing of the Hindu property.[4] It was observed that during 27 years since 1964 to 1991 more than 50 lacs Hindus left Bangladesh. Even the Hindu burning ghat was not spared. Salam Azad specifically mentioned that Zaffarabad burning ghat at Royer Bazar was occupied by one of the local residents an Advocate Mohammed Ali Khan son of Ismail Khan alias Tokani of 28 Zaffarabad occupied the encroached road leading to the burning ghat. The President of BNP Party Mohammad Abdur Razzak occupied the entire land of Radha Binod Jeu-temple at Tipu Sultan Road in old Dacca.[5] In this way many lands of the Hindu religious property have been forcefully grabbed by the local Muslim *Matabbars*. It is calculated that in 14 crore population the Hindu population is 1,24,19,195. Since 1974 to 1991 the Census Report of Bangladesh estimated that everyday about 475 Hindus quit Bangladesh which is accounted to 1,73,375 annually left East Bengal forever.[6] The author exclaimed that if the Hindus did not leave East Bengal then the population in Bangladesh would have been about 3.25 crores and the country would have enriched and prospered in the field of Economy, Politics, Cultures and intellectual activities. His mission would be successful if amity overcomes the enemity.

In fact the partition of India created more harm than solving the communal hatred for which it was needed. The Kashmir problem has been a serious obstacle to the peaceful and purposeful pursuit of our national agenda. The diplomatic efforts of Pakistan are likely to drag to another partition. The Kashmir Pundits are ousted from their own hearth and home. The dividend of Partition pays in hard reality. The division of the Sub-Continent not only deprived us of much of our history but geographically we have lost the Indus, part of the Brahmaputra and the Gangetic delta. The Kargil incident is a great slur to our border security. The continuous ISI sabotage deplores the country's peaceful existence. The recent unpleasant incident of Bangladesh wherein the "gruesome killing of 16 BSF officers and Jawans in Boraibari by Bangladesh Rifles and civilians was nothing but a conspiracy.

The undercurrent communal forces who were responsible for the Partition of the Country are still active in disguise. In an editorial of the Statesman (13 May, 2001), it has been mentioned "Sheikh Hasina has many Trojan horses in her party. Their acts and deeds in recent months have tainted the party's image."[7] The discovery of a car bomb outside Sheikh Hasina's residence in Dhaka, a powerful explosion device found at her native place Kotalipara are the incidents of involvement of fundamentalists. Since January 20 people were killed by two major blasts at Dhaka. The first blast at a Communist Party rally claimed 8 lives and the second 12 lives at the Pahela Baisakh function at the 'Batamool'.

There were not only Islamists in the opposition parties in Bangladesh but also quite a few fifth Columnists in Hasina's own party. Her father's most confidants in the party like Khondokar Mushtaque Ahmed, Taheruddin Thakur and Shah Moazzem Hussain hatched the conspiracy along with a section of the military staged the bloody coup for liquidating Mujib's family. A section of the country's Islamists vowed to Talibanise Bangladesh. The defeat of Awami league brought a change in the government of Bangladesh, triggered a violent back lush on minorities. Such organised conspiracy of atrocities are still continuing even after 50 years of partition. While Punjab had exchange of population neither the British nor the ruling Congress Party demanded exchange of population in the eastern Bengal. The heart rending reports of continuing persecution and the killing of a Principal of a Chittagong College in broad day light by supporters of Jamat-e-Islami have been a great concern to the minorities of Bangladesh. Since one and half month about 20,000 Bangladeshis flocked to West Bengal and Tripura. A Government confidential note indicates that "Muslim activists from various fundamentalist organisations of Bangladesh have decided to induct cadres in towns and villages on the Indo-Bangladesh border to assess the opinion of Indian Muslims and mobilised them against US design." The cadres from Bangladesh were likely to interact with the Muslims population in India to organise the popular "Hujur Saheber Mela."

A veteran Journalist (RGK) once said, he heard some Pakistanis boasting in 1947 - *Hanske Liya Pakistan, Ladke Lenge Hindustan.* This was confirmed by Collins and Lapierre – "In Ukarna, Moslem-dominated mill-town on the Lahore/Karachi railway, Madanlal Pahwa, a stocky 20-year-old Indian Navy veteran, cowered inside the home of his aunt. Through the windows he could see the town's jubilant Moslems dancing, singing, waving flags, chanting their newest slogan : *Hans ke liya Pakistan, Ladkelenge Hindustan* – We got Pakistan by laughing, we'll get India by fighting."[8] Recently, a new slogan is heard in Agartala, Tripura 'Ghuske Lenge Hindustan' (India will be conquered by sending intruders). Moreso, tupi (cap) on head and burkha clad Muslim women are gradually increasing.

The Partition also led to the rise of seperatism among sections of the population who had been part of the main stream. In reality we have lost our national unity. The consequences of the Partition will be felt even for centuries. The disturbed political situation if prevails in such a manner it would encourage the Islamic fundamentalists who are supported by Pan-Islamic forces. Thus the effects of the Partition are likely to pay for unending period.

Prakash Chandra Dey wrote a letter in the daily *Bartaman* on 16th April, 2005, wherein he informed a conspiracy has been hatched for further division of India. He wrote an area '*Mughalstan*' like Pakistan is likely to evolve occupying a vast area from India. A map has been chalked out which was shown through Website Kashmir Herald-Web Edition, June-2004. It has been prepared by revealing a plan for racial division in South Asian peninsula. This was prepared by one Jahangir Khan of the Mughal Research Institute. Their address, as was mentioned Jahangir Nagar. It was shown in the map that the North-West Frontier Province of Pakistan to the Northern part of India including Jammu-Kashmir which was known in the ancient India as the '*Aryabarta*' and including the Bangladesh will be formed *Mughalstan*. Apart from the existing Kashmir, Punjab, Ayodha there will be new provinces, such as, *Bangistan. Khalistan, etc.* Besides *Mughalstan* there will be division of India which will appear in a new shape i.e. Rajputana, Braja, Dalitstan, Bangal etc. It has referred from the sixteen Mahajanapada of Ancient India which has been said Nepal as Mithila, Koushala in Orissa etc. Assam, Manipur, Mizorm, Nagaland, Tripura and Khasia instead of Meghalaya has been left outside of *Mughalstan.*[9] Outwardly it may be ludicrous to hear such a plot but we cannot ignore it. The Pakistan may be a lesson in this context.

Prof. Saradendu Mukherjee in an overview of the Indo-Bangladesh situation drew the conclusion that "India is beginning to look like a defenceless David before the Bangladesh Goliath." He established his logic by stating - "The traditional subservience of the Indian ruling class to the Islamic *ummah* and the abundant availability of the petro-dollar for the committed – while useful in vote-bank politics – led to the adoption of two suicidal policies. One was the open encouragement to the influx of Muslims from Bangladesh, beginning with the Bihari-Muslim collaborators of Pakistani regime. The second was the once vigorous protest over the treatment of the hapless Hindu, Christian and Buddhist minorities, voiced from time to time by the likes of Shyama Prasad Mukherjee, Nirmal Chatterjee, Babasaheb Ambedkar, Jadunath Sarkar, Atulya Ghosh and Jayaprakash Narayan, turned into mild murmurs, as newer definitions of secularism were churned out. A creative people, who had sacrificed so much for the Renaissance and India's freedom movement, were thrown to the wolves. In 1947, they were 29 per cent of the state's population, today they comprise less than 10 Per cent. In few countries have the minorities been so systematically eliminated, as the Hindus, Buddhists and Christians in Bangladesh. The substantial contribution to this mind-boggling and self-destructive policy came from the media and intelligentsia of West Bengal, who were wholly backed by the political leadership."

An unprecedented sequence of this capitulation by India is the continuous firing by Bangladesh Rifles on Indian security forces, the sheltering of insurgent groups on Bagladesh soil, the movement of illegal immigrations from Bangladesh into India, rampant smuggling, the mushrooming growth of madrasas and a vigorous religious propaganda of nefarious kind. Thus "India today is beginning to look like a defenceless David before the Bangladesh Golialth."[10]

NOTES AND REFERENCES

1. Jogen Mandal's Letter of Resignation to Liaquat Ali Khan, the Prime Miniter of Pakistan, October 9, 1950.
2. Carter, Lionel, Mountbatten's *Report on the Last Viceroyalty*, p-395
3. Sengupta, Sukharanjan, *Banga Sanhar Ebong*, p-204. Source : Letter of Shri Siva Rao, Journalist Member, CA, 1946-50 : Lok Sabha 1952-57, Rajya Sabha 1957-60, enclosed in a letter to Dr. Rajendra Prasad to Sardar Vallabhbhai Patel, Dy. Prime Minister dt. 7. 6. 1950.
4. Salam Azad, *Hindu Sampraday Keno Bangladesh Tyag Kareche*? P-132.
5. Ibid, p-140.
6. Ibid, p-152-53.
7. The Statesman, 13 May, 2001.
8. Collins, Larry and Lapierre, *Freedom At Midnight*, p-286.
9. Letter of Prakash Chandaa Devi, Bartaman, Kolkata 16th April, 2005 and Swami Juktananda, Banga Bhanger Satabarsha – Sarthakata Kishey? Pranab, 79th year, No.6, September 2005.
10. Mukherji, Saradindu, Bangla Policy is out of Kilter, The Indian Express, 15 November, 2005.

7

Sense of Realisation

A sense of realisation seems to have developed among the intellectuals in Bangladesh. The High Court of Bangladesh issued notices to the Government, the intellectuals protested atrocities on the minorities.[1] The NGO and the media raised their voice of protest. Countless letters written by the affected Hindus are published in the Dacca daily newspapers. Saifur Rahman insisted that the Government to suppress communal elements with drastic action.

The Amensty International took note with grave concern about the situation of members of the Hindu Community in Bangladesh over the past several months. The current wave of attacks against the Hindu community began before the general elections of 1st October 2001 when the Hindus were threatened by BNP-led alliance parties not to take part in elections for fear of votes in favour of Awami League. The backlash after the election was systematic and severe. Reports indicated that the worst affected areas have been in Barisal, Bhola, parts of Pirojpur, Khulna, Satkhira, Gopalganj, Bagerhat, Jessore, Commilla and Narshingdi. The attackers have reportedly entered the Hindu homes, beaten members of the family, looted their property and in some cases raped the Hindu women. It was also mentioned in the report that in an affected village Ziodhara several Hindu villagers left for fear of being attacked and their children could not attend schools. In another village, Deuatala Bazar, gangs of youngmen wielding sharp weapons reportedly went door to door telling the Hindus to "go away". In the village of Daspara in Mithanala Union, Mirersarai Upazila, a gang of about 25 youths reportedly attacked homes of the Hindus around midnight on 5th November. One Sri Sunil Das Sandhu (28) was reportedly hacked to death and 16 others were injured, some seriously. They ransacked houses, looted them, dragged family members out of their homes and beat them. Hundreds of the Hindu families have fled across the border into India because they have been attacked or threatened. They have been trickling into India reportedly either by paying bribes or crossing along the remote unmanned border areas. According to news agency AFP of 29th October, 2001 they have either ended up in camps or gone to their distant relatives. On an interview by the Journalists they have disclosed that they have been targetted to have been the supporters of the defeated Awami League.

In regard to allegations of rape, the Human Rights Organisations in Bangladesh noted over 100 women have been subjected to rape. The perpetrators have been mainly members of the BNP or its Coalition partners Jamaat-e-Islami'. The information mentioned some specific instances. In Azimnagar. Bhanga of Faridpur district a college student was reportedly raped in front of her mother at her home. The attackers entered her home on 6th October at about 9 PM ransacked the house, looted valuables and raped the student. On October 8, in Delua, Ullapara, Sirajganj a schoolgirl was reportedly gangraped by the attackers and ill-treated the members of her family.

Two Hindu women were reportedly raped in front of their husbands on 11th October in Khanzapur Upazila in Gopurnadi, Barisal because they had voted for the Awami League. On 6th October, in Bashkandi, Chorfashon, Bhola the attackers entered the home raped the girl and her mother. On 11th October 2001, a gang of armed men reportedly abducted at midnight three Hindu girls at the village of Nohata in Shreepur in Magura district. Another girl was reportedly abducted from her home at Razarchor, Sadar Barisal after the attackers were not paid a large sum of money which they had demanded for leaving the family alone. They also molested the girl's mother and her aunt.

The Amenesty International issued an Urgent Action on 15 October, 2001, expressing concern at reports that the Hindus and other religious minorities have been attacked since the general election, allegedly by supporters of the BNP-led coaliton.[2] But the reaction of the Government was initially not encouraging. Altaf Hossain Chowdhury, the Bangladesh Home Minister, said that the news of the attacks on members of the Hindu minority in Bangladesh were "baseless, exaggerated and politically motivated." However, the Agence France-Presse reported on 9th November, 2001, that the Bangladesh Government had set up a Committee headed by the principal Secretary to Prime Minister Khaleda Zia to investigate the alleged atrocities committed against members of the Hindu community and their exodus to India.[3] The Committee does not appear to be independent of the Government, as the Home Minister reportedly has a supervisory role. The Committee was to submit a report within a week but there has been no further news about the progress of the Committee.

Meanwhile a number of BNP members have reportedly been arrested due to attacks on the Hindus. *The Daily Star* reported on 15th October, 2001 the arrest of Abdur Rouf, President of the BNP Unit at Purba Delua village, Ullapara Thana, Sirajganj. He had reportedly led some 16 BNP activists who attacked Anil Seal, beating him as well as his wife, Basanti Rani and their two daughters Purnima and Gita Rani in an attempt to secure land belonging to the family.[4]

This time the Bangladesh press covered atrocities against the Hindu communities widely, raising awareness in Bangladesh. This has attracted the National human rights organisations as well as International reactions. In rural areas, some 30 Hindu families in Reeshipara village of Boraigram Upazila in Natore have allegedly been threatened by armed men identifying themselves as members of the BNP to either provide them with 300,000 Taka (Dollar 5,317) or leave the village.

On 16th November, 2001, Gopal Krishna Muhuri, Principal of Nazirhat College in Chittagong was shot dead at his house. The prominent journalist and writer Shahriar Kabir was arrested on 22nd November 2001, as he sent message to the human rights defenders in Bangladesh and throughout the world.[5]

Another significant development in Bangladesh was noted when the Bangladeshi scholars in Diaspora said in a statement that "We shall not be silent on the plight of our Brothers and Sisters" and signed by Dr. Ansar Ahmed, Baldwin-Wallace College, Ohio, USA and twenty two scholars abroad for ensuring the full rights of citizens which is the prime responsibility of the authority.[6]

A 2-Day International Conference on Civil Society, Human Rights and the Minorities in Bangladesh (22-23 January, 2005) held in Kolkata organised by Campaign Against the Atrocities on the Minorities in Bangladesh (CAAMB), in association with the Bangladesh Hindu Buddhist Christian Unity Council (BHBCUC, International Chapters). The participants were Representatives from the Bangladesh Hindu Buddhist Christian Unity Council (International Chapters), Human Rights Congress of Bangladesh, Parbatya Chattagram Jana Samhati Samiti, Hot Line Bangladesh, Bangladesh Tribal Forum, Representatives from the USA, Canada, Great Britain as well as Journalist from France, Intellectuals, writers and Journalists from West Bengal etc. During the 2-day Seminar there were various speakers who narrated the alarming situation prevailing in Bangladesh and the reasons for ethnic cleansing by Islamisation in the State.[7]

Prajnalankar Bhikkhu observed that although Bangladesh is the fourth largest Muslim-populated country in the world, racially and culturally it is still a diverse nation. The total populaton is about 141 million. Muslims constitute nearly 88% of the total population, while Hindus and others (Buddhists and Christians) constitute 11% and 1% respectively. There are 45 distinct indigenous peoples in Bangladesh. They follow Buddhism, Christianity and Hinduism beside their indigenous faiths. Their total population is around 2 million. Their ethnic identity, language, culture, traditions, and way of life are totally different from that of the majority Bangla-speaking Muslims. The largest group of the indigenous peoples known as *Jumma* live in the three Hill districts – Rangamati, Khagrachari and Bandarban – of the Chittagong Hill Tracts. Their total population is around 700,000.

Shri Ushatan Talukdar, Secretary for Poltical Affairs, Parbatya Chattagram Jana Samhati Samiti (PCJSS), said that from time immemorial, the CHT had been the home to eleven indigenous ethnic peoples. They collectively identify themselves as the Jumma people (High Landers), the first people of the CHT. They are the Bawm, Chak, Chakma, Khumi, Khyang, Lushai, Marma, Mro, Pangkhua, Tanchangya and Tripura. The Jumma people are distinct and different from the majority Bengali people of Bangladesh in respect of race, language, culture and religion.

Like indigenous peoples in other parts of the world, the indigenous Jumma people of the CHT have been suppressed for centuries. Before the British annexed the region to Bengal, CHT was independent. Even during the colonial period, the CHT was regarded as an "Excluded Area", in order to protect the indigenous Jumma people from economic exploitation by non-indigenous people and to preserve the indigenous peoples' socio-cultural and political institutions based on customary laws, community ownership of land and so on. In fact, several provisions of the CHT Regulations of 1900 functioned as a safeguard for the Jumma people and it prohibited immigration into the region and land ownership by non-indigenous people.

However, during the Pakistani period and even after Bangladesh became independent in 1971, the entire CHT region was thrown open for unrestricted migration and acquisition of land titles by non-indigenous people, in violation of the letter and spirit of the 1900 Regulations. Although generally Bangladeshi and CHT laws acknowledge the CHT peoples as "indigenous", this was not formally acknowledged in the national Constitution of Bangladesh, which was adopted in 1972.

The Constituent Assembly members were so cruel they even adopted an Article which made all the citizens of the country to be known as Bengalis. So there had been no provision for the CHT and its Jumma people in the Bangladesh Constitution passed in November 1972. When all democratic avenues had been failed and the Jumma people had nothing left they opted for armed struggle.

He also said that the CHT Accord which was signed between the government of Bangladesh and PCJSS on 2nd December 1997, had ended the decades long fierce armed conflict between the Jumma people and Government of Bangladesh. But it was painful to note that the Government of Bangladesh, in particular the then Awami League government, signed the Accord, but it had no sincerity to implement the Accord. The BNP led present coalition government also followed the same policy. As a result, though more than seven years have been passed after signing of the Accord, most of the provisions, especially the main issues of the Accord remain unimplemented. There is not only lack of government sincerity in implementing the Accord, but a vested group of the government, military and civil administration in CHT, Islamic fundamentalist groups have been trying to make impediments to it from the very beginning. The BNP and the Jatiya Party (Manju) with two hard-core (Jamat-E-Islam and Islamic Oikya Jote) Islamic fundmentalist parties, from the very first day of their formation of the sitting government have been violating the basic clauses of the Accord. So nothing was expected from the Government except gradual violation of the clauses of the Accord. Moreover, after the arrival of this new government, the minority and indigenous peoples, particularly the Hindu community in Bangladesh has been suffering enormously.

He also said that their lands, forests and territories have been and are still being taken away without their free, prior and informed consent, to build so-called “Reserve Forests”, “Protected Areas”, “National Parks”, “Eco-parks”. Tourism, and even for establishing military bases and training centres. In 1960, the Kaptai Dam flooded their lands and homes and even today many of their people remain un-rehabilitated.

In 1979 the Government of Bangladesh undertook drastic programme to settle Bengali Muslim population from other plain districts of Bangladesh to CHT for outnumbering the Jummas and evicting them from their ancestral land. Consequently thousands of indigenous people were displaced from their ancestral lands. The government-sponsored Bengali settlers have been occupying the settled and possessed lands of the Jummas and committing series of ethnocides upon the Jummas with the direct help of government machineries. This is one of the tactics adopted by successive Governments to drive out the Jumma peoples from their ancestral land for expansion of Islamisaation in the region. Even after the signing of the Accord, land grabbing process is continuing throughout the CHT. The CHT region once a pre-dominant non-Bengali Muslim area is fast becoming a Bengali Muslim area by Islamisation policies of the governments. The influx of outsider Bengali Muslim settlers into the CHT region had been started since the creation of Pakistan. Later on, Bangladesh government's vigorous Islamisation policies had made the situation worse than ever before.

Dr. Nimchandra Bhowmic, a Professor of Dacca University and Secretary, Bangladesh Hindu Buddhist Christian Unity Council said that Bangladesh got its freedom with the blood of Hindus, Muslims, Christians, Buddhists and other religions. It is evident from the history of independence movement that the minorities suffered during the struggle against the British, the torture of the Pakistanis and so on. Did the minorities get their proper rights in 1971 when Bangladesh got freedom? However, in the concluding session of the CAAMB it was resolved that the united minorities of Bangladesh will not leave their ancestral birth place and their mother land and rather they will resist the planned atrocities for ethnic cleansing. The proposed International Seminar for Campaign Against Atrocities on the Minorities in Bangladesh is a primary step for creating general opinion against the planned Islamic Democracy.

The CAAMB having successful in their first International

Conference, arranged the Second International Conference on 11-12 February, 2006 at Kolkata. The Conference was inaugurated by General Sankar Roychoudhury, Ex-MP and Chief of Army Staff (Retd.) and attended by various dignitaries from all over the country and abroad, especially those who fight for the Human Rights. Among them were Dr. Ajoy Roy of Dhaka, Ms Rosaline Costa of Hotline Bangladesh, Mr. Rabindra Ghosh, President, Human Rights Congress of Bangladesh Minorities, Dhaka, Mr. Samaresh Baidya of Bhorer Kagaz, Dhaka, Mr. Rana Dasgupta, BHBCUC, Chittagong. The delegates attended from USA were Mr. Pabitra Chowdhury, Indian American Intelletuals Forum Inc. New York, Mr. Nicholas Shikdar, BHBCUC, USA, Mr. Aloke Chaudhury, Canada. Mr. Arun Barua of BHBCUC attended from Switzerland. The delegates represented from England were Mr. Debabrata Chowdhury, BHBCUC, Mr. Ramen Dam, BHBCUC, London, Dr. B. B. Chowdhury, BHBCUC, London, Mr. Sisir Majumdar, BHBCUC, London etc. From the Indian side Shri Amitabha Choudhury (Nirapeksha), Prof. Sunanda Sanyal, Ms Maitreyi Chatterjee, Writer, Women Rights Activist, Dr. Esha Dey, Prof. Saradindu Mukherjee, Hansraj College, Delhi and former member of the ICSSR, Mr.Sarat Mukhopadhya (Poet), Mr. Bimal Paramanik, Director, Centre for Research in Indo Bangla Relations, Mr. Samir Adhikari, Mr. Subodh Roy Chowdhury, Mr. Ratneswar Sarkar, General Secretary, All India Refugee Front, Mr. Susanta Saha, Udbastu Sangram Parishad, Mr. Gopal Saha, Secretary, Indian National Forum etc.

During the two days conference the Speakers narrated the horrible conditions of the minorities and the atrocities on them still continuing. The minorities in Bangladesh are living a 'life of second class citizens.' The proportion of Hindus in population has now come down to mere 9 percent. The Buddhists indigeneous people of Chittagong Hill Tract are being forced out of land and the place is being taken over by Islamists. .. … … Bangladesh now is in the grip of Islamic Fundamentalism. The simultaneous hurling of as many as 500 bombs in 63 of the 64 districts of Bangladesh by the militants of Jamaiatul Mujahideen on 17 August, 2005 clearly testifies to the iron grip of the Islamic militants over the country. Such a horrendous incident only goes to show how well-equipped the religious militants of Bangladesh are, in terms of technical and strategic skills. The Islamic militants who wrecked havoc to the western world by detonating bombs in Madrid (2004) or in London (2005) are nothing compared to their counterparts in Bangladesh. The Speakers expressed their concern at the rising intolerance and extent of physical violence against the sane and secular voices of the civil Society in Bangladesh.

The culture of intolerance is spreading in West Bengal too. Hundreds of Madrasas in West Bengal have cropped up. The Speakers lamented that even after the mass attacks on minorities, the ethnic cleansing, rape of hundreds of women, killing of people, destruction of temples-churches, imposition of Enemy Property Act. West Bengal is not bothered. And strangely least bothered are the refugees themselves from East Bengal who have fled to escape the Islamic rule. This horrible violation of human rights have been always ignored by majority intellectuals in West Bengal – writers, painters, film and theatre personalities, journalists and others – in the name of secularism. All Human Rights Groups ignore the issue and try to silence others under the garb of so called secularism.

The Speakers requested the well-settled refugees from East Pakistan/Bangladesh to take up their moral responsibility and raise their voices in support of their brothers and sisters across the border. They also desired that the human and women's rights' organisation should protest against the worst cases of violation of the rights of the minority population and especially their women. The attention of the Govt. of West Bengal was sought up and demanded to prevent the ongoing demographic disaster. They appealed to the media to support the most oppressed people of the world so that the minorities in Bangladesh could live in dignity with secular values.

NOTES AND REFERENCES

1. On a petition filed by Bangladesh legal aid organisation, Ain-O-Salish Kendra, the High Court ordered the Government on 26 November 2001 to explain why it has not done more to protect the country's Hindu religious minority.

2. Ratneswar Bhattacharya, *Sankhyaloghu Bitaran*, p-95. Source: Amensty Report – Bangladesh Attacks on Members of the Hindu Minority.

3. Agency Report of Agence France-Presse dt.29 October, 2001.

4. *The Daily Star*, dated 15 October 2001.

5. Ratneswar Bhattacharya, *Sankhyaloghu Bitaran*, p-798. Source : Report of the Human Rights Organisation in Bangladesh.

6. Ibid,p-100.

   Statement of Bangladeshi Scholars in Diaspora – "We Shall Not Be Silent on the plight of our Brothers and Sisters". Signed by 1. Dr.Ansar Ahmed, Baldwin-Wallace College, Ohio, USA. 2. Mr. Arif Ahmed, Ikonami Limited, U.K. 3. Dr. Raisuddin Ahmed, International Food Policy Research Institute, Washington DC, USA. 4. Professor Syed M. Ahsan, Concordia University, Canada. 5. Professor Sheik A. Akbar, Ohio State University, Ohio, USA. 6. Mr. Tanweer Akram A. T. Kearney, Virginia, and Columbia University, New York, USA. 7. Dr. Imam Alam, University of Northern Iowa, Iowa, USA. 8. Professor Syeed Saad Andaleeb, Pennsylvania State University, Pennsylvania, USA. 9. Mr. Syed Abul Basher, York University, Canada. 10. Professor A. R. Chowdhury, Marquette University, Winsconsin, USA. 11. Professor Ahsan Habib, Adrian College, Michigan, USA. 12. Professor Kabir Hassan, University of New Orleans, New Orleans, USA. 13. Professor Anisul Islam, University of Houston-Downtown, Texas, USA. 14. Dr. Selim Jahan, United Nations Development Programme, New York, USA. 15. Professor Azizur Rahaman Khan, University of California-Riverside, USA. 16. Professor Farida Khan, University of Wisconsin-Parkside, Winsconsin, USA. 17. Dr. M.G.Quibria, Asian Development Bank,Tokyo, Japan. 18. Mr. Selim Raihan, University of Manchester, U.K. 19. Professor Salim Rashid, University of Illinois-Urbana Campaign, Illinois, USA. 20. Mr. Adnan Rubai, State University of New York-Binghamton, New York USA. 21. Professor Omer S. Sher, Algonquin College, Canada. 22. Fazley Siddiq, Dalhousie University, Canada. 28 November 2001.

7. International Conference on Civil Society, Human Rights and Minorities in Bangladesh – Organised by Campaign Against Atrocities on Minorities in Bangladesh (CAAMB) in association with Bangladesh Hindu Buddhist Christian Unity Council (BHBCUC, International Chapters), held in Kolkata on 22 – 23 January 2005. Second International Conference held in Kolkata on 11-12 February, 2006.

8

EMERGENCE OF BANGLA BHAI

In consonance with the constitution, the government of Bangladesh pursues a policy of integration of the indigenous peoples and their territories and resources with the "Islamic democracy'.[1] This policy known as "Islamization" encourages forcible land-confiscation and settlement of Bangla-speaking Muslims in territories traditionally controlled by indigenous peoples, militarization, religious persecution, and human rights violations against the indigenous peoples. Under this policy, the government of Bangladesh secretly sponsored the settlement of over 400,000 Bangla-speaking Muslim settlers in the CHT region in the late 1970s and early 1980s and militarised the traditional homeland of the Jumma indigenous people with 80,000 army personnel, 25,000 BDR (Bangladesh Rifle – a paramilitary force) personnel, 8,000 Ansars (Islamic guards), and 1,500 navy servicemen. It resulted in massive human rights violations in which more than 15,000 indigenous people were killed, thousands of indigenous families were displaced from their ancestral lands and nearly 70,000 indigenous people were forced into refugee camps in the neighbouring Indian state of Tripura in the late 1980s. No perpetrators of these human rights violations have been brought to justice.

The 2001 general elections in Bangladesh mandated a four-party coalition consisting of the Bangladesh Nationalist Party

(BNP), Jamat-e-Islam, Islami Oikyo Jote and Jatiya Party (M) to power. It helped Islamic hardliners gain a strong ground in the "Islamic democracy". Islamic hardliners are widely believed to have opened up their facilities for many Taleban and Al-Qaeda operatives, who were facing a serious threat of survival in Afghanistan and Pakistan following the US-led strike on Afghanistan and the General Pervez Musharaff's anti-terrorist drive in Pakistan under the US pressure.[2]

Bangladeshi Islamic hardliners got a new impetus when they came in touch with the highly trained and sophisticated foreign Islamic terrorists. Bangladesh became a meeting point of international Islamic terrorists including the ones suspected for the Bali bomb blast in Indonesia.

Now there has been an emergence of the "Bangla Bhai" and other Islamic 'Terrorist organisations.' This is popularly known as "Bangla Bhai" (Hero or Brother of Bangladesh), Ajijur Rahaman A.K.A. Siddique Islam is the self-styled Islamic militant fundamentalist leader of the Jagrota Muslim Janata of Bangladesh (JMJB – Awaken Muslim People of Bangladesh), the national militant Islamic fundamentalist group of the four-party coalition government of Bangladesh launched on 1st April 2004. The BNP-led coalition government uses this group to crash its political opponents and free thinkers often in the name of eliminations of "crimes" and "corruptions" from the society. In an interview with Hasibur Rahman Bilu, Bogra correspondent of *The Daily Star*, Bangla Bhai recently said, "Our goal is to root out Sarbahara men (Leftists) and corruption from society, seize illegal weapons and establish the ideal of the Rasul (Prophet Hazrat Mohammed)".[3]

Quoting an article by Haroon Habib in the *Frontline* (19th June – 2nd July 2004), Joanna Kirkpatrick writes – Bangla Bhai's men levy protection tolls on villagers, order them to wear *tupi* (cap), go to mosque regularly, and force women to wear *burqa* or *hijab*. Those who defy it in any way are subjected to physical abuse and/or their property is wasted. "They usually kill their victims in gruesome ways and often mutilate their bodies. In the last week of

May, one of the three supposedly Left extremists caught by Bangla Bhai's 0peratives was beaten to death and hanged upside down from a roadside tree in Bogra. The main Dhaka newspapers deny such goings on, and the government of Khaleda Zia pretends that the police have been notified to capture him. However, in four northwestern districts – Rajshahi, Naogaon, Natore and Bogra – police are collaborating with this gang and justify what they do by saying they are undermanned and cannot control all the criminal elements. Not only does the government turn a blind eye, Prime Minister Begam Zia also appointed a Jama'ati as the Agriculture Minister, thus ensuring Islamist influence and a free rein for Bangla Bhai and other Islamist forces in the rural areas."[4]

Jahangir Alam Akash, a Bangladeshi journalist, in Rajshahi told in an exclusive interview with the *Voice of America*, Bangla Service on 24th July, 2004 that Bangla Bhai has a "likely link" with the Al-Qaeda. The US administration has blacklisted the University of Chittagong for its alleged links with national and international Islamic terrorists. Two other Islamic terrorist organisations in North Bengal supported by "Bangla Bhai" are Jamaitul Mujahidin and Shahdat-e-al-Hiqma. The Islamic terrorist organisations which are active in Bangladesh include, among others, the Jehad-e-Islami, Islamic Chhatra Shibir, Al Badar, Bangladesh Islamic Manch, Harkat-ul-Jihad-al-Islami of Bangladesh, Harkat-ul-Mujahideen, Islamic Majlis, Islamic Madrasa Musadereen and Quami Madrasa Musadereen. There have been bomb blast on British deplomat in Sylhet, on opposition Awami League party rally in Dhaka and in the Mymensingh cinema hall. It is also noted that there have been Secret Islamic terrorist training camps in the country, particularly in inaccessible terrains in the Chittagong Hill Tracts.[5]

The latest development in Bangladesh has been reported by Press Trust of India from Dacca, on 17th August, 2005, wherein it is stated that "Serial explosions rock Bangladesh". "Over 400 small bombs, suspected to have been planted by a banned Islamic militant outfit, exploded near simultaneously almost all over Bangladesh today, killing two people, including a child, and injuries at least 140."[6]

Police said that 63 of Bangladesh's 64 districts were hit by the bombings, which occurred between 11 a.m. and 11.30 a.m. (local time), targeting government offices, courts and Press clubs in the first such attack in this politically volatile South Asian country, prompting Dhaka to sound a security alert.

A private NTV television channel showed at least 140 people were injured in more than 400 explosions of crude bombs. A rickshaw puller died of his injuries in western Chapainawabganj, while a boy died in a hospital in nearby Savar area, police said.

At least 40 suspects have been arrested from different parts of the country, sources said. Police suspected the involvement of the outlawed militant outfit Jamiat-ul-Mujahideen Bangladesh after recovering leaflets under its name from the blast sites which demanded implementation of Islamic law in the country. The outfit is led by "Bangla Bhai", who has been on the run since his outfit was banned last year.[7] (*The Statesman*, 2005-08-18).

It may be recalled that immediately after the assassination of Sheikh Mujibar Rahaman on 15 August 1975, the Islamization in Bangladesh started openly. Abu Sadat Muhammad Sayem, who had become Chief Martial Law Administrator on 7 November 1975, issued a proclamation repealing the provision of Article 38 of Bangladesh's Constitution which forbade the formation of parties on a religious basis. This was made possible for political parties like the Jamat and the Muslim League, which had earlier been declared illegal, to participate in politics again.

Dr. Muhammad Asadulla al-Galib who was then a student of Dacca University left an organisation called Jomiyat-e-Ahle Hadith in 1978 and set up another organisation Ahle-Hadith Juba Sangha (AHSS). Galib expressed the need to wage jihad against Islamic fallacies, including the *mazar* culture, to establish Islamic rule in the country. In 1980, he joined Rajshahi University as a lecturer and he made it a base of the AHJS and launched its public activities in 1990. In 1994, Galib formed AHAB, its women's wing, a welfare organisation called Tawhid Trust, and a publication wing called Hadith Foundation Bangladesh.

Having received huge funds from Arab countries, Pakistan, the AHAB, JMB and JMJB expanded both the organisational infrastructue and followers. "According to Maulana Abdur Rahman, Sheikh of JMJB, the latter's highest decision-making body was the Majlis-e-Shura. He was the Ameer while Bangla Bhai was one of the seven members. Its members and supporters formed three tiers. The first comprised of Ehsars recruited as full-time activists whom it had trained all over Bangladesh and on whom it spent Tk 700,000 per month and who acted according to the direction of the higher echelons. The second tier comprised Gayeri Ehsars, part-time activists who numbered over 100,000. The third tier was made up of those who cooperated indirectly with the JMJB".[8]

Galib advocated armed struggle for an Islamic revolution in the country. He said – 'At every village, there will be a team of mujahids committed to reconstituting the Society and reforming their personal, family and social lives according to the dictums of the Holy Quran and Hadith.'[9]

According to a report in the *Janakantha* of 1 March 2005, since 1992 Galib had built nearly 650 mosques, madrasas, orphanages and other such institutions across Bangladesh.[10]

Intelligence reports assessed by *INDIA TODAY* suggest that since 2001 over 75,000 Madrasas have cropped up in Bangladesh. Most of them are funded by Saudi Arabia, Pakistan and Indonesia. Many of them belonging to the Harkat-ul-Jihad (HUJI). Bangla Bhai's Jagrata Muslim Janata Bangladesh (JMJN) and Jamatul Mujahidin Bangladesh (JMU) in Rajshahi train militants for Jihad. They are taught to use sophisticated weapons.[11]

Investigation by the Intelligence Branch of West Bengal Police revealed that Galib visited several madrasas in the border district of North 24-Parganas, Malda and Murshidabad without valid visas. "He had links with the banned Students' Islamic Movement of India (SIMI) and also perhaps the Jamaatul Mujahideen in India. … … Clearly, the border areas of West Bengal and Assam are in danger of becoming in the parlance of guerrilla warfare, safe rear areas for Bangladesh's fundamentalist Islamist militants. This is yet another indication of the planned and highly methodical way in which the latter, led by the Jamaat, are going about to capture power in Bangladesh with the aim of turning it into an Islamist state like Afghanistan under the Taliban, and making it the staging ground for the Islamization of the whole of South and South-east Asia."[12]

The Statesman, in an editorial on 20th August, 2005, stated – "The most disturbing aspect of the serial blasts in 63 of Bangladesh's 64 districts is that it reveals the bread of the net-work this jihadi group has been able to set up. It clearly can not only spread terror and mayhem in every nook and corner of Bangladesh but also work towards its objective of an Islamic state. Already the outfit has decreed that Bangladesh's current judicial system and the Constitution are in conflict with divine dictate. It has told Bangladeshis that until Shariat laws are enforced they should go to khatib of mosques and mohaddis of the *madrasas* and also to scholars of Islamic law for adjudication. It has warned that if the government refuses to promulgate Islamic law, the soldiers of Allah will teach the enemies of Islam "appropriate lessons of their life."

Undoubtedly all these pronouncements are an open challenge to Khaleda's government and seek to undermine its authority. But this should not surprise her. When she embraced the Jamat-e-Islam and the Islamic Oikya Jote as her coalition partners in 2001 to defeat the Awami League, she had been warned this would be politically suicidal. She also ignored suggestions to distance herself from pro-Pakistan elements who wanted to implement the Pakistani Jamat-e-Islami agenda through the government. In the past four years, these elements have infiltrated not only various layers of government but also built a vast network of operatives who last Wednesday bared their fangs. "Bangladesh is paying a heavy price for allowing 8,000 Afganistan-returned, Taliban-trained

Mujahiddeen to operate from heavily armed camps in the Chittagong Hill Tracts, and also for refusing to arrest the Islamic terrorist Bangla Bhai who since May last year has spread terror and mayhem to north-western Bangladesh. ... ..." [13]

The Centre For Policy Studies, Chennai conducted a study on Religious Demography of India by A.P. Joshi, M.D.Srinivas and J. K. Bajaj, wherein it was mentioned that "Islamic naval and land expeditions began exploratory incursions on Indian borders from as early as 636 AD. But Islam could obtain a foothold in India only in 713 AD, with the victory over Sind. India successfully resisted further spread of Islam into Indian territories for the next three centuries. From the beginning of eleventh century AD, India began rapacious Islamic invaders of Turkish origin. Mahmood Gazhni invaded India several times from 1000 to 1026 AD and annexed Punjab to his empire. The Ghur successors to the Ghazni Empire were finally able to extend Islamic conquest into the heart of India after defeating the valorous Prithvi Raj Chauhan in 1192.

"Thus, in contrast to the easy conquest the Islamic forces had in many other parts of the world, it took them more than five centuries to break the defence of India. From 1192 to around the end of the seventeenth century, various Islamic dynasties, derived from the Turko-Afghans and later the Central Asian Mughals, ruled over large parts of India. These about five centuries of Islamic rule constitute the first period in the long and unbroken history of India, when India was ruled by a group that did not subscribe to the fundamental civilisational and religious principles of India.

"Islamic rulers, even those who were relatively tolerant of the Indian beliefs and practices and did not attempt to forcibly propagate Islam, were committed to retaining distinct Islamic identity and presence within the larger and otherwise homogenous civilisation of India. Unlike all those who came into India before them, the Islamic rulers, consciously and perhaps conscientiously, resisted acculturation into the timeless civilisational and religious milieu of India. This thus became the first source of heterogeneity in India, dividing the Indian population mainly into two distinct religious communities, Hindus and Muslims, as reflected in the 1881 Census figures. In time, this demographic heterogeneity led to the Partition of the country into Indian and two separate Islamic enclaves."[14]

It was also mentioned in the Preface of the Study that "in the areas that form Pakistan now, the proportion of Indian Religionists rose considerably during the pre-Partition period, from 15.93 percent in 1901 to 19.69 percent in 1951. This is the only region of India, where Indian Religionists registered any gains in the course of the twentieth century. Partition immediately negated these gains; the proportion of Indian religionists declined to 1.60 percent in 1951, and has remained around that figure since then.

"In the areas that form Bangladesh now, Indian Religionists formed 33.93 percent of the population in 1901; their proportion declined to 29.61 percent by 1941 and further to 22.89 in 1951 as a consequence of Partition. Between 1951 and 1991, proportion of Indian Religionists in Bangladesh has been declining precipitously; they form only 11.37 percent of the population in 1991, less than half of their share in 1951."[15]

The Partition of India resulted in a huge influx of religious minorities, mainly Hindus from East Pakistan to West Bengal. During the liberation struggle in East Pakistan in 1971, around 10 million fled to India. Although after the war, a majority of these migrants went back to their homeland, but a sizeable residue stayed back in West Bengal, Assam, Trpura and other north-eastern states. After the liberation of Bangladesh, both Hindus and Muslims have been migrating in droves to West Bengal and other bordering states of India."[16]

It is also mentioned in the said article – "Of the estimated 15 to 20 million illegal migrants, approximately eight to 10 million have settled in West Bengal, six to eight million in Assam and the rest in Tripura and other north-eastern states and in such major cities as Delhi, Mumbai and Ahmedabad.

"During the period 1991-2001, the average growth of

population in the interior districts of West Bengal is considerably lower than the state average growth rate at 18 per cent (Burdwan 14 per cent, Hooghly 16 per cent, Bankura 14 per cent, Purulia 14 per cent, Howrah 15 per cent and Midnapore 16 per cent for example), whereas in the border districts the growth rate is much higher (Nadia 22 per cent, North 24-Parganas 23 per cent, South 24-Parganas 34 per cent, Murshidabad 28 per cent, Malda 31 per cent and Uttar Dinajpur 34 per cent).

"The same trend was noticed in the earlier inter-census decades 1971-81 and 1981-91 as well. The 1991 Bangladesh census report identified migration of Hindus since 1947 as the main cause for the decline in Hindu population in the country. The 1991 Bangladesh and India census reports threw significant light on the demographic dynamics on both sides, proving phenomenal migration from Bangladesh to India, particularly West Bengal.

"Higher growth in the Indian districts bordering Bangladesh and significantly lower growth rates in the adjoining Bangladeshi areas, extremely low growth rates (in some cases negative growth) in Hindu-dominated districts of Bangladesh and population explosions in some urban pockets of West Bengal confirmed this phenomenon.

Concentraton of Bangladeshi migrants has completely changed the demographic profile of the border districts of Assam and West Bengal. That has effectively shifted the frontier of Bangladesh, as it were, 10 to 15 km inside India. While striking down the illegal Migrants' Determination by Tribunal Act recently, the Supreme Court likened the enormity of the demograhic changes in Assam with "external aggression".

While the Chief Minister of West Bengal said "Bangladesh is a threat" to India, the West Bengal Governor Gopal Krishna Gandhi said illegal immigration is "a time bomb". The distinguished Journalist and writer Hiranmoy Karlekar, Consulting Editor of the Pioneer and Member of the Press Council of India wrote a book wherein he asserted – Bangladesh : The Next Afghanistan?

The most alarming state of the affairs has been the forecast by Bimal Pramanik who said that not only the intruders but the unplanned parenthood of the Muslims, there will be explosion of children who will be after 13 years i.e. by 2018 will enhance the Muslim population in West Bengal by 33.17 per cent. He has quoted from the Italian Writer and Diplomat Niccolo Machiavelli who said during Sixteenth century- "Sending immigrants is the most effective way to colonise countries because it is less offensive than to send military expeditions and much less expensive."[17]

NOTES AND REFERENCES

1. Paper on "Islamic Democracy" Vs Indigenous Peoples And Religious Minorities, presented by Prajnalankar Bhikku at the International Conference on Civil Society, Human Rights and Minorities in Bangladesh – organised by Campaign Against Atrocities on Minorities in Bangladesh (CAAMB), in association with Bangladesh Hindu Buddhist Christian Unity Council (BHBCUC, Internationl Chapters) held on 22-23 January, 2005, at Ballygunge Sikhasadan, Kolkata.
2. Ibid. This fact is well-known to those who are aware of "Deadly Cargo", *Time Magazine*, 21 October 2002 Issue, New York, USA and Bertil Lintner's "BANGLADESH; A Cocoon of Terror", the *Far Eastern Economic Review*, 4 April 2002.
3. Ibid
4. Ibid
5. Voice of America, Bangla Service dt.24 July 2004.
6. Press Trust of India, *Report from Dacca on 17 August 2005.*
7. *The Statesman*, Calcutta, dt.18 August 2005.
8. Hiranmoy Karlekar, *Bangladesh : The Next Afganistan*? p-188.
9. Ibid.
10. Ibid.
11. Saurav Shukla, *India Today*, Neighbour Bangladesh New Hot Spot of Terror, Sept. 2005.
12. Hironmay Karlekar, *Bangladesh : The Next Afganistan*? P.198-99.
13. *The Statesman*, Calcutta, dt. 20 August 2005.
14. *Religious Demography of India*, Ed. A. P. Joshi & others, The Centre for Policy Studies, Chennai.
15. Ibid.

16. Bibhuti Bhusan Nandy, Delimitation Can Wait, *The Statesman*, 8 September 2005.
17. Bimal Pramanik – Bangladeshi Anuprabesher Sudurprasari Fal Maratwak *Dainik Statesman*, September 13, 2005.

9

THE TRAGEDY

How many lives were lost during the Punjab massacres can never be established with any pretence at accuracy. The propagandists gave a slogan of 'A million dead'. G. D. Khosla estimated 4-5 lacs, Ian Stephens 5 lacs, Humphrey Trevelyn estimated 'less than a quarter of a million'; Chandulal Trivedi, first Governor of the Punjab estimated 225,000. Probably the most systematic attempt to work out a correct figure was that of Penderel Moon, who suggested that the most likely total was 200,000. However, "the partition of the Punjab caused untold misery to several million refugees and left a scar of pain across the surface of Mountbatten's Indian achievement."

At a speech in the India House when Mountbatten was on a visit to London in November, he said – 'Only' a hundred thousand people had died and only a small part of the country had been affected. Ismay told his wife 'I was horrified at Dickie's speech.' ... "It seems to me immaterial whether one hundred thousand or a million have actually died; or whether only 3% of the country is in turmoil. The essential facts are that there is human misery on a colossal scale all around one and millions are bereaved, destitude, homeless, hungry, thirsty – and worst of all desperately anxious and almost hopeless about their future."[1]

The history of the migration of the Hindus from East Pakistan after the Partition is one of the tragic episodes of contemporary history. Prior to the Partition the costs of the 'Great Calcutta Killings' which continued during 16th to 19th August, 1946, alone were 4000 dead, 10,000 injured.[2] "In Bengal it was an agonizingly protracted process. It started before the partition with the Noakhali riots of 1946 and continues down to this day. The migrants came in waves. At times the migration hit West Bengal in the shape of formidable breakers and often subsided into a trickle. But, except for a very brief period, it never stopped. It will not stop until the last of the non-Muslims is driven out of that country."[3]

The greatest tragedy of the British who thought themselves as an excellent champion of victory by dividing India, had lost all the Colonies. "As early as the turn of the century, Maud Diver commented, that 'more than half of the Anglo-Indian women of India today (1900) have spent their girlhood and early childhood in the country' (qtd. In Bailey 33). Ann Lind writes that approximately 8648 of the 45,418 British females in India in 1931 were born in India. And, although by 1939 there were only 759 Britishers in the Indian Civil Service (compared with 540 Indians), there was a substantial English population in India constituted of Army Officers, Planters, Businessmen, Journalists and the like, many of whom had a tradition of service in India going back many generations. Numbers of officials began to decrease around the time of the Second World War, when the British parliament decided to cease recruitment for the ICS.[4]

According to the *Star,* in May 1947, there were a little over 50,000 British still in India. Lord Wavell's estimate was 90,000 foreigners in India. There were, of course, a few who planned to stay on in India. The majority left.

What is learnt from a few books, most notably those by Allen Greenburger, Philip Woodruff, Susan Bailey; and Mary-Ann Lind that there were business classes, missionaries, novelists, labourers etc. Gordon Shepherd mentioned the category, he locates ex-majors whom he noted sleeping on railway platforms and women reduced to begging or abandoned, some by Indian husbands. There were

British Marxists sent to India to spread "Communism in the Colonies".[5]

Allan Mooreheed, the Special Correspondent for the *Observer* in India at that time speaks feelingly about "the British" in India : Strange New World" (9 November) : "The British also find themselves in a Special case. Nobody really attacks them now; they are the new Untouchables – for the moment. Most of them, in disgust, want to go. In places like Kashmir you find little pockets of old English couples who retired to spend their last pensioned years free of European income tax, and to die. Some of them have been there for 20 years. All around them are the shuttered houses, the forlorn little English Churches, the deserted clubs. In some places the Indians have moved in, but for the most part the gardens are going to ruin, the paint is peeling from the walls, and the museum-like atmosphere is hard to bear."

There was an instance where an old couple have decided to emigrate – where? Perhaps Malta or Cyprus. Perhaps England. But England with very little money, and no friends and no servants, and no home? Can anyone take such decision at the age of 70, after living 40 years in India?

"There were probably many more like the prominent General Auchinleck, who returned to England and found it impossible to live there, kept wishing to return to 'his men' and 'home' in Pakistan and settled finally in Morocco."[6]

Just after the Partition in Simla, "Mrs. Maude Penn Montague refused to leave the home in which she had given so many grand balls and dinners. She considered herself in mourning." She was born in India, of a father who'd also been born on the sub-continent and as such India has become her home. "With the exception of five years schooling in England, her whole life had been spent there. To friends who suggested it was now time to leave, she replied: 'My dear, whatever would I do in England? I don't even know how to boil the water for a cup of tea.' And so, while the former summer capital of the Raj celebrated, she sat at home weeping, unable to bear the sight of another nation's flag going up that pole where her beloved Union Jack had flown."[7]

Lord Mountbatten always thought himself a happy man. He had a delightful family, and all ten of his grandchildren were absolutely enchanting. Philip Zieglar mentioned in his book *Mountbatten* that "He wrote his manifesto of contentment at the end of the Broadlands Christmas, one of the two immutable tribal ceremonies when each year children and grandchildren rallied in force to celebrate together. On Christmas morning adults and children lined up in the hall and the senior staff of household and estate would file past to shake hands and receive their presents. The children abhorred this ritual; Mountbatten delighted in it. There followed a rally in the family pew of Romsey Abbey for the morning Eucharists, a visit to the old people at Edwina Mountbatten House, a massive luncheon for eighteen or more with 'crackers and general excitement', the ceremonial exchange of presents, the Boxing Day shoot." During 1977 he said 'I am indeed a very lucky person.'

The other gathering, longer and more relaxed but equally rich in ritual delights, was August at Classiebawn. Mountbatten as *pater familias* was seen all his splendour in his fastness. Building dams across the mouth of the stream, lobster-potting, prawning, he was always attended by a trail of devoted grandchildren, each performing an allotted task, all delighted to play their part in the unvarying routine, yet none of them even slightly intimidated by this formidable ancestor who ordered them about, bellowed at them, yet patently adored them. Classiebawn was a place for family reunions: a few old friends were asked to stay but only if it was known that they would fit in happily with the established pattern of existence. Mountbatten was more happy there than anywhere else on earth. He enjoyed 'a traditional Victorian-type family holiday, in a modern setting, or rather a timeless one.'

Mountbatten always paid much thought before his visit to Ireland. In 1974 he was concerned about the kidnapping of Lord and Lady Donoughmore. Robert Mark established the views of the Garda and told him that they strongly recommended that the visit should take place. 'We cannot show the white flag to the I.R.A.

and although we do not think there is any real danger, we feel obliged to assure you that as many men as are needed will be applied to the task.' Mark told Mountbatten that, speaking personally, he would prefer him not to take the risk, 'or, some might say, offer the challenge', but he could not formally reject the advice of his Irish opposite number. The twelve-man guard of 1972 was raised to fifteen the following year and to twenty-eight in 1974. Each year Mountbatten continued to consult Scotland Yard, but as time passed it seemed more and more of a formality. ..... Curiously enough, the previous year it had been at Broadlands that he had seemed in danger. His distant cousin, Prince Moritz of Hesse Kassel, had been kidnapped in Germany. He had quickly been released, but his abductors had boasted that Lord Mountbatten was another of their targets.[8]

The Prince of Wales wrote in mid August 'I hope you are having a decent rest in Ireland and are not working unnecessarily hard.' Whether necessarily or unnecessarily, Mountbatten was always working hard; but the work was concerned with schools or charities, not national defence, still less the affairs of Ireland. Why kill or kidnap an old man of nearly eighty? The family had noticed that the twenty-nine-foot fishing boat, *Shadow V,* in which they went out most days was left unguarded for long periods; they had even spoken to the police about it but they did not want to seem importunate. Surely there was no real danger?[9]

Mountbatten climbed down into *Shadow V* in the little harbour of Mullaghmore at about half past eleven on the morning of 27th August 1979. There were Lord and Lady Brabourne, Lord Brabourne's mother Doreen, and the Brabournes' fourteen-year-old twin sons, Nicholas and Timothy. An Irish boy from the neighbourhood, Paul Maxwell, came along to help with the boat. A police car had escorted them from the castle to the harbour and proposed to follow them along the coast road, surveying operations from the shore. Until recently a member of the Garda had always come out with them on their expeditions. The last policeman to accompany them, however, had been violently seasick and

Mountbatten has suggested that there was no need for anyone to put to sea.[10]

"As the boat cleared the harbour wall Mountbatten raced the engine furiously. John Brabourne benignly watched his father-in-law as he applied himself to his task with all the concentration he had lavished on the great enterprises of his prime and remarked how much he seemed to be enjoying himself. He was wearing a T-shirt designed to commemorate H.M.S.*Kelley* – bearing the words 'The Fighting Fifth'. It was something his family had never seen him in before. All his other clothes were familiar favourites, twenty year old or more. *Shadow V* slowed down as she approached the first of the lobster-pots which were the object of the expedition. Before Mountbatten had time to cut the engine the bomb, which had been placed beneath his feet, exploded and the boat disintegrated. Probably it was detonated by remote control from the shore, but some sort of timing device may have been used."[11]

Paul Maxwell and Nicholas Knatchbull were killed, eighty-three-year-old Lady Brabourne fatally injured. Timothy was blown some distance from the boat and was picked up with serious injuries but paddling strongly. John and Patricia Brabourne were taken from the water badly hurt, their legs broken, their skin lacerated by splinters of wood and metal. Mountbatten's body was found floating face downwards in the water a few yards away his limbs remarkably, unscathed. He had been killed instantly by the blast.[12]

Ziegler wrote – what had induced the I.R.A. to decide that 1979 was a suitable year in which to kill a distinguished old man and his family may never be known. The fact that the murder was almost simultaneous with the massacre of eighteen paratroopers on the other side of Ireland at Warrenpoint suggests that the decision was taken at a high level. It was, pronounced an I.R.A. bulletin, 'a discriminate operation to bring to the attention of the English people the continuing occupation of our country. We will tear their sentimental, imperialist heart,' the statement continued. The 'execution' was a way of 'bringing emotionally home to the English ruling-class and its working-class slaves ..... that their government's war on us is going to cost them as well'. The size of the bomb – claimed as fifty pounds and certainly no smaller – makes it evident that the intention was to kill not only Mountbatten but everybody else on board.[13]

NOTES AND REFERENCES

1. Ziegler, Philip, *Mountbatten*, p-437. Source :17 November 1947, Ismay Papers, III/8/22b).
2. *Transfer of Power*, Vol-VIII, p-302, Foot Note – Parliamentary Debates 5th ser. H of C, Vol.430, written Answers to question by Mr. R. A. Butler, Mr. Henderson gave the casualty figures for Calcutta Disturbances, 18 November 1946, Cols. 13-14).
3. Prafulla K. Chakrabarti, *The Marginal Men*, p-1
4. Sukeshi Kamra, *Bearing Witness : Partition, Independence, end of the raj*, p-238.
5. Ibid.
6. Ibid. p-242.
7. Collins Larry and Lapierre Dominique, *Freedom At Midnight*, p-269.
8. Ziegler Philip, *Mountbatten*, p-696-98.
9. Ibid.
10. Ibid. p-698.
11. Ibid. p-699.
12. Ibid.
13. Ibid.

10

Jinnah Defeated

Mohammad Ali Jinnah (1876-1948) started his political career as an ardent nationalist with a deep and sincere commitment to secular democracy. He was the champion of the Hindu-Muslim amity. "He abhorred religious obscurantism and sectarian politics and shunned both until he discovered a destiny for himself in the evening of his life. He once told Motilal Nehru, another secularist, that he disliked the Mullahs; and believed in 'none of their nonsense', although he had somehow 'to carry these fools along!' Most of his intimate friends, lawyers and politicians, were Hindus, the rest being Parsis. Gokhale, a man endowed with superlative political wisdom, was his guide, philosopher and friend. Indeed it was one of his most cherished ambitions to 'become the Muslim Gokhale' ... Jinnah had genuine admiration for all these nationalists who came forward to serve their motherland."[1]

Jinnah was not only able to win for himself a leading position at the Bar, but soon he made his debut in Indian politics in 1906. "His own political views had been shaped by association with Gokhale, Dadabhai Naoroji and Surendra Nath Banerjea" and his ambition, as he himself admitted, was to become the Muslim Gokhale".[2]

Initially the Muslim League party was pre-eminently a body of what Khaliquzzaman calls "Jee-huzoors" or "yes-men" whose main concern was to receive the favour of the British Government.

In the name of the Muslim Community they had only made their demands and the foreign Government was willing to meet them only because of their own interest. Jinnah took the charge of moribund state of the Muslim League in end of nineteen thirties. The Party was looked after for many years by men like Aga Khan and Sir Fazl-I-Hussain.

Pakistan was obtained by a 'nod'[3] and it was the one-man achievement of Mohammed Ali Jinnah. But the cost of India's Partition was not insignificant. "In August 1947 since nine months about fourteen and sixteen million Hindus, Sikhs and Muslims were forced to leave their homes and flee to safety from 'blood-crazed mobs'. In the same period over 600,000 of them were killed. But no, not just killed. If they were children, they were picked up by the feet and their heads smashed against the wall. If they were female children, they were raped. If they were girls, they were raped and then their breasts were chopped off. And if they were pregnant, they were disembowelled."[4]

Jinnah was proud of his singular achievement and arrived in Karachi 'in the midst of the holocaust all around with gruesome tales of plunder, rape and killings in several parts of the Sub-continent'. While Margaret Bourke-White, Photographer of the American Journals *Time* and *Life* congratulated Jinnah for creating the world's largest Islamic Nation, Jinnah corrected her : "Oh, it is not just the largest Islamic nation. Pakistan is the fifth largest nation in the world." Bourke-White commented, "The note of personal triumph was so unmistakable that I wondered how much thought he gave to the human cost : more Muslim lives had been sacrificed to create the new Muslim homeland than America, for example, had lost during the entire Second World War."[5]

The first act of the Constituent Assembly of Pakistan which met on 11th August 1947 was to elect him as its President. In the course of his Presidential address Jinnah said : You are free; you are free to go to your temples, you are free to go to your mosques or to any other place of worship in this State of Pakistan. You may belong to any religion or caste or creed – that has nothing to do with the fundamental principle that we are all citizens and equal citizens of one State. Now, I think we should keep that in front of us as our ideal, and you will find that in course of time, Hindus would cease to be Hindus, and Muslims would cease to be Muslims, not in the religious sense, because that is the personal faith of each individual, but in the political sense a citizens of the State.[6]

The Constituent Assembly passed a resolution conferring on Jinnah the honorific of "Quaid-i-Azam" (great leader), a title for which he had been called by Muslim Leaguers for some years. Liaquat Ali Khan in moving the resolution, hailed Jinnah as "the Ataturk or the Stalin of our State." The Constituent Assembly also decided that the Muslim League flag, with a white strip near the mast, should be the flag of the Pakistan Dominion.[7]

Though Jinnah exploited Islam to achieve Pakistan, there was no trace of his involvement in his religion in practice. A few days before the inauguration of Pakistan when Iskandar Mirza, who later became the head of the new state, enquired of Jinnah : "What kind of polity are you going to have? Are you going to have an Islamic state?" Jinnah replied, "Nonsense. I am going to have a modern state."[8]

After a few days when a group of leading Ulama asked him whether to apply the Shariah to the functioning of the new state. Jinnah told them sternly : "Whose Shariah? Hanafis? Hambalis? Sha'afis? Ma'alikis? Ja'afris? I don't want to get involved. The moment I enter this field, the ulama will take over for they claim to be the experts and I certainly don't propose to hand over the field to the ulama. I am aware of their criticism but I don't propose to fall into their trap."[9]

Jinnah wanted to dissolve the Muslim League and transform it into Pakistan National League. The speech of Jinnh advocating secularism has been strongly criticised by religious divines, confessional sects and right-wing political parties because of its opposition to the creation of an 'Islamic State'.... If Pakistan was the culmination of the struggle for a "Muslim Nation, then clearly secularism was a somewhat inappropriate ideology for it. A 'Muslim

Nation' should have a 'Muslim Constitution'.... If its aspiration could be implemented in Pakistan, then surely they could equally have been put into practice in a united India. In reality if the the Subcontinent had not been divided on a religious basis, the Muslims would actually have been a stronger force..."[10]

Jinnah was not sure of the future of the Muslim League and rather worried after Pakistan. He convened a meeting of the Governing Council after four months which met in Karachi on December 14-15, 1947. Out of 300 members about 160 came from divided India. Jinnah presided over the meeting and told his devotees that "the League would have to be split and the Indian part would have to function independently without his leadership. The separation was permanent and he was extremely sorry about it."[11]

One of the Indian members shouted : "We never thought this would be our fate; you have divided brother and brother. And left us completely in the lurch."[12]

Jinnah replied, *"But that was inevitable; it could not have been avoided." (Italics mine)*[13]

Another member from India interjected, "But you never warned us about it; you said we would be rid of Hindu domination; you have chained us to them forever."[14]

Naturally there was pandemonium, shouts and cross-words etc. Maulana Jamal Mian angrily rose to protest that "Pakistan could hardly take pride in calling itself a 'Muslim State'. He found many un-Islamic things in the State from top to bottom ...... The behaviour of the Minister is not like that of Muslims. The poor cannot enter the houses of the Ministers, the needy and the lowly cannot see them. Only the courtiers can enter, those who possess large bungalows can enter. The name of Islam has been disgraced enough."[15] Jinnah tried to pacify the agitators and soothe their frayed nerves. He took pains to assure them that as time passed everything would be all right. There was no need, he said, to be so pessimistic. "God willing we shall overcome our difficulties. Have patience and have faith in yourself."[16]

Jinnah maintained the laws of British which he did not change. In fact he desired to transfer Pakistan into another Turkey on the lines of Kamal Ataturk. He used to follow the British style of life. In his daily routine, he enjoyed his bacon and eggs for beakfast, ham sandwiches for lunch and two or three pegs of whisky before dinner... He wore Sherwani and the black cap (Jinnah cap) for public appearance in the evening of his life, he was always more at home on his Saville Row suit and hat... His outlook and thinking were deeply influenced by western ideas and principles. He had neither read Ghazali nor Rumi nor any of the other classic thinkers of Islam. He was quite ignorant of Islamic teachings.[17]

As a Governor-General of Pakistan, Jinnah continued hardly for over a year. He had to be confronted with many state problems. Due to severe strain and tension he was loosing his weight and his health was gradually deteriorating reduced to a skeleton. He felt dejected with what he witnessed; all that he had obtained after a hard struggle turning into a mess and his newly created 'homeland of Muslims' harbouring evils like corruption, nepotism and fanaticism. "He was disillusioned by the performance of his trusted collegue like Liaquat Ali Khan... Jinnah had also started suspecting Liaquat's loyalty. Likewise he was unhappy with the Chief Minister of Punjab, the Nawab of Mamdot who had no control on administration nor any idea of dealing with problems. He called the Governor, an Englishman by the name Mudie, and ordered him to sack Mamdot and appoint Mian Mumtaz Daulatana in his place. Mudie called the Mian and offered him the job but he refused. He told Jinnah that had he accepted the chief ministership 'Mamdot would have just cut my throat.' Quaid-i-Azam could not believe his ears; he was shocked to learn that his Pakistan was almost being taken over by a mafia."[18]

Jinnah realised that his so-called lieutenants whom he had patronised, turned out to be self-seekers who would not even mind resorting to murder to usurp power; they lacked character and would even conspire against their Quaid-i-Azam if need be. Someone who was in his full confidence warned him that many politicians had no scruples whatsoever; they were capable of instigating the army to overthrow him.

Before Partition Jinnah had been cautioned by several experts that it would be difficult to manage both western and the eastern wings separated by twelve hundred miles of foreign territory and 'inhabited by people different in their habits, customs and lifestyle'. But he had such confidence in the supremacy of his leadership that he believed that he would be able to put everything right. Now he became aware that neither he nor the bond of Islam would be able to knit together two such diverse peoples. The gulf in every respect – political, economic and social – was so wide that even Islamic brotherhood could not keep them together. He received the biggest set back when the Bengalees in the eastern wing rose *en masse* against his Goverment's decision to make Urdu as the only official language of the dominion. They demanded that as they constituted more than half the population of the new state, their language, Bengali, should also be made an official language.

The situation was so explosive that despite his ill-health Jinnah rushed to Dacca to pacify the agitated Bengalis. On March 21, 1948, he arrived in the capital of the eastern wing amidst in a cold reception. There were no slogan of "Quaid-i-Azam Zindabad".

Jinnah had been told that the Islamic bond would be strong enough to silence the opposition; he was, however, taken aback to find that language was proving to be a much more powerful link than religion. More than three lakhs people had gathered in Dacca Racecourse maidan to hear him, expecting he would concede their demand, but Jinnah was in an aggressive mood. That was his last major public address; ironically, he delivered it in English, though he spoke to a Bengali-language audience and informed them "in the clearest language" that "the State Language of Pakistan is going to be URDU and no other language." This was, of course, the most volatile, divisive issue in Pakistan politics. During the deliberation of his speech he said :

Any one who tries to mislead you is the enemy of Pakistan. Without one State Language, no Nation can remain tied up solidly together and function. Look at the history of other countries, Therefore, so far as the State Language is concerned, Pakistan's language shall be URDU..... I tell you once again, do not fall into the trap of those who are the enemies of Pakistan. Unfortunately you have fifth-columnists and I am sorry to say they are Muslims – who are financed by outsiders ... you must have patience. With your help and with your support we will make Pakistan a mighty State ... No amount of trouble, no amount of hard work or sacrifice is too much or to be shirked .... I wish you God speed.[19] The audience reacted vehemently and angrily they heckled him. There was pandemonium. Jinnah lost his calm and tried to admonish the unruly crowd.

Jinnah returned to Karachi from Dacca, his first and last visit to turbulent East Pakistan exhausted, depressed and forlorn; he confided to his sister Fatima, "I am sorry the game is lost. I backed the wrong horse."[20]

The Frontier grew more restive as well. Pathans continued talking about a state of their own "Pushtunistan", and even the Baluchis kept murmuring about a "Greater Baluchistan". So Jinnah was flown to Peshwar in the month of April where he had to speak at Islamia College and to air force cadets at Risalpur, and to the Civil Officers at the Government house, and then at an open-air meeting in Peshwar, where 'he was drenched to the bone", Fatima recalled. "That night it was obvious that he had caught a chill, but he refused to send for a doctor. 'Its nothing', he said to me, 'just a cold'. This cold was the beginning of the end. In Karachi, his cough continued, and only when I forced a doctor on him did we learn that he had bronchitis..."[21] Jinnah knew it was much worse than either a cold or bronchitis but did not wish to alarm Fatima more than was absolutely necessary. He understood too well by then that there was no cure for his sickness, no simple patent medicine to take his pain away or make the coughing stop.[22]

The relations with the closest collegues of Jinnah deteriorated rapidly in the end part of his life. Liaquat Ali Khan offered to 'resign' as Prime Minister because of Jinnah's dissatisfaction with his work. Jinnah expressed equal frustration and disgust at the way the Nawab of Mamdot was moving, then Chief Minister of the Punjab, "who was uninterested in the fate of the refugees."

However, in the month of June, Jinnah and Fatima flew to Quetta. The change of climate in the Baluchistan mountain country suited him comfortable. Fatima recalled "with few days of our arrival... he was able to sleep and eat well; the coughing subsided and his temperature came down to normal." This was the first time after many years he seemed relaxed.[23] On June 14th, Jinnah addressed the officers of Quetta's Staff College, reflecting perhaps his own deepest anxieties about the growing strain in his relations with the cabinet and other colleagues:

"You along with other Forces of Pakistan, are the custodians of the life, property and honour of the people of Pakistan. The Defence Forces are the most vital of all Pakistan Services and correspondingly a very heavy responsibility and burden lies on your shoulders... I want you to remember and if you have time enough you should study the Government of India Act, as adapted for use in Pakistan, which is our present Constitution, that the executive authority flows from the Head of the Government of Pakistan, who is the Governor-General, and, therefore, any command or orders that may come to you cannot come without the sanction of the Executive Head."[24]

He also told them that there was no need to modify the existing administrative set-up and warned them that they should not listen to the Mullahs who had no idea about how to run a State. If they were to be followed, Jinnah said, there would be nothing but chaos everywhere and Pakistan would be thrown back into the Middle Ages.

Jinnah attended a gathering of the Quetta Municipality. They presented him a handsome Relief Fund purse. He said "luckily Baluchistan was spared the tragedy which the Punjab went through on the establishment of Pakistan... Quetta may be as great a civil station as a Cantonment... For a large part of Western Pakistan it will be the natural Summer resort... It naturally pains me to find the curse of Provincialism holding sway over any section of Pakistanis. Pakistan must be rid of this evil. It is a relic of the old administration... British control .. we are now all Pakistanis – not Baluchistanis, Pathanis, Sindhis, Bengalis, Punjabis and so on... And we should be proud to be known as Pakistnis and nothing else."[25]

On 1st July, 1948, Jinnah went to Karachi to speak at the opening ceremony of the State Bank of Pakistan. The journey of the flight exhausted him so much that "he could hardly get out of bed" to deliver the speech that was written by him.

Jinnah was not passing well as he was suffering from sickness. His voice was feeble and paused and caughed his way through his speech. Fatima noted "when we returned home he collapsed into bed with his shoes on."[26] The doctors advised moving him to even more rarefied an atmosphere as he continued to run "a slight fever".

On July 6th, Jinnah and Fatima flew back to Quetta. As he was continued to run "a slight fever", the doctors advised moving him to even more rarefied atmosphere. Ziarat, a lonely Baluchi hill station forty miles and several thousand feet above Quetta, boasted a residencey bungalow built by the British. The hill station was perched like an eagle at the top of the timber line. It was Jinnah's last retreat in the search of air pure enough to save his dying lungs. Fatima recalled – "A cluster of fruit trees and beds of flowers add to the beauty of the place her brother liked its quiet charm."

On receiving an urgent call from the Secretary General to the Government of Pakistan Muhammad Ali from Karachi on July 21st, 1948, Lt. Col. Ilahi Bakhsh of the Indian Medical Service who was then "sitting out on (his) lawn" in Lahore after dinner immediately went to Quetta along with Major General M. A. Khan and Col. K. Jilani and drove to Ziarat in the Governor-General's car.

Next morning Fatima took Lt. Col. Ilahi Bakhsh to the great

leader's bed room where Quaid-i-Azam lying in bed facing the door. Dr. Bakhsh recalled – He looked shockingly thin and weak and had an ashen grey complexion … his appearance that morning frightened him. Jinnah must have guessed what was in his mind, for he diverted his attention by motioning him to a chair and enquiring if he had a pleasant journey. Dr. Bakhsh sat down and asked for detailed account of his illness past and present.

..."There is nothing much wrong with me" he told me, "except that I got stomach trouble and exhaustion due to overwork and worry for forty years. I have worked for 14 hours a day, never knowing what the disease was. However, for the last few years I have been having annual attacks of fever and cough. My doctors in Bombay regarded these as attacks of bronchitis, and with the usual treatment and rest in bed, I generally recovered within a weak or so. For the last year or two, however, they have increased both in frequency and severity and are much more exhausting." While I was listening to him I found him losing breath after every sentence and sometimes pausing in the middle. His mouth was dry and he moistened his lips many times while talking. The voice lacked tone and was ... almost inaudible. He had a couple of fits of coughing.....which left him exhausted .... After a short pause during which he closed his eyes and looked more dead than alive, he continued, "About three weeks ago I caught a chill and developed fever and a cough for which the Civil Surgeon of Quetta prescribed penicillin lozenges. I have been taking these since; my cold is better, the fever is less, but I feel very weak I don't think there is anything organically wrong with me .. ....if my stomach can be put right I will recover soon. Many years ago I had a rather bad stomach trouble for which I consulted two or three London Specialists, but they failed to diagnose my illness, and one of them even advised operation .... I didn't submit to the operations and on the advice of another London doctor went to Germany and consulted a famous doctor. He told me that I had no organic trouble and only needed rest and a regulation of diet. I stayed in his clinic for a few weeks and recovered completely. In 1934 I was diagnosed by the Bombay doctors to be suffering from heart disease, but a heart specialist in Germany assured me that my heart was perfectly normal.[27]

After thorough examination of the Quaid-i-Azam Dr. Bakhsh rang up the Civil Surgeon who drove up to Ziarat next morning with his clinical pathologist and brought along his microscope and reagents to test Jinnah's blood sputum etc. Their findings confirmed the Colonel's suspicions. So Bakhsh wired his own hospital staff in Lahore ordered three of its best Specialists to fly to Ziarat, telling one of them to bring his portable X-ray machine along. Then he wired Karachi for special medicines. Within the week most of Pakistan's advanced medical experts were flown or driven 8,500 ft above sea level to Ziarat; then concentrated on the dying old man who coughed without respite in that remote spot, whose strange name means "burial tomb", like the ancient Ziggurat mound of Mesopotamia erected at the dawn of civilization to house the remains of a god-king.[28]

Dr. Bakhsh recalled – while I was telling him the grave news I watched him intently. He ... ... remained quite calm and all he said after I had finished was, "Have you told Miss Jinnah?" I replied, "yes, Sir ...... I had to take into confidence." The Quaid-i-Azam interrupted me and said, "No, you shouldn't have done it. After all she is a woman." I expressed regret for the pain caused to his sister.... The Quaid-I-Azam listened patiently and in the end said, "It doesn't matter, what is done is done. Now tell me all about it. How long have I had this disease? What are the chances of my overcoming it? How long will the treatment last? I should like to know everything and you must not hesitate to tell me the whole truth." .... I replied that I .... felt confident that with the aid of the latest drugs there should be a fair chance of a considerable improvement.[29]

The situation turned into so grave that Ispahani flew in from New York and offered all sorts of medical aid from America. Bakhsh tried everything what the American could do. In fact "no cure had been discovered for the tuberculosis-turned-to-lung-cancer that had by then almost totally consumed both of his lungs."[30]

Liaquat Ali Khan arrived after Ispahani left and spent about half an hour alone with Jinnah. He might have observed that the Governor-General was dying and the burden of leading Pakistan would fall upon him. Fatima Jinnah never liked either Liaquat or his Begum. After Liaquat left, Jinnah told her with trembling voice, "Do you know why he has come? He wants to know how serious my illness is, how long I shall last."[31]

Liaquat Ali Khan, who held a vast property and a leader of the Muslim community was a displaced person from the United Provinces and who was then fifty-three years old, realised the uphill task he had to perform that "a nation to be run – millions of displaced persons to be fed and cared for, an undeclared war in Kashmir to be fought, a constitution to be drafted, dissident Bengalis, Pathans, Baluchis, Punjabis and Sindhis somehow to be satisfied.

Dr. Bakhsh remarked of Liaquat Ali Khan: Downstairs in the drawing room I met Prime Minister. He anxiously enquired about the Quaid-i-Azam, complimeted me on having won the first round by securing the patient's confidence, and expressed the hope that it would contribute to his recovery. He also urged me to probe into the root cause of the persistent disease. I assured him that despite the Quaid-i-Azam's serious condition there was reason to hope that if he responded to the latest medicine which had been sent for from Karachi he might yet overcome the trouble, and that the most hopeful feature was the patient's strong power of resistance. I was moved by the Prime Minister's deep concern for the health of his Chief and old comrade.[32]

The 'miracle' drug Streptomycine though administered could not achieve the impossible, nor did the "Id prayers from every mosque in Pakistan and elsewhere throughout the Muslim world on August 7th, suffice to turn the inexorable tide of the insidious disease that silently consumed his lungs." The medical team decided on August 9th to remove him to a lower altitude. The coramine injection and ultraviolet therapy proved unsuccessful. Jinnah was reluctant to move to Karachi carried by a stretcher, especially on the eve of Independence Day of Pakistan.

However, on August 13th at 3-30 pm Jinnah started his final journey to home. Fatima recalled "he insisted on wearing a brand new suit with a tie to match, and a handkerchief in his vanity pocket." Also she helped him put on his polished pump shoes. He was brought down on a stretcher and was placed in a semi-reclining position in the back of the big Humber car, in which they travelled to Quetta.[33] Inspite of the journey kept 'top secret' cheering crowds lined the road along their winding descent. It was quite a convoy with the Governor-General's handsome blue flags flying.

The convoy reached Quetta just before Sunset after about four hours' driving. The Residency was cleared of all visitors, and Jinnah was shifted on a stretcher to his bed-room on the first floor. Dr. Bakhsh examined him immediately and observed that "every tenth or fifteenth beat was missing …" Next day, August 14th, was the Anniversary of the establishment of Pakistan. Jinnah glanced the morning newspaper which was composd in Karachi, in the name of a message from Quaid-i-Azam to the Citizens of Pakistan which was written as :

Today we are celebrating the first anniversary of our freedom. We have faced the year with courage, determination and imagination, and the record of our achievement has been a wonderful one in warding off the blows of the enemy…… I congratulate you all – my Ministers under the leadership of the Prime Minister.[34]

Jinnah was getting better in the third week of August. But his doctor was 'shocked' to find that he weighed only eighty pounds. The doctors were confused if they would be able to return to his capital alive. Jinnah was again unwilling to go 'home' to the Governor-General's mansion as an "invalid". He said to Dr. Bakhsh : "Don't take me to Karachi on crutches … I dislike being carried on a stretcher from the car to my room." He wanted none of his Karachi staff to see him that he was too week to stand up.

Jinnah practically stopped eating after August 28th. … He lived on a few cups of tea and coffee, and some plain water to swallow his pills. He "lay in bed quietly all day," listless, apathetic, depressed. "Fati, I am no longer interested in living. The sooner I go the better," he confessed before the month ended. "It does not matter whether I live or die" he told Bakhsh on August 29th. Baksh "noticed tears in his eyes, and was startled by this manifestation of feeling in one generally looked upon as unemotional and unbending ….. I had always felt that he had been kept going, despite his low vitality, by and indomitable will ….. I knew from experience that when a patient gave up the fight no treatment, however perfect, could achieve much, and was, therefore, greatly distressed to find that the man of iron will had given up the fight.[35]

By September, Jinnah had pneumonia as well as tuberculosis and cancer of the lungs. His temperature rose high with his pulse disproportionately higher and his heartbeat was irregular, occasionally missing. Oxygen was required to help him breathe. Ispahani was cabled to call Dr. Hinshaw of the Mayo Clinic in Minnesota to fly immediately to Quetta for consultation. Dr. Bakhsh also sent for Dr. M. A. Mistry from Karachi…. After examining the patient, Mistry confirmed his friend's diagnosis, treatment, and advice, judging that there was really nothing more any American doctor could do.[36]

The Governor-General's Viking and two Dakota airplanes to carry his staff and luggage arrived at Quetta airport and were ready to take off by 2.00 P.M. on September 11, 1948. Fatima recalled : As his stretcher was taken into the Viking's cabin the pilot and crew lined up and saluted him. He in turn lifted his hand feebly .. A bed had been improvised in the front cabin and I sat with him, along with Dr. Mistry …. Oxygen cylinders and a gas mask were ready …. After about two hours flying, we landed at the Air Force base at Mauripur at 4-15 PM. Here he had landed just over a year ago, full of hope and confidence that he would help build Pakistan into a great nation. Then thousands had thronged to welcome him. But today, as instructed … there was no one at the air-port. Colonel Knowles … greeted us as we came out of the plane."[37] Knowles was Jinnah's military Secretary and had brought the army ambulance into which the Governor-General was carried on his stretcher. Fatima and a Quetta nurse, Sister Dunham, sat inside the rear of the ambulance with Jinnah, while the doctors followed in the Governor-General's new Cadillac Limousine.

After they had covered hardly four or five miles, the ambulance came to a sudden stop. Five minutes later Fatima reported, "I got out only to be told that it had run out of petrol, but the driver was also fidgeting with the engine ….. There was no breeze, and the humid heat was oppressive. To add to his discomfort, scores of flies buzzed around his face, and he did not have the strength to brush them away …. Sister Dunham and I fanned him in turns, waiting for another ambulance to arrive…. Every minute was an eternity of agony. He could not be shifted to the Cadillac as it was not big enough for the stretcher."[38]

"Wondering what had happened," wrote Bakhsh, "I got out and found that there had been a breakdown due to engine trouble. The driver assured us that he would soon put it right, but he fiddled with the engine for about twenty minutes, and the ambulance would start. Miss Jinnah sent the Military Secretary to fetch another ambulance. Dr. Mistry went with him. … … I examined him (Jinnah) and was horrified to find his pulse becoming weaker and irregular. I ran … and brought back a thermos flask containing hot tea. Miss Jinnah quickly gave him a cup … what a catastrophe if, having survived the air journey, he were to die by the road-side."[39]

It was a lonely stretch of highway leading south toward Karachi. "Nearby stood hundreds of huts belonging to the refugees", noted Fatima, "who went their business, not knowing that their Quaid, who had given them a homeland, was in their midst, lying helpless. Cars honked their way past, buses and trucks rumbled by, and we stood there immobilized in an ambulance that refused to move an inch …. we waited for over one hour, and no hour, in my life has been so long and full of anguish."[40]

The trip from the airport to the Government house took half as long as the entire flight from Quetta. They reached the Governor-General's mansion at 6-10 pm. "He slept for about two hours", Fatima noted, "then he opened his eyes and … whispered,

'Fati......' His head dropped slightly to the right, his eyes closed. I ran out of the room crying. 'Doctor, doctor. Come quickly. My brother is dying. Where are the doctors?' In a few moments they were there, examining him and giving him injections. I stood there, motionless, speechless. Then I saw cover his body, head to foot, with the sheet .... And fainted on the floor."[41] Quaid-i-Azam Jinnah died at 10.20 pm. on September 11th 1948.

Pravash Chandra Lahiry said "Pakistan is born out of deep-seated Hindu-hatred antipathy for India which according to the Muslims, was termed as Hindustan – a land for the Hindus. This idea pushed into and fomented by the imperialist Britishers who were the occupiers and rulers of India, for the purpose of holding a permanent subjugation of India for their nefarious imperialist designs."[42] The British found out in Mohammad Ali Jinnah a true exponent and vehicle of this narrow reactionary communal ideology.

Prof. R. K. Dasgupta while reviewing a book *Bangasanhar Ebong* written by Sukharanjan Sengupta, stated – "Jinnah's absurd Two-Nation Theory created Pakistan on 14th August, 1947, few realised that what made that possible was not the crooked diplomacy of the Bombay barrister, but his policy of Direct Action which had led to the Calcutta killing of 16 August, 1946."[43] This had obliged the British Government to submit to Jinnah's Muslim League for its fulfilment of diplomacy through communal violence in Bengal. Prof. Dasgupta also stated "The battle which the League fought in Bengal, a kind of Fourth battle of Panipat for Muslim power, was really fought in Kolkata, which was the scene of the worst British perfidy in the history of British Rule in this country. Unfortunately, this is not understood by historians, Indian or foreign, who make Delhi the centre of political activity which ended in Partition."[44]

Rafiq Zakaria writes in his book *The Man who Divided India* that "Jinnah died a disheartened man. He had no doubt won Pakistan ..... but he could not run it as he wanted. It turned out to be a hybrid – neither Secular nor Islamic."[45]

Three years after Jinnah's demise Liaquat Ali Khan, the first Prime Minister of Pakistan was assassinated. This had created a threat to destabilise the newly born Pakistan. The former Chief Minister of undivided Bengal Khwaja Nazimuddin succeeded him. Though Khwaja Nazimuddin was appointed as Prime Minister, he was too weak to control the situation and as such the politicians in West Pakistan, especially the Punjabis, openly defied him. After some time the Governor-General Ghulam Mohammad dismissed him. It may be noted the men who were governing the affairs of Pakistan whether politicians, bureaucrats or army commanders, were hardly practising Muslims; "they were the products of Anglo-Saxon training; their administrative approach was so oriented. Their living and thinking was also anglicised."

Iskandar Mirza became the first President of the Republic. He sacked Choudhury Mohammad Ali and appointed Suhrawardy as Prime Minister. In East Pakistan Fazlul Huq who was the Governor dismissed the Cabinet of Ataur Rahman Khan. Iskandar Mirza being annoyed dismissed Fazlul Huq and appointed Abu Hussain Sarkar as Chief Minister. But "within twelve hours he was also dismissed and Ataur Rahman Khan was brought back as Chief Minister. There were fist-fights among members of the Assembly; chaos prevailed; the Speaker was declared of "unsound mind" and removed; the hapless Deputy Speaker being a nonentity was beaten to death on the floor of the House."[46]

In such a chaotic state President Iskandar Mirza handed over power to the Army by ending the civilian rule. For the first time martial law was imposed in Pakistan. Ayub Khan became the supreme arbiter of the state. In a broadcast he said to the people on October 8th, 1958 : "Ever since the death of the Quaid-i-Azam and Mr. Liaquat Ali Khan, politicians started a free-for-all type of fighting in which no holds were barred. They waged a ceaseless and bitter war against each other regardless of the ill-effects on the country, just to whet their appetites and satisfy their base motives ... ... Having nothing constructive to offer, they used provincial feelings, sectarian, religious and racial differences to set a Pakistani against Pakistani.They could see no good in anybody else. All that mattered was self-interest. In this mad rush for power and acquisition, the country and people could go to the dogs as far as they were concerned."[47]

As Pakistan could not finalise their own Constitution perfectly, Ayub Khan drafted a Constitutioin based on the recommendations of a Commission appointed and briefed by him. On March 1, 1962 he announced the salient features of the new Constitution through broadcast. It replaced parliamentary democracy by Basic democracy. He rejected the ulama's pleas to make Islam the State religion..."[48]

The Scheme of Ayub Khan failed and could not satisfy all. He was ousted by handing over power to General Mohammad Yahya Khan. He held general elections on the basis of one-man one-vote. In East Pakistan Mujibur Rahaman's Awami League party secured a majority vote in the Nationl Assembly. But this was the reason of resentment of Zulfiqar Ali Bhutto of Pakistan People's Party who obtained the majority of seats in West Pakistan. The Punjabis were not prepared to play second fiddle to the Bengalis. There was political deadlock. "Yahya therefore promulgated a Legal Framework Order which enjoined that since Pakistan was created in the name of Islam, the constitution must adhere to Islamic ideology. This was a clever move to subordinate the forces of Bengali nationalism which propagate the predominance of language over religion. In order to suppress the revolt in East Pakistan, Yahya resorted to the worst form of repression and the army indulged in the genocide of Bengali agitators who resisted the onslaught and with the help of India seceded from Pakistan and became the free, separate state of Bangladesh. The conflict exhibited the ironic spectacle of Muslims killing Muslims; West Pakistani personnel behaved in the most inhuman manner, committing atrocities and sadism to defend their hold on East Pakistan. There could have been no greater betrayal of the so-called Islamic brotherhood which Jinnah had so relentlessly and stubbornly proclaimed; it negated the whole basis for the formation of Pakistan."[49] Our history reveals that when Muslims ruled India before the British, they lived together as good neighbours. But Jinnah divided Indian Muslims splitted into three nations-- Pakistani Muslims, Indian Muslims and Bangladeshi Muslims who now have no connection with each other. He has destroyed all the ties which had once knit them together. And all this he had done in the name of Islam.

It may be noted that after Jinnah's death, the politicians of Pakistan were like "a flock of sheep without their shepherd. From the date of its birth till the Governor-General Iskander Mirza, handed over the country's Government to General Ayub Khan in October 1958, there were as many as seven Prime Ministers" and none of them were bold enough to tackle the difficult situation.[50]

NOTES AND REFERENCES

1. Kulkarni, V.B., *Pakistan : Its Origin and Relations with India*, p-55.
2. Ikram, Dr. S.M., *Indian Muslims and Partition of India*, p-357. Source: M.H. Saiyad, *Mohammed Ali Jinnah: A Political Study* (1st Ed.), p-39.
3. Hodson, H.V., *The Great Divide*, p-312.
4. Mosley, Leonard, *The Last days of the British Raj*, p-243.
5. Zakaria, Rafiq, *The Price of Partition*, p-166.
6. Menon, V.P., *The Transfer of Power in India*, p-410.
7. Ibid.
8. Khan, Wali, *Facts are Facts – The untold story of India's partition*, p-158.
9. Zakria, Rafiq, *The Man Who Divided India*, p-102. Source: Iqbal, Afzal, Islamization of Pakistan, p-25.
10. Ibid, P-163, Source : Tariq Ali, *Can Pakistan Survive? The Death of a State*, Middlesex, 1983,pp-42-43.
11. Ibid, p-163.
12. Ibid.
13. Ibid.
14. Ibid.
15. Wolpert, Stanley, *Jinnah of Pakistan*, p-355.
16. Zakaria, Rafiq, *The Man Who Divided India*, p-164.
17. Ibid.

18. Ibid, p-167.
19. March 21, 1948, Quaid-I-Azam Speaks.
20. Zakaria, Rafiq, *The Man Who Divided India*, p-170.
21. Wolpert, Stanley, *Jinnah of Pakistan*, p-360. Source: Jinnah, My Brother.
22. Ibid.
23. Ibid.
24. Wolpert, Stanley, Jinnah of Pakistan, p-361; Source: Quaid-i-Azam speaks, June 14, 1948, pp.154-55. Speeches of Quaid-I-Azam Mohammad Ali Jinnah, Karachi: Ministry of Information & Broadcasting, 1950.
25. Ibid.
26. Ibid, p-362.
27. Wolpert, Stanley, *Jinnah of Pakistan*, p-363.
28. Ibid,p-364.
29. Ibid. Source : Ilahi Baksh, With the Quaid-I-Azam During His Last Days (Karachi: Quaid-I-Azam Academy, 1978), p-8. The following quotes are from Ibid, pp.9-10).
30. Wolpert, Stanley, *Jinnah of Pakistan*, p-364..
31. Ibid, p-365; Source Pirzada, *Last Days of the Quaid*, p-6.
32. Ibid; Source : Ilahi Baksh, With the Quaid-I-Azam During His Last Days, p-11.
33. Ibid, p-366, Source: *Jinnah My Brother*.
34. Ibid, p-366, Source : August 14, 1948, Quaid-i-Azam Speaks pp.247-49.
35. Ibid, p-368, Source : Ilahi Bakhsh, With the Quaid-I-Azam During its Last Days, pp.32-33.
36. Ibid. Source: Baksh, p-40.
37. Ibid. p-369. Source: Jinnah, My Brother.
38. Ibid.
39. Ibid. Source : Ilahi Bakhsh … *Last Days*, pp.47-48.
40. Ibid. Source: *Jinnah, My Brother.*
41. Ibid. p-370.
42. Lahiry, Pravash Chandra, *India Partitioned And Minorities in Pakistan*, p.3-4.
43. *The Statesman*, Kolkata, 6 November,2002, R. K. Dasgupta, Looking Back at Tragedy.
44. Ibid.
45. Zakaria, Rafiq, *The Man Who Divided India*, p-171.

46. Ibid. p-180.
47. Ibid. p.181-82. Source:Jahan, Rounaq, *Pakistan : Failure in National Integration;*, New York, 1972, p-55.
48. Ibid. p-184. Source : Iqbal, Afzal, *Islamization of Pakistan*, Delhi, 1984, pp.80-81.
49. ibid. p.184-185.
50. Kulkarni, V.B., *Pakistan, Its Origin & Relations with India*, p-110-111.

POSTCRIPT

In analysing the whole episode of our struggle for Independence it seems that the foreign imperialist after loosing the colonies in America where by imposing unjustified taxes and control over the democratic Government, the colonies were united and took arms in hand and on 19th April 1775 "First shot fired at Lexington. British retreat."[1] The British took a great lesson from this incident and they applied a secret Diplomatic policy to retain India in their fold. Strategically, India became the centre of imperial defence whose limbs were stretched from "Hong Kong to the Middle East, From East Africa to the Northern passes of Burma." Winston Churchill once expressed his view on India in the House of Commons in February, 1931 that "the loss of India would be final and fatal to us. It could not fail to be part of a process that would reduce us to the scab of a minor power."

While the English were trading in India there was not much concern about them. Even when they were ruling, people did not care as Indians had in the past many rulers who never interfered with the local self-government. The East India Company took the advantage of the situation due to the down-fall of the Mughal Empire and encroached further area for the benefit of trading as well as ruling. They attempted to 'anglicise' every sphere of life of the Indian people. The missionaries became very active in propagating their religion and educational institutions on the British model and extended to different parts of Bengal. In fact, inaugurating the new educational system, the British deliberately stated that their object was to train up a nation who would be English in everything except in race and who would be pro-British.

Realising the menace of being swallowed up by a new religion and a new culture, the soul of the people revolted. The first visible embodiment of the revolt was Raja Rammohan Roy and the movement of which he was the father of the Brahmo Samaj movement. Raja Rammohan Roy stands out against the dawn of the new awakening in India as the prophet of the new age. He advocated an all-round regeneration of the social and national life and the acceptance of all that is useful and beneficial in the modern life of Europe.

The Brahmo Samaj was founded in 1828. Raja Rammohan Roy was succeded by Devendranath Tagore, father of Rabindranath Tagore. His successor was Keshav Chandra Sen. By the time the British rule in India had spread throughout a large portion of the country and people had began to realise slowly that the new invaders were quite different from the others. They had come merely not for trade and commerce or to preach religion, but to conquer and to rule. They were also likely to rule our country as foreigners. *Baniker mandanda dekha dilo Rajdanda rupe pohaley sarbari* (Traders become the Rulers overnight). The realisation of this national menace quickly roused the masses to a sense of the danger that threatened them. Thus occurred the revolution of 1857. It was a revolution in which both the Hindus and the Mohammedans unitedly fought and as such it was thought that the English would be thrown out of the country. Unfortunately the revolution failed and the British followed a reign of terror and punished thousands of rebels killed by Fire Squads and by an enactment under Section I Act.XVII of 1857. The Act empowered the Civil Authorities "to sentence to death any man identified as having belonged to, or been present with a Regiment in Mutiny at the time of its Mutiny and to carry the sentence into the immediate execution." The entire country was disarmed.[2]

The Mutiny was a turning point in the history of British India. The Board of Directors of the East India Company was taken over by the British Government. Queen Victoria was proclaimed the Empress of India and the Governor General was designated the Viceroy and Governor General. Next the British Indian army was reorganised and enhanced the British personnel in the Army. The paramountcy of the British Government was proclaimed – all ruling kings and titular princes of India were declared the feudatories of the British Crown.

The Brahmo Samaj had considerable influence on the new generation of English-educated Indians and even those who did not become converts to the Brahmo Samaj accepted the spirit of reform and progress for which it stood. About this time two prominent religious personalities appeared on the scene who were destined to have a great influence on the future course of the new awakening. They were Ramakrishna Paramhamsa, the Saint, and his disciple Swami Vivekananda. Ramakrishna preached the gospel of the unity of all religions and urged the cessation of inter-religious strife – *Jato math tato path* (There are many ways to God).

In the Western India the renaissance unlike that in the Northern India, appeared more in the form of a movement for educational and social reform than as a religious movement. The originator of this awakening was Justice M. G. Ranade who, later on, found a worthy disciple in Mr. G. K. Gokhale. In 1884, Mr. B. G. Tilak, Mr. G. G. Agarkar and Mr. V. C. Apte, founded the Deccan Education Society.

In the South the Theosophical Society founded at Adyar near Madras in 1886 by Madame Blavatsky and Col.Olcott, played an important role in social and public life. Mrs. Annie Besant joined the Society in India in 1893 and became the President in 1907. She continued in the office till her death in 1933.

When the foreign government ruled by the bureaucracy, the people realised for the first time in their history what a foreign rule really meant. In South Africa the Boers fighting against the British for their freedom, the newly-awakened Japanese fighting the Russians for their existence and safety and the Russian masses fighting the all-powerful Tsar for their bread and their liberty. "The

Indian middle class, steeped in English literature and history, gorged themselves with the ideas of *liberty, equality and fraternity* which the American War of Independence (1773) and the French Revolution (1789) had glorified." All these incidents opened the eyes of the Indians and they were encouraged by the movement of the masses.

The protest against the oppression of the Indigo planters and the agitation of the ryots acquired a greater momentum in resentment against the British. Meanwhile the spread of English education brought into being a new generation imbued with liberal ideas and willing to fight a long drawn battle with the British for independence and accordingly, a vernacular press was slowly took shape to express Indian aspirations.

During 1875 there were as many as 475 newspapers, mostly published in the provincial languages. The British Indian Association in Bengal was started in 1851 by Dr. Rajendra Lal Mitra and Ramgopal Ghose. In Bombay there was Bombay Association under the leadership of Sir Mangaldoss Nathubhai and Mr. Naoroji Furdunji. The association owed its origin to Dadabhai Naoroji and Juggannath Sankar Seth. In the South public life was inaugurated by *The Hindu.* The founders were messrs. M. Veeraraghavacharian, Hon'ble Rangiah Naidu etc. In maharashtra, the Poona Sarvajanik Sabha was set up. In Bengal the Indian Association was founded in 1876 by Surendra Nath Banerjee and Ananda Mohan Bose as first Secretary.

The Vernacular Press Act of 1878 was promulgated by the Viceroy Lord Lytton to supress the native press for their provocative rebellion. The whole masses of India protested against the Act. As such the Act was repealed at last by Lord Ripon in 1882. In this manner the people protested the Arms Act, Ilbert Bill etc. In West Bengal there were large parts engulfed agrarian unrest during the period 1870s and early 1880s.

To subdue the growing discontent among the masses which was likely to lead towards a popular and violent revolution, A.O. Hume, a retired English ICS officer under the direction adn guidance of the Viceroy Lord Dufferin took the initiative of formation of an Indian Association to provide a safe, mild, peaceful and constitutional outlet of the grievances of the people which could be a safety volve. With this end in view one day i.e. on the 1st March 1883, Hume addressed the graduates of the Calcutta University wherein he asked "for fifty men, good and true, men of unselfishness, moral courage, self-control and active spirit of benevolence ... if joined as founders the thing can be established and further development will be comparatively easy.[3] Thus in 1885, the Indian National Congress was formed by A.O. Hume at a conference held in Bombay under the Presidentship of W.C. Banerjea, a veteran lawyer of Calcutta. It was attended by 72 delegates from all over India.

In 1899 Lord Curzon came to India as the Governor General. Under his regime the administration reached new levels of efficiency. No Viceroy, before or after him, initiated administrative measures so numerous and so far-reaching. Some of these measures roused great resentment and opposition. The Partition of Bengal, in particular, was vehemently resisted. Lord Curzon sought to justify the Partition of Bengal in the interests of better administrative efficiency. But the dividing line was so crudely drawn that it meant the splitting of the Province into two Communal blocks – the one in which the Hindus were in the majority, and the other in which the Muslims pre-dominated. This measure was construed as an attempt on the part of Lord Curzon to cripple the new renaissance in Bengal and, for the first time, agitation went beyond the accepted methods, namely, of prayer, petition and protest. A new programme of resistance was launched which included the boycott of British goods.[4] After the Independence of India, it was revealed from the Government secret reports that "the real purpose of the Partition was to reduce the Bengalee Hindus to political impotence".[5]

Lord Curzon's perfidy did not end here. He took measures to alienate the Muslim leaders from the anti-Partition movement. He encouraged communal dissensions by telling the Muslims that they would be in a majority in the new Province. The Nawab of

Dacca was given a loan of Rupees fourteen lakhs to launch an anti-Hindu campaign which led to serious communal riots, bloodshed and loss of life and property.

The final decision on the Partition was announced in July 1905. The Plan was to be operational from 15th October 1905. A wave of indignation passed over Bengal. The students were on war-path. There was vehement protest all over the Province. Boycott of the Government and boycott of British goods were suggested in the newspapers like *Amrita Bazar Patrika, Sanjibani* and *Sandhya.* The most remarkable feature of the movement was its spontaneity.

The movement that ensued cannot be called as a mere political agitation. This was 'an upsurge of the people on all fronts.' This was a moment of destiny for the Bengalees. A large number of Primary schools were organised, often in remote villages, to impart education to boys and girls of all castes and creeds. The rich and poor alike contributed money. Eventually the National Council of Education was set up on 14th August 1906 to extend educational facilities all over Bengal. A large number of industrial concerns grew up all over the Province for indigenous manufacture of goods to meet the needs of the people. There were some places where trade unions were sponsored to protect the interests of labour and enhance their bargaining power following a wave of strike in Government establishments, in railway workshops and factories of the European business houses.

There was brisk literary activity in Bengali in the form of patriotic songs of great national fervour and beauty. Those were composed by many eminent poets including Rabindranath Tagore. Unknown bards of rural Bengal composed songs expressive of the spirit of this age. There was an intense movement for self-development and self-realisation developed in all spheres of life. The Bengalees for a time were lifted to a higher level of thought and action. Gokhale said : "What Bengal thinks today, India thinks tomorrow."

The Boycott resolution was adopted in several meetings all

over the District towns, Sub-divisional towns and even in remote villages of Bengal. The leaders of different shades of opinion also met privately almost daily in Calcutta. A public meeting was called at the Town Hall, Calcutta on 7th August, 1905. The students were gathering in College Square from 2 PM with black flags and shouting slogans against the proposed Partition of Bengal. In this gathering in College Square the slogan '*BANDE MATARAM*' was adopted as a battle cry of Indian nationalists in their fight for freedom.[6]

The students thereafter moved in procession towards the Town Hall. A large number of people including representatives from the districts assembled in the meeting. The gathering was so vast that eventually two meetings were held – one inside the Town Hall and the other in the adjacent ground outside. The resolutions passed in the two meetings were identical. The first two resolutions condemned the proposed Partition of Bengal and the manner in which it was decided upon in complete disregard of public opinion. The third and fourth resolutions laid down the programme of action to be pursued against the Government's move and urged the people unequivocally to boycott all British goods and to carry on the movement ceaselessly till the decision on the Partition was annulled.

As the day of the actual Partition i.e. 16th October, 1905 advanced, the tempo of the people in the shape of revolt rose high. The eminent persons of non-political activities forsook their normal avocation and joined the movement thereby upgrading the national honour and integrity. The most remarkable personality among them was the poet Rabindranath Tagore. He came forward to give a lead to the national fight against the Partition of Bengal. He suggested that everyone should suspend normal activity and observe fasting, there should be no cooking of food (Arandhan) on the same day and in spite of Government's administrative action, every Bengalee should refuse to accept the artificial division and vow for the eternal unity of the Bengalees. Sarala Ghoshal, the poet's niece suggested that everyone should tie up a Rakhi (sacred red thread) which is the religious custom of the Hindus for affinity and integrity of brotherhood. Many people from various localities marched in procession to Kali temple at Kalighat on 28th September 1905 and offered prayers desiring the blessings of the Mother Goddess Kali.[7]

On the 16th October, 1905, thousands of people of all ranks of the society marched in a huge procession to the Ganges with Rabindranath Tagore. They were all barefooted as is customary for bereaved Hindus. After ceremonial ablution in the Ganges, they tied 'Rakhi' to each other's wrist. Rabindranath composed a song in Bengali which was chanted by the people :

Let the soil of Bengal, its waters, its airs, the fruits of its trees be all holy, Oh God!... Let the soul and mind of Bengal, be one, let the brothers and sisters in homes of Bengal remain united!

About fifty thousands men and women assembled in the afternoon and joined a meeting in the Parsibagan grounds (where the Brahmo Balika Shikshalaya is now situated). The meeting was presided over by Anando Mohan Bose who was brought from his sick bed on a stretcher. A resolution was passed in the meeting both in English and Bengali version. The Bengali version was read by Rabindranath Tagore. The resolution expressed the determination of the people of Bengal, "to oppose the parliamentary decision on partition of Bengal and to fight its ill effects and expressed their resolve to preserve the unity of Bengalees by all means in their power." The progress of the movement created a thrilling and enthusiasm among the politically conscious people all over India. The fight in Bengal against the imperialist – the Swadeshi movement, the revolutionary movement – often ignited the imagination of the ignorant masses as well. The militant nationalism in India moved a step forward.[8]

To subdue the student movement, the Chief Secretary of Bengal Government R. W. Carlyle issued a confidential circular in October 1905, to all District Magistrates laying down the policy of the Government. It was clearly stated that the Government will not tolerate any anti-Partition agitation by the students of the Government-controlled or Government aided Institutions.

The student community of Bengal reacted sharply. Immediately they formed an Anti-Circular Society. Sachindra Prasad Bose, an under-graduate student of the City College led the students for Anti-Circular agitation. He was assisted by some senior leaders, notably Krishna Kumar Mitra, Editor of *Sanjibani* and Liaquat Hussain. The Anti-Circular Society within a short while became very effective orgnisation and flourished in number of Branches in the districts. Sachindra Prasad Bose by his dynamic leadership was able to co-ordinate the work of the students over a wide area.

The Anti-Circular Society set up National Schools for extending educational facilities to expelled students. Accordingly, the first school was established at Rangpur and the next one at Calcutta. Subsequently, this activity of the Society discontinued when the National Council of Education was formed.

The Anti-Circular Society although formed to meet a specific situation, was in fact an association of students embodying the true ideals of Youth Movement. Really, it was the first step of conscious youth power in Bengal in modern times to shape our history. "It consistently maintained a secular and non-communal stance and abjured the Hindu imagery and religious symbols. It supported the right of the Muslims to ceremonial slaughter of cows – a matter of great courage in those days. It had a large number of Muslim members and at least on one occasion averted a communal riot at Jessore."[9]

The import of British goods declined due to the movement of boycott. The British industrialists from England put pressure on the Government of India. Hence repression became wanton and inhuman. The Lt. Governor of newly created Eastern Bengal Mr. Fuller took repressive measures beyond the limit of law. Almost all the districts suffered from his revengeful actions.

Out of several volunteer orgnisations in Bengal the Swadesh Bandhab Samity was founded by Ashwini Kumar Datta. His unique achievement was to establish the Braja Mohon Institution where he not only followed the University curriculum but took real efforts to bring out the young men of character. The Swadesh Bandhab Samity initially set up before the Swadeshi movement to render services to sick and poor, to people in distress and to extend primary educationl facilities into remote villages. Further, the Samity tried to inculcate a sense of self-help, to improve community life and arrange for the settlement of disputes through local arbitration so as to save the ignorant rural people from ruinous litigation. At the heyday of its activities, the Samity had about 200 branches and set up numerous primary schools, over 250 arbitration courts functioned under its aegis. The members of the Samity rendered valuable service when famine conditions prevailed in Barisal during 1906. On March 11, 1906, the National Council of Education was established.[10]

The Bengal Provincial Conference held in Barisal on April 1906 gave it a distinctive place in the annals of the freedom movement. The conference was an annual event and was a forum for discussion on the social, political and cultural problems. The participants were men of various shades of opinion and besides the political leaders, there were men of various professions, educationists and other men of letters. It was never a platform from which a rebellion could be proclaimed, yet the Government was in a belligerent mood right from the beginning and a prohibitory order was issued on the 13th April banning the shouting of '*Bande Mataram*' in the streets.

On the scheduled date of the Bengal Provincial Conference on 14th of April, 1906, the President-elect Abdul Rasul and several other delegates along with local volunteers proceeded to the conference pandal in a procession. The President-elect and his British wife were seated on a horse-drawn carriage but the others, including Surendra Nath Banerjea, Motilal Ghosh (Editor, *Amrita Bazar Patrika*) and Bhupendra Nath Bose proceeded on foot. The Police contingent present did not interfere in the movement of the leaders; but all of a sudden fell upon other delegates and volunteers and indiscriminately assaulted them. There was no shouting of slogan '*Bande Mataram.*' After the assaults the yougmen violently and boisterously raised the slogan '*Bande Mataram.*' Chittaranjan Guha Thakurata who was then quite young was severely beaten up by the police and then thrown him down into a way-side pond. Surendra Nath Banerjea protested to the European Officer-in-Charge but he was arrested and summarily sentenced to a fine of rupees two hundred.

Surendra Nath Banerjea and other delegates on their way back to Calcutta received spontaneous grand ovations by the people assembled in the steamerghat and Railway stations. At last when they reached the Sealdah station there were about ten thousand gathering received them by thunderous cheers. Surendra Nath Banerjee's carriage was drawn by enthusiastic youngmen to College Square where he addressed a vast assembly. The incidents at Barisal were all widely covered in the newspapers. The issue was discussed in a series of public meetings. The Swadeshi movement thus gained in momentum. The administration imposed oppressive measures to subdue the movement but their attempts were in vain.[11]

The Swadeshi movement urged forward while the Hindus and Muslims fought unitedly. But after a year the seeds sown by Lord Curzon began to bear fruits. The Muslim henchmen gradually alienated and serious Hindu-Muslim riots broke out in East Bengal. The boycott movement was not effective outside Bengal. The leaders of the extremist youth put forward a new programme. Bepin Chanra Pal first put forward his doctrine of passive resistance and it was furher elaborated by Aurobindo Ghosh who proposed to systematic and more extended boycott of British goods. They advised to boycott of the Government educationl schools and colleges, boycott the Court of Justice, Non-cooperate with the Executive authority, Setting up of arbitration Courts, Disobedience of all repressive laws and punitive measures and finally social boycott of those who co-operate with the Government.

Sri Aurobindo while formulating the above programme thought it would eventually lead to the next stage of aggressive resistance and he took it to a stage of open insurrection. As the machinery to carry out the programme was inadequate it flopped. There was no central organisation and naturally some youths joined the secret movement.

The Government took serious action and enforced excessive repressive measures. Firstly, the '*Bande Mataram*', the '*Jugantar*' and the '*Sandhya*' were forced to cease publication.

In December 1908, the Anushilan Samity and Atmonnati Samity of Calcutta were banned. In January 1909, Suhrid Samity and Sadhana Samity of Mymmensingh, Anushilan Samity of Dacca, Brati Samity of Faridpur and Swadesh Bandhab Samity of Barisal were banned and declared as unlawful organisations.

Next the eminent nationalist leaders were arrested in December 1908 and confined without trial for about fourteen months in different jails outside Bengal. Some of them were – Aswini Kumar Datta, Manoranjan Guha Thakurata, Satish Chandra Chatterjee of Barisal, Krishna Kumar Mitra, Raja Subodh Mallick, Sachindra Prasad Basu and Shyamsundar Chakrabarty of Calcutta, Bhupesh Chandra Nag, Pulin Behari Das of Dacca.

Further a crop of revolutionary leaders emerged – Brahma Bandhab Upadhaya, Lajpat Rai and Bal Gangadhar Tilak etc.. Tilak led the people from Maharashtra. In Bihar, Khaparde emerged as the leader and Lala Lajpat Rai led Punjab.

The Lt. Governor Fuller of the new East Bengal Province exploited Hindu-Muslim differences of opinion to create factions. He openly supported the muslim majority and discriminated heavily against the Hindu minority in the province. The Muslims formed a political organisation *Muslim League* which published anti-Hindu and pro-government pamphlets. Thus communal riots occurred at Comilla in Tipperah district in 1907 and Jamalpur taluk of Mymensingh district and the riots occurred in everywhere as a regular feature.

In 1908, while the Government imposed heavy repression on the revolutionaries the infuriatd people resisted with all their might and sacrifices. The leaders were either imprisoned or deported. Bipin Chandra Pal and Lala Lajpat Rai went into self-imposed exile, Aurobindo escaped to Pondicherry, a French enclave and Tilak remained incarcerated in Mandalay.

However, at the (Royal) Coronation Durbar held on December 12, 1911, two important announcements were made. One was the annulment of the partition of Bengal and the other the transfer of capital from Calcutta to Delhi. The transfer of capital to Delhi evoked no reaction as everybody was happy with the annulment of the Partition.

"The Partition of Bengal provoked a storm of protest which culminated in the first organised uprising against the Crown's rule in this country. It took different forms : from the peaceful boycott of British goods to the organised revolutionary activities calculated to ovcerthrow the British from the seats of power. Two Bengals were placed under a Lieutenant-Governor."[12]

In contrast, after fortytwo years of the 'Bengal Partition' movement Pravash Chandra Lahiry, an active freedom fighter who was in Rajshahi on the day of the 'Partition of India' in 1947, narrates the flag hoisting ceremony of Pakistan on "Fourteenth day of August, Nineteen Forty Seven. The day dawns with mirth and hilarity on all sides. Every face of the vast population shows signs of radiant glow of fulfilment of a long cherished desire of winning freedom from foreign rule.[13] This was the day when Pakistan was born out of India after a major British diplomacy.

He also writes – India bleeds and the nationalist fighters for Independence weep in their heart of hearts. Many of them came into the political arena after the Partition of Bengal in 1905 and fought for its annulment but today they are powerless – they are mere spectators of the gruesome operation, as their leaders accepted and submitted to it, and the rank and file also accepted it with all humility and dignity. The Bengal revolutionaries who had the bright record and reputation of playing with the bombs and revolvers had not fired a shot or burst a bomb on this heinous operation of mother-India but could hardly become hilarious over this achievement of freedom; hence they kept away far from the flag-staff in a moody and dejected state of mind. Yes, freedom has come but not the freedom they fought for.

Further he states – Group of persons – young and old, boys and girls – parade the streets with hilarious shouts of 'Pakistan Zindabad', Quaid-i-Azam Zindabad'. Pakistan national flags, newly designed with white and green pieces of cloth joined together with crescent and stars on the green, representing the minority and the majority communities respectively, flutter on every house-top with the morning breeze.

While the day advanced, the rural people in their hundreds and thousands poured in the town with same spirit of mirth and festivities, the railway authorities allowed free journey on this august day. The District and the Divisional headquarter towns of Rajshahi 'wears a gala look with newly improvised decorated gates on the roads and streets and flags and festoons running across them.' The whole day passed on in gaity. All sections of people gathered in the College ground to hold a public meeting and "national flag of Pakistan ceremoniously hoisted jointly by the then Presidents of the two premier political organisations of the District Muslim League and the District Congress Committee. The President of the District Congress Committee, so to say, rather roped in to hoist the flag with the President of the Muslim League, it seems, only to humiliate the Organisation which stood for the independence of United India as a whole in its relentless struggles for it."[14]

The incident certainly grieves the fighters for freedom. Shri Jitesh Chandra Lahiry, Shri Sudhangshu Mohan Choudhury alias Cheru, Shri Biresh Chakrabarty, Shri Birendra Nath Sarkar and Shri Pravash Chandra Lahiry and few others who were the actual freedom fighters and who had the scars of their struggles on their foreheads were seen to sit in a corner of the madding crowd – far, far away from the Flag-staff in a moody and dejected manner.

It would be surprising to note that even Pandit Jawaharlal Nehru was not happy at the final deal. He suffered from 'personal embarrassment of a rebel'. M. O. Mathai writes – "At the Viceroy

House at 11 A.M., on 2 September 1946, on the installation of the interim government, an acute personal embarrassment awaited Nehru." Nehru affirmed allegiance to King George VI, Emperor of India and also to affirm that he would well and truly serve 'our Sovereign.'[15] With the extreme annoyance he went through the affirmation of allegiance as follows : "I, Jawaharlal Nehru, do solemnly affirm that I will be faithful and bear true allegiance to His Majesty, KING GEORGE THE SIXTH, Emperor of India, His Heirs and Successors, according to law."

In affirmation of office he read as follows: "I, Jawaharlal Nehru, do solemnly affirm that I will and truly serve our Sovereign, KING GEORGE THE SIXTH, Emperor of India, in the office of Member of the Governor General's Executive Council, and that I will do right to all manner of people after the laws and usages of India without fear or favour affection or ill-will."

For several days Nehru went on murmuring like a child and lamented "I had not bargained for these". When dominion Government came into force on 15 August 1947, the Emperor of India automatically stepped down to become King of India; and Nehru, the Prime Minister, corresponded directly with the King. The British Government went out of the picture.

Nehru soon discovered that his communications to the King had to be in third person and in the form of "humble duty submission." Mathai writes – when the first such submission was placed before him for his signature, Nehru was annoyed and said, "Oh Lord" and pushed away the signature pad. After some time he signed "the wretched thing." Mathai also enclosed a photo copy (enclosed as Annexure-7) of a letter for approval of His Majesty which is as follows:

Prime Minister	*GR*	New Delhi
India	*appd*	28th April 1948

JAWAHARLAL NEHRU presents his humble duty to your Majesty and has the honour to submit, for Your Majesty's approval, this proposal of Your Majesty's Ministers in the Dominion of India that Sri Chakravarty Rajagopalachari, Governor of West Bengal, be appointed to be the Governor General of India on the demission of that Office by His Excellency Rear Admiral the Earl Mountbatten of Burma, K.G., P.C., G.M.I.E., G.C.V.O., K.C.B., D.S.O.

Sd/-

Jawaharlal Nehru
PRIME MINISTER
OF THE DOMINION OF INDIA

The rebel leader's embarrassment reminds us the remarks of Winston Churchill who said that 'In handing over the Government of India to these so-called political classes we are handing over to men of straw of whom in a few years no trace will remain.'[16]

It may also be noted that the rebel leader after his release from imprisonment was a guest of Lord and Lady Mountbatten at Singapore. Mountbatten 'asked Wavell to permit Nehru to leave India in order to help him placate the still restless and disturbed overseas Indian communities in Burma, Malaya and Singapore'....Nehru flew out of Delhi headed for Singapore ....Dickie sent his own open-topped Limousine to the airport to pick up Pandit Jawaharlal Nehru, whose Royal Air Force plane touched down shortly after noon on March 18, 1946. Captain Ronnie Brockman was waiting to drive Nehru to Government House, where the handsome, charming Dickie welcomed him warmly. They hit it off beautifully at first handshake and had a most civilized chat, Nehru magically transported back to his 'halcyon' years at Cambridge and in London as they drove through lines of cheering, flag-waving crowds of adoring Indians, Malays, and rather startled English troops, who lined the road six deep as they rolled passed the high open gates into Singapore's YMCA compound, where 'Forty-four-year-old Edwina Cynthia Annette Ashley Mountbatten who was one of the richest, thinnest, fastest, most fearless women in Great Britain' awaited them upstairs.[17] Lord Mountbatten also told Pandit Nehru that he could go anywhere he liked and could do what he liked but to refuse the invitation of local Indians to lay a wreath on the memorial to the Indian National Army.[18]

Lord Mountbatten was not only the supreme Commander of Southeast Asia but second cousin to the King and Krishna Menon's first choice to be the last British viceroy of India. The three who were soon to rule India dined together that evening. Lord Mountbatten recalled "and we made lifelong friends,".[19]

Thus there were so many promises, spoken and unspoken throughout that night "in the eloquent language of trust and love from Nehru's hypnotic eyes to the beautiful faces of Dickie and Edwina, each so sensitively attuned and receptive to the other that words were almost redundant". The next morning Dickie and Edwina flew off to Australia; Jawaharlal back to India. Their rendezvous in Singapore, though brief, proved most potent.[20]

An instance of the role of Krishna Menon can also be cited here. Prior to the departure of Lord Mountbatten to India as the last Viceroy of India, hardly ten days ahead i.e. on 13th March 1947, Krishna Menon suggested by a hand written note how to tackle the situation in India. Krishna Menon stated that Mountbatten should accept the demand for 'Pakistan' as Muslim 'Home lands' to those areas where the Muslim population was "predominant" and where the League had won "an appreciable majority of elected seats". In regard to the "Western Pakistan" he told Mountbatten to include only the Muslim-majority districts of the Punjab, together with Muslim districts of Sind, allowing an "approach to the sea at Karachi. He also suggested the "Eastern Pakistan" would contain the Muslim districts of Eastern Bengal, without Calcutta. Calcutta should be retained for India's West Bengal but offered the need of a Port for Eastern Pakistan which should be Chittagong after investing a huge amount of money. (An excerpt of his secret suggestion letter has been enclosed in Annexure-6).

Now I draw the attention of my countrymen to the Leaderless movement during 1942. In response to Gandhiji's call of 'Do or die' *(Karange yea Marenge),* the AICC appealed to the people of India to 'face the dangers and hardship that will fall to their lot with courage and endurance, and to hold together under the leadership of Gandhiji and carryout his instructions as disciplined soldiers of Indian freedom." Finally the "AICC wishes to make it quite clear to all concerned that embarking on a mass struggle, it has no intention of gaining power for the Congress. The power, when it comes will belong to the whole people of India."[21] Immediate after the arrest of the leaders on 9th August 1942 - "A hot gush of mass anger had welled to the surface and overflowed in violent and non-violent protests."[22] Despite country-wide arrests, thousands of people demonstrated against the repression of the Raj. There were peaceful hartals and protest meetings, there were outbreaks of mob violence, arson, murder and sabotage. Students and workers launched demonstration and for several days all activities ceased to function. In Ballia in the United Provinces crowds were machine gunned from the air. For six months the police and military had opened fire on demonstrating crowds as many as 538 times, killing 940 and wounded 1,630 persons. Later it was revealed that 10,000 persons killed and 60,000 arrested. In Dacca central jail there was no room to accommodate any further revolutionary and the arrested persons were sent to different jails in Bihar and other provinces. The agitation was first confined to Bombay, Ahmedabad and Poona but soon the demonstrations spread throughout the country and in certain districts in Bihar and Bengal the function of the normal life had been seized for several days. Tamluk of District Midnapur declared freedom as a result severe repression imposed on the people of that district.

The initial damage and destruction of the government property done by the violent mob, as estimated by the Govt. officials – there were 250 railway stations damaged or destroyed, 550 post offices attacked, 50 offices burned, 200 post offices damaged, telegram and telehone wires cut at 3,500 places, 70 police stations burned and many Govt. buildings destroyed.

The Government had repressed with a heavy hand all the discontented elements in India; it had picked out all the people who could reorganise the dispersed forces of revolt and give a new lead to these in welcoming the Army of Liberation marching towards India and under the leadership of Subhas Chandra Bose. By the time when the Azad Hind Government was organised at Singapore, forces of economic disruptions had been released over the country. Specially, in the province of Bengal which would be the gateway of the attack on India, man and nature comprised to disrupt the normal economic life. The attempt of the Government to "deny" food and boats even bicycles to the prospective Japanese invaders helped to upset Bengal's economic life. "There was communalism in the Nazimuddin Ministry that exercised certain of the powers of the State in Bengal and the functions of the State that touched the every day concerns of the people's life. Thus did State policy, communalist Ministry, profiteering and black-marketing, cooperate with one another to drive people in Bengal to famine and starvation, thereby turning their attention from thoughts of political rights from the fight for their assertion."[23]

Frank Moraes writes that "the public reaction was undoubtedly strong, widespread and in many places violent. But the authorities also struck ruthlessly and with a heavy hand." Apart from the aerial machine-gunning on crowds in Ballia, there were harrowing tales of repression in Midnapur and of military excesses on villagers in the hamlets of Ashti and Chimur in the Central Provinces. Nehru also recalls there were cases where "the whole villages were reported to have been sentenced to all manners of punishment from flogging to death." The Benares Hindu University being closed it was occupied by the military forces. In Bengal the local Government admitted that "Government forces burnt 193 Congress camps and houses in the subdivisions of Tamluk and Contai before and after the cyclone of 1942." Among the few organisers the emergence of Mrs. Aruna Asaf Ali, Achyut Patwardhan, Nana Patel, Jayaprakash Narayan were most prominent activists. Mr. Amery declared in the British House of Commons that collective fines were imposed on towns and villages as punitive tax which amounted to 9,000,000 rupees ($ 1,800,000) to be realised mainly from indigent, often starving villagers. Winston Churchill, in September 1942, had boasted "The disturbances were crushed with all the weight of the Government."[24]

Thus after so many sacrifices, oppression, repression, humiliation and sufferings of the people 'India Wins Freedom' which was not desired. After the 1942 movement the rebel leaders surrendered and preferred negotiations and compromise than movement.

Dhirendranath Sen wrote that "at the very outset the change in the political scene of 1947 was due not to capture or seizure of power but to a transfer based on compromise, and that the compromise was a tripartite agreement between the British Government, the Congress leadership and the League High Command. It was not a popular, democratic deal. *And a compromise, mind you, presupposes, on the one hand, agreement on fundamentals and, on the other, excludes any revolutionary social change*"[25] *(italics mine).*

The Transfer of Power is the greatest Tragedy of mankind and the Partition of India is the most unfortunate event of history.

NOTES AND REFERENCES

1. Sarkar, Prof. S.C., Burke, Edmund – *American Taxation. Chronological Summary*, 1775, 19 April.
2. Archive Papers – Fort William, the 10th August, 1857. Proceedings of the Lt. Governor of Bengal, No.662.
3. Sitaramayya, B. Pattabhi, *The History of the Indian National Congress*, Vol.I, p-14.
4. Menon, V.P., *The Transfer of Power in India*, p-7.
5. Roy, Amarendra Nath, *Bengal's Turbulant Years*, 1905-40, p-7.
6. Ibid, p-10.
7. Ibid, p-13.
8. Ibid, p-14,
9. Ibid, p-17.

10. Sarkar, Sushobhan, *On the Bengal Rennaissance*, p-124.

11. Roy, Amaarendra Nath, *Bengal's Turbuland Years*, 1905-40, p-21.

12. Sen, Dhirendranath, *From Raj to Swaraj*, p-219.

13. Lahiry, Pravash Chandra, *India Partitioned land Minorities in Pakistan*, p-1.

14. Ibid.

15. 15. Mathai, M.O., *Reminiscences of the Nehru Age*, p-21.

16. Menon, V.P., *The Transfer of Power in India*, p-343.

17. Wolpert, Stanley, Nehru : A Tryst With Destiny, p-361.

18. Lord Mountbatten delivered lectures in memory of Jawaharlal Nehru in the University of Cambridge on 14th November 1968.

19. Wolpert, Stanley, *Nehru : A Tryst with Destiny*, p-361. Source : Mountbatten to Earl of Listowell, Broadlands, October 3, 1978.

20. Ibid.

21. *Transfer of Power*, Vol.II, No.469, p-621.

22. Moraes, Frank, *Jawaharlal Nehru – A Biography*, p-301.

23. The Indian Annual Register, Vol.II, 1945, p-62.

24. Moaes, Frank, *Jawaharlal Nehru – A Biography*, p-302.

25. Sen, Dhirendranath, *From Raj to Swaraj*, p-219.

Annexure-1

The Hindu Mahasabha observed the All India Independence Day and the anti-Pakistan Day on 10th of May, 1942, when a resolution passed by hundreds of meetings held at Bombay, Poona, Calcutta, Nagpur, Luknow, Amritsar, Peshwar, Patna, and hundreds of other cities and towns all over India and were attended altogether by not less than a couple of millions of Hindus. Dr. V. D. Savarkar, by sending the resolution to Marquess of Linlithgaw, apprised the Government the intensity of the determination of Hindudom as a whole to oppose any scheme like the Pakistan one which seeks to allow freedom for any Province to secede and thus to break up the Unity and integrity of Hindusthan as a consolidated Nation and a Centralised State.

THE RFESOLUTION PASSED AT THE ANTI-PAKISTAN MEETINGS ON 10TH MAY, 1942

1) We, Hindus, reassert our determination to continue the Battle of Freedom which began on this memorable day, the 10th of May, on the eve of our National Rising in 1857, and has been handed down to us from Sire to Son.

Our methods and means may tactically change from time to time even as they are restricted today to the constitutional and peaceful sphere. But our ideal remains unchanged – the achievement of *Swarajya,* the absolutely Political Independence of Hindusthan! And we will continue the fight till this goal is ultimately won!

2) But the independence of Hindusthan does and must

inevitably imply in itself the Unity and integrity of it. This Unity of Hindusthan, our Motherland, and Holy Land from the Indus to the Seas, had been through a thousand generations of our people, the vision of our seers, the theme of our poets, the mandate of our law-givers and the battle-cry of our warriors – till at last it got identified with the oneness of our Nationl Being itself. To us, Hindus, today this Unity of our Motherland is an article of faith, the very life-breath of our Nationl Being.

We, Hindus take up therefore, a solemn vow today that we will resist, defy and defeat any attempt on the part of the Muslims to curve out any independent Pakistan federation by breaking up this Unity of Hindusthan as an integral Nation and a centralised State.

3) Nevertheless, we also made it clear once more that we, Hindus, are willing to share a common citizenship with all other non-Hindu minorities like the Parsees, Christians, Jews and others who bear patriotic and undivided loyalty to our common Country, and stand by its Unity as an integral Nation and a Centralised State. There shall be Constitutional safeguards guaranteeing to all citizens alike the liberty of worship, of language, of script and even in representation in proportion to population if it be insisted on by any cultural group. We hope that all our countrymen, irrespective of caste or creed or religion, will realise before long that the interests of everyone of us demand that we should all merge, on such sound and honest, democratic lines and on the basis of such rights and duties of equal citizenship, into a United and independent Hindusthan!

But if in spite of our earnest desire to meet all these requirements which true Nationalism demands, the Muslims try to browbeat the Hindus into yielding to them more than what is due to them in common with all India Citizens, we, Hindusabhaites in particular and Hindu Sanghatanists in general shall resist them and even to British Government, in case it sides with the Muslims in pursuance of an anti-Hindu Policy. The Hindu Mahasabha does not claim today an inch more for the Hindus than what is due to them on Nationl grounds, and in relation to their population proportions. But we are resolved and proclaim that we shall fight to the bitter end any effort on the part of any one to deprive an inch of what is due to the Hindus in virtue of their population strength and their equal rights held in common with all other Indian citizens. (Transfer of Power, Vol.II, p.86-87).

ANNEXURE – 2

HOW HUMANITY ATTACKED UNDER LIAQAT-NURUL AMIN REGIME?

Below is the statement of Sm. ILA MITRA made before the court of Rajshahi with regard to Inhuman treatment meted out to a lady, only because she holds a political opinion other than that of Liaqat-Nurul Amin Feudal class :-

Smt. Ila Mitra in her statement pleading 'not guilty' to the charges said : I know nothing about the case. On 7. 1. 50 last I was arrested in Rahanpur and taken to Nachole the next day. The police guards assaulted me on the way and thereafter I was taken inside a cell. The S.I. threatened to make me naked if I did not confess everything about the murder. As I had nothing to say all my garment were taken away and I was imprisoned inside the cell in stark naked condition.

No food was given to me, not even a drop of water. The same day in the evening the sepoys began to beat me on the head with butt ends of their guns, in the presence of the S.I. I was profusely bleeding through the nose. Afterwards my garments were returned to me, and at about 12 midnight I as taken out of the cell and lead possibly to the quarters of the S.I., but I was not certain.

In that room where I was taken they tried brutal methods to bring out confession. My legs were pressed between bamboo sticks, and the people around the cell was being administered a 'Pakistani injection'. When this torture was going on they tied my mouth with a napkin. They also pulled off my hairs, but as they could not force me to say anything. I was taken back to the cell carried by the sepoys, as after the torture it was not possible for me to walk.

Inside the cell again the S.I. ordered the sepoys to bring four hot eggs, and said, now she will talk. Thereafter four or five sepoys forced me to lie down on my back, and one pushed a hot egg through my private parts. I was feeling like being burnt with fire, and became unconscious.

When I came back to my senses in the morning of 9. 1. 50, the S.I. and some sepoys came into my cell and began to kick me on the belly with boots on. Thereafter a nail was pierced through my right heel. I was then lying half conscious, and heard the S.I. muttering : we are coming again at night, and if you do not confess, one by one the sepoys will ravish you. At dead of night, the S.I. and his sepoys came back and the threat was repeated. But as I still refused to say anything, three or four men got hold of me, and a sepoy actually began to rape me. Shortly afterwards I beame unconscious.

Next day on 10. 1. 50 when I became conscious again, I found that I was profusely bleeding and my cloth was drenched in blood. I was in that state taken to Nawabganj from Nachole. The sepoys in Nawabganj jail gate received me with smart blows.

I was at that time in a prostrate condition and the Court Inspector and some sepoys carried me to a cell. I had high fever then and I was still bleeding. A doctor, possibly from the Govt. Hospital at Nawabganj had noted the temperature of my body to be 105. When he heard from me of the profuse bleeding I had he assured me I would be treated with the help of a woman nurse. I was then also given some medicines and two pieces of rugs.

On 11.1.50 the women nurse of the Govt. Hospital examined me. I do not know what report she gave about my condition. After she came, the blood strained piece of cloth I was wearing was changed for a clean one. During all this time I was in a cell of the Nawabganj P.S. under the treatment of a doctor. I had high fever and profuse bleeding, and was unconscious from time to time.

On 16. 1. 50, a stretcher was brought before my cell in the evening and I was told that I would have to go elsewhere for examinations, on my protest that I was too ill to move about. I was struck with a stick and forced to get on the stretcher after which I was carried on it to another house. I told nothing there, but the sepoys forced me to sign a blank paper. I was at that time in a semi-conscious state with high fever. As my condition was going worse, I was next day transferred to the Nawabganj Govt. Hospital and on 21. 1. 50 when the state of my health was still very precarious, I was brought from Nawabganj to Rajashahi Central Jail, and was admitted to the jail hospital.

I had not under any circumstances, said anything to the police, and I have nothing more to say than I have stated above.

ANNEXURE - 3

Brief accounts of the incidents and casualties submitted by a Memorandum to the Prime Minister of Pakistan on 20 March, 1950.

SYLHET

The burden of the speeches of different speakers at a public meeting on the eleventh February was, "Blood will flow down the rivers of Sylhet." A local paper "Ansar" clearly reported some misdeeds and attempts in rural areas on the part of a section of Muslims led and supported by some maulavis at converting Hindus under coercion.

The troubles started in Sylhet town on the 13th February and continued till the 16th. According to official version in Sylhet town itself there were 50 to 60 cases of stabbing of which six proved fatal. In this town some ten or twelve houses are reported to have been looted and burnt. Almost simultaneously the troubles started in the rural areas within P.S. Sadar, Biswanath, Chatak, Fenchuganj, Balaganj and Gopalganj. In all these places a large number of Hindu Villages were attacked and have been completely destroyed and some Hindu girls were abducted and raped. Reports of mass conversion of Hindus of several villages have also been received. The modus operendi in these places was as follows :-

A few Mullahs first visited the village and asked the Hindus to save themselves by embracing Islam. Brahmins were made to tear their threads and recite Kalma. Wherever there was resistance the Muslim mob attacked the village and the entire village was looted and burnt and persons killed and women abducted.

In the first part of February 1950 several Muslim leaders of Sylhet town were openly preaching that communal acts of violence and lawlessness were prevailing in West Bengal and Karimganj sub-division of the Cachar district and as a result of that the Muslims of Sylhet must take revenge upon the Hindus. On the 10th February, which was a bazar Day and a Friday, a big placard was hung up in a prominent light-post on the Bander Bazar Road of the Sylhet town under the caption "Julums in Hindusthan on Muslims" and depicting on it hand-drawn picture showing the Muslims being dragged by ropes by the Hindus with weapons in their hands and pool of blood, coloured prominently in red, flowing. This placard attracted the attention of the passerby and soon an angry mob gathered round it. On the 11th February there was a public meeting in which some Muslim leaders delivered highly inflammatory speeches. On the 12th February there was a rumour in the town that Maulvi A. K. Fazlul Haq had been killed in Calcutta. The whole atmosphere was thus surcharged and trouble broke out from the 13th February and spread into rural areas.

At Manikpur some 25 houses of Naths (weavers) have been looted. In Jalapur area all the Hindu houses in village Senagram, Ajmatpur and Daspara were looted. Deities and idols were destroyed. At Lalbazar all Hindu shops have been looted and all the Hindu houses in neighbouring villages have been burnt. At the Hindu shops at Rakhalganj Bazar were looted. Most of the Hindu houses in villages Jhapa and Samalsasan were looted. All the Hindu houses of the Steamer Workshop at Fenchuganj have been burnt. At Majigaon and Machnabahar within the same P.S. several Hindu houses were looted and burnt. In Bagalganj P.S. several Hindu houses in villages Sukanpur, Madhurai and Kathalkair were looted. At Kathalkair and in its neighbouring villages there were mass conversions of the Hindus. In Golapganj P.S. large number of Hindu houses were looted. In villages Fulsain, Dakshinbhag, Purkayesthapara and Sribahar a large number of Hindu houses were looted and two girls of Bharat Choudhury were abducted from the village Dakshinbhag in Golapganj P.S. These girls were returned on the following day in a precarious condition and admitted into hospital. All Hindu houses in Dandapanipur under Biswanath Thana (within half a mile from the thana) were looted. Most of the Hindu houses under Biswanath Thana villages, Krishnapur, Kurma, Rajaganj-Akhra, Singerkatch-Akhra, Bulchandergaon, Satpara, Mahabatpur, and Tukerkandi were looted. A large number of murders were also committed in all these places and people were forcibly converted on pain of death.

MYMENSINGH DISTRICT

In Mymensingh district the worst affected parts are within the Jamalpur and Kishoreganj sub-divisions. Several incidents of arson and stabbing took place in Mymensingh town too. One teacher was stabbed to death. Trouble started in Jamalpur sub-division from the 13th February and continued till the 18th. The worst affected parts are within P.S. Jamalpur, Dewanganj, and Islampur. Quite a large number of stabbings, arson and loot took place within the Jamalpur town. Stray cases of arson, loot and stabbing also occurred in other thanas of this sub-division. At least 25 villages in Jamalpur and Sherpur P.Ss. and almost an equal number of villages of Diwanganj and Islampur P.Ss. were seriously affected. At those places 4 Hindu villages were completely burnt down. At Kursha within a mile of Jamalpur town all the 24 Hindu houses were completely looted and at Kochgar 20 Hindu houses were looted and 6 persons including 2 women were killed. Almost all the Hindu shops of Jamalpur town were looted. In and around Jamalpur town itself as many as 18 deaths took place and some 305 houses in 15 villages and all the Hindu houses in 10 other villages have been completely looted. In Kishoreganj sub-division P.S. Kishoreganj, Kotihadi and Astagram were the worst-affected. More than 20 villages in these thanas besides a few other villages in other thanas were raided and Hindu houses looted and burnt. There were also a number of stabbings in these places. The most dastardly murder was committed at the house of Babu Prafulla Dutta Roy, President, Kastul Union Board. Prafulla Babu was murdered in his own house by some Muslim friends whom he had called to tea to form a Peace Committee. His daughter aged about 18 years, who came to her father's help was carried away by the miscreants and her dead body was found in the field on the following morning. It is suspected that she was raped before she was done to death. During this holocaust even Hindu officers of the East Bengal Government were not spared at some places. Out of a number of such cases to mention only one, Babu Nagendra Nath Chatterjee, an Inspector of Civil Supplies of East Bengal Government with his son aged 7 years, a daughter aged 4 years and a nephew aged 27 years were all killed in the train at Bhairab Bazar while he was proceeding to his station in Bakerganj district. His wife and another daughter aged 1.1/2 years were also stabbed and thrown into the river below Bhairab Bridge. Thereafter they were rescued under very thrilling circumstances wounds on their persons. The whole story has been obtained with from the wife. Some more murders under such circumstances took place. The house of Sri Rohini Choudhury of Rahoulpur in Sadar Sub-division was raided. Altogether five members of the family including Rohini Babu's daughter who was to be married next day were killed. The girl was taken way first and raped before killing.

BAKARGANJ DISTRICT

At Barisal town the disturbances started on the 13th February following a rumour that Mr. A. K. Fazlul Haq of Barisal and his nephew were killed in Calcutta. Twentyfive Hindus were stabbed on the 13th and 14th of whom six died. About a dozen houses were burnt and looted including a Government Civil Supply Godown and the rest belonging to the Hindus. The flare spread to the rural areas in Sadar sub-division and continued till the 22nd. Total number of villages affected are about 50. Some of the worst affected villages are Lakulia, Sarshi, Madhabpasa, North Kashipur, Kalasgram, Rahamatganj, Kaunia, Khanpur and Khanpura. Most of the Hindu houses in these villages were looted and some burnt. More than a thousand Muslims on the morning of the 16th February attacked the Lakuta Rajbari and set fire to the heaps of straw and branches placed around the house. Compelled by the smoke and fire the Hindus who took shelter there came out and ran toward their homes. A large number of them were then killed, whose number is estimated at about 100. Fifty females after abduction were recovered from one village another 50 taken away. At Sarshi 50 dead bodies were found in a pit in the village, and a dead body of a woman was hanging near her house even on the 4th March. Vultures were seen eating the dead bodies. In this village the total number killed were estimated to be 80. The worst happenings took place at Muladi which is a thana Headquarters in the Sadar-sub-division. When loot and arson broke out in this village hundreds of Hindus ran for shelter to the thana premises where they stayed on the 18th and 19th February. On the 20th they were driven out from there and they took shelter at Muladi Bunder, half a mile from the thana where they were robbed and killed. The total number killed at the Bunder is estimated at five hundred and about 200 more dead bodies were lying scattered in the village. A considerable number of abduction of women and forcible conversion are reported to have taken place in these areas. Even as late as 3rd March Hindu shops in Bhandaria in the Ferozepur sub-division of the same district were looted. Under Rajapur thana in village Kaibartakhali about 37 were killed, and in village Rajapur 17. The total number of persons killed in areas under this thana will be about 150. At Ilshaghat in one family eleven were killed. Unwarranted arrests of respected leaders like Sj. Satindra Nath Sen, M.L.A. and some other leaders of the minorities during the riot period have added to the existing great panic in the minds of the people.

CHITTAGONG DISTRICT

In the Chittagong town the disturbances broke out on the 13th February, which continued till the 16th with a few cases of stabbing. On the 14th and the 15th disturbances spread out to the rural areas, Patenga, Kumira, Fatikchari, Rouzan, Hatazari, Anyara, Boalkhali Patiya and Sitakunda. Amongst these places the loss of life and property was considerable in Patenga, Kumira, Fatikchari and Sitakunda. Hindu pilgrims numbering about 130 who had gathered at Sitakunda fair during the Shivaratri festival are also reported to have been killed. In Patenga 27 Hindu families and in Kumira 47 Hindu families lost their all. At Patenga women were abducted, 3 of whom were recovered later on by the police, one being recovered on payment of ransom money.

During these disturbances Mrs. Nellie Sengupta, M.L.A. who was at Chittagong at the time and wanted to visit the disturbed areas was not allowed by the District Magistrate to go out for 4 days. Definite names have been received of the killed numbering 143.

NOAKHALI DISTRICT

At Feni on the 2nd February 7 Hindus were murdered and their shops looted. On the 13th February disturbances broke out throughout the sub-division. At Feni town itself 15 Hindu houses were burnt. In a single village Banspara, P.S. Chagalnaiya, the houses belonging to 42 families were burnt down. The number killed in the sub-division is reported to be 15 and one is missing. At Noakhali town 3 persons were killed on the night of the 10th February.

TIPPERA DISTRICT

On the night of the 11th February and the following day 7 Hindus were stabbed to death and 11 others injured in the town of Brahamanbaria. On the 12th February all the Hindu houses except one and all the Hindu shops at Talshahar Bazar were looted. This was one of the richest Hindu localities in the Brahamanbaria sub-division. Loss of property here is estimated to be very high.

DACCA DISTRICT

The disturbances in the city of Dacca have already been dealt with above. Looting and arson on a large scale also took place in P.S. Joydevpur, Tejgaon, Kapasia, Sripur, Rupganj, Sibpur, Monohardi, Narsindi, Fatulla and Narayanganj of the Sadar and Narayanganj sub-divisions. Harirampur and Shivalaya P.S. in Manikganj sub-division covering about 150 villages including Hats and Bazars. At Kotabari a village adjoining Mirpur all the Hindu houses were looted and completely razed to the ground. Most of the Hindu houses of villages Mirpur and Ghosepara were similarly looted and Hindu temples desecrated. In this area seven Hindus including a woman were killed. At these places even the corrugated iron sheets, door and window leavers and posts were uprooted and taken away. At Tongi and Pubali Bazars all the Hindu shops were completely looted on the 12th February. Other worst affected villages in the Sadar sub-division were Dattapara, Baradewara, Jazhar, Dakshinpara, Sataish, Gatcha, Harbaid, Udhur, Joynagar, Patertek and Gusain. At Harbaid alone as many as 40 Hindu houses were burnt on the 12th and 13th February. On the 13th February local Muslim Matbars spread the rumour that the Biharis were coming to attack the village and unless the Hindus embraced Islam their lives could not be saved. On the following day a meeting was called in the compound of the local Zamindar where about a hundred Hindus were forced to recite Kalma and say the Namaj.

In Rupganj P.S. of the Narayanganj sub-division nearly all the Hindu houses of 10 villages including Majhina, Baruna, Nowrah, Nagari, Pashi and Icchapura, were looted and many of them burnt on the 13th night. Several thousands of Hindu refugees flocked to the thana premises for shelter but the police did not take any action to stop the loot and arsons which continued till the 14th. The dead bodies in the Nowrah village lay in the houses for two days and two nights but the police took no action to take charge of the bodies and they visited the spot after the bodies had been disposed of by the Muslims.

At Jatrapur on the outskirts of the city of Dacca large number of Hindus were killed. In one house alone a woman with her 4 children were killed and their dead bodies were thrown into a well and were left there for a few days. For more than 10 days no police officer visited this area, which is a suburb of the Dacca city and was one of the worst affected areas. In Dacca city several Hindu temples were desecrated and idols were broken. The 70-year old priest of the Anandamoyee Ashram at Dacca which is within a stone's throw from the Prime Minister's residence was stabbed to death in broad day light and the Ashram was looted.

KILLINGS IN RAILWAYS AND STEAMERS

Besides these killings in town and villages of different districts a very large number of Hindu passengers travelling by train, steamer and buses during this period were killed. Most of such killings took place at Talshahar and Bhairab Bazar stations where trains were stopped and armed goondas got into the compartments and butchered the Hindu passengers. At Bhairab Bazar the trains were stopped on the bridge to allow the murderers to throw the dead and injured into the river below. At other places the dead and the injured were just thrown out into the fields alongside the railway line. There is a large number of eye witnesses to these cold-blooded murders. To cite only two, we may mention the names of widows of Professor Jyotish Chandra Das of the Kishoreganj College and Babu Nagendra Nath Chatterjee, an Inspector of Civil Supplies of the East Bengal Government posted at the time of his death in Bakerganj district. Similarly a large number of Hindu passengers on board the steamers as well as those waiting at different steamer stations were killed.

Apart from the above killings on trains steamers and buses three passenger trains were attacked by armed mobs, one at Surjanagar near Rajbari station on the 25th February and two at Santahar on the 28th February. The attack on the last two trains were made within an hour of each other and in all cases in the presence of armed guards travelling in these trains. The casualties caused in the first train are reported to be seven dead and 25 injured and those on the other two trains nearly 200 dead and injured.

INCIDENTS AND HARRASSMENTS STILL CONTINUING

Before the situation could settle down to normalcy reports of fresh outbreak of lawlessness in isolated way and in trains are pouring in ... unauthorised and humiliating searches and harassments of persons and belongings of the travellers in railway and steamer stations and on the way persist everywhere. Gold ornaments and other valuables are seized and taken away. The ladies are subjected to personal searches by males, customs, police, Ansars and other non-official elements in almost all places in an objectionable manner. Extortion of money from the passengers by threats or other coercive methods takes place. Snatching away of articles is often reported. Unnecessary oppression by prolonging searches is being indulged in so that the travellers may fail to pursue the normal journey, while their belongings are thrown pell-mell. No remedy from any quarters – Station staff was found generally callous and indifferent. There is also the unchecked high-handedness of the coolies, cooly hire charges varying from Rs.5 to Rs.10/- for each load. Accommodation in and guarding of railway compartments reserved for minorities is insufficient. Similar is the case with ferry steamer – at different points.

Economic boycott has also started. Hindus are not allowed to sell their movables or other articles or properties. Houses vacant or otherwise, are being forcibly occupied in rural areas also.

Generally persons leaving the province are not finding any safe passage yet. On 13. 3. 50, Daughter-in-law of Sri Umes Dev of Mymensingh town was robbed of her trunk and sewing machine at Pradyotnagar station on her way to Mymensingh. Gopal Chandra De was attacked just near the Narudi railway station and robbed of his suit-case and wrist-watch. On 14. 3. 50 Jatindra Karmakar of Mymensingh town went to railway station with a platform ticket to see off his daughter. He was subjected to search by customs official unnecessarily and Rs.43/- in Pakistan currency was taken away. On other's intervention money was later on returned but in Indian currency.

On 15.3.50 – About 30 to 40 persons of Halija village in Jamalpur sub-division of Mymensingh district were searched by a 'Daroga' at Dharmakura railway station while coming to Mymensingh. The Daroga extorted Rs.300/- from them.

The wife of Lalit Karmakar of village Paratala under Sibpur P.S. in Dacca district was taken away and returned next morning after ravishing her. Six Hindu houses in village Shampur under P.S. Melandah in Jamalpur sub-division were raided and looted twice on 14.3.50 and 15.3.50.

Robbery took place in the house of Jamini K. Paul of Manki under P.S. Melandah in Jamalpur sub-division in Mymensingh district and two unmarried daughters of Jamini Babu carried away. A girl from Noapara under P.S. Kendua (Mymensingh) was forcibly taken away in the evening and returned in the morning after rape. Some incidents of looting and murder were reported from Kaorai locality (Dacca District) on 16.3.50.

On 17.3.50 – Members of the family of Sri Jitendra Chakrabarti, teacher of Jubilee School, Dacca, were robbed of all belongings by Muslims on the way while coming to Dacca from Outshahi between Betka and Outshahi.

On 18.3.50 – Three or four days back the house of a Hindu widow in village Kumargata under P.S. Muktagacha (Mymensingh) was raided and looted. The widow was stabbed to death.

A telegram from Bar Library, Jamalpur (Mymensingh district) sent which reads : *Lawlessness Rampant in Villages, Spreading Daily. Evacuees Passing Raided on Way. No Stern Action.*

The above account of complete lawlessness throughout a large part of the province for a period of nearly 15 days is merely illustrative and not exhaustive. The magnitude of the loss of life and property can be correctly estimated only by a thorough enquiry by an independent tribunal. The aftermath of this widespread disturbances is more terrific. Vast masses of people have been rendered destitute and homeless within a few hours and they are now either moving about from door to door to eke out a miserable existence or are so panic-stricken that they are trying to leave this country for places of safety. The problem of restoring confidence and sense of security among these millions and rehabilitating them in their original homes needs the immediate attention of the Government. Up till now nothing tangible appears to have been done in this direction. A rehabilitation grant of Rs.10/- to Rs.20/- per family which was doled out to some of the inmates of the refugee camps in the city of Dacca was insufficient even for the purpose of their daily existence for a week.

The circumstances surrounding us are so bewildering that we naturally feel a bit hesitant to offer any suggestions as to the way out of the crisis... Politically judged, all the present maladies in our opinion, are traceable to the theocratic (Islamic) concept of the State, in which an idea of discriminating between different elements of the state on religious basis is inherent. Such an outlook has already been engendered in the minds of the general people (whether administrative personnel or not) much to the detriment, of the interests of the minorities resulting in treating the minorities as mere 'Jimmies' with all its obnoxious implications and humiliations. Unless this outlook is fundamentally got rid of, there seems to be no possibility of any change for the better being effected in the lot of the minorities. Constant and unremitting emphasis on the character of the state an Islamic one, evokes the proselytising and general communal zeal of the dogmatically minded members of the majority community. From our bitter yet long experience we can make bold to say that this outlook has inevitably created prejudices against the minorities and has its extensive and intensive and baneful reaction in all spheres of our public life, political, economic and administrative. Particular mention in passing may here be made of the evil effects of this outlook as reflected in the actual application of the policies of education, gun-seizure, house-requisitioning, detention and arrests.This outlook requires a radical change to prevent any recurrence of troubles, major or minor.

So, we humbly suggest that the state should be declared to

be "secular democratic" and further that the minorities should be treated as equal citizens with equal rights and obligations as the members of the majority community.

... In conclusion the members had suggested some measures for permanent solutions.

The Memorandum was signed by – Basanta Kumar Dass, Ganendra Nath Bhattacharjee, Munindra Nath Bhattacharjee, Haran Chandra Ghosh Choudhury, Monoranjan Dhar.

Annexure - 4

The evidences of more victims are mentioned below :-

Kulodini Sangma(Witness No.MN-646), Nalitabari, P.S. Bisgiripara said that she was a widow and was staying in the village with her daughter. The Muslims used to come and ask to marry her daughter with them. They used to trouble her every day and night. They took away her paddy, rice and other things. Being oppressed she left Pakistan and came to India.

Jisu Sangma (Witness No.MN 648), said – The Muslims used to trouble them by taking whatever they wanted without the house owner's permission. Every thing was taken in this way from their houses. When he used to go out for work they used to come to his house and harass his wife and daughters. The Muslim miscreants tried to abduct his daughters. They wanted to marry his daughter Kona Sangma. In order to be free from this harassment he had to pay Rs.300/- to the miscreants.

He said that the police of Nalitabari used to go to their village and say that all the Garos were leaving Pakistan and going to India so those villagers also should move and go to India. As there was no alternative left he had to leave Pakistan and came to India. He crossed the border on February 8, 1964.

Ganendra Hajong (Witness No.MN 651), said – "On Februrary 6, 1964, Muslims, Ansars, Pakistan police and E.P.R. armed with weapons entered our village, group by group, and looted our paddy, rice, cattle and other things. Then they drove us out of our houses and took our houses by force and gave them to Muslim deportees from India. After a few days, we received news that there was firing by E.P.R. on the group of people who were leaving Pakistan. Muslims and Government officers saying, 'Hajongs, Garos and Dalus have no faith, they must leave Pakistan' started looting in our village and in nearby villages. Having no alternative left, we left Pakistan."

Phulchand Hajong (Witness No.MN 668), said that his village was very near the Pakistan-India border. The shots were fired by E.P.R. on the people going from Pakistan to India, on 21 Magh 1370 (February 1964). Many people were injured and killed. On the same day his village was attacked by a large mob of Muslims, armed with various kind of weapons who looted everything from their houses.

Rai Mohan Sangma (Witness No.MN 626), Deodara, said – "One day, on the last week of January, 1964, Haik and 2 sepoys coming to our village tried to take away my brother's (Manjur Sangh's) wife by force but failed. We brought it to the notice of the Officer-in-Charge of Hatipagar Camp. This was also reported to Officer-in-Charge of Nalitabari P.S., but no action was taken.

On February 6, 1964, the East Pakistan Rifles, assisted by a large number of Muslims armed with guns, lathis and other weapons, fired on the people who were crossing the border at about 4 p.m. I personally witnessed this incident. An injured person named Nisal Patheng went to our village for shelter and he reported that due to firing about 2 hundred refugees were killed."

Rejot Sangma (Witness No.760) of Kakorkandi said – "On February 6, 1964, the Ansars set up their camp in the middle of our village and other Muslims also came and joined them. At last, when they were in a very large number they began to loot our houses continually.

After that on the same day at about 3 p.m., when we started for India because of their unbearable oppression, the East Pakistan Rifles fired on us without any warning at the Pakistan border. As a result, my father-in-law died along with many people and many were injured."

Sridam Dio (Witness No.MN 761), said – "On February 6, 1964, a party of Ansars set up a camp in front of my house under the pretext of helping us. Local Muslims joined them and when they became large in number, they bgan to loot our houses and took away all the properties of our houses.

Being harassed, we started for India on the same day. At the border we were fired upon by the E.P.R. Many people died and many were injured. I was also injured."

Several other witnesses have told the similar incidents that shots were fired by E.P.R. and Ansars at the border when the people who were harassed and driven out by the Muslims while crossing the border and coming to India. Some of the witnesses have described the looting of Kakorkandi, Jayramkura and Gobrakura villages in the month of April, 1964.

KALAKUMA – IN THIS VILLAGE THE MAJORITY OF THE PEOPLE WERE GARO CHRISTIANS.

Maru Marak (Witness No.MN 1015), said that the E.P.R. always troubled them in various ways. They used to impose heavy work on the villagers and used to pay very little. He said that Morzina Rechil, daughter of Suven Sangma, was raped by the Havildar Asfan Ali of the E.P.R. Ramchandra Kura B.O.P. Camp. Suven Sangma, her father, appealed to the court for justice but with no result. He also mentioned that Suruni Mankin, daughter of Mialy Marak, was raped by Abdul Joban.

Roykhan Marak (Witness No.MN 1021), said that Md. Meer Bux of Nalitabari tried to abduct his sister Chinmoy Marak by force. When witness resisted he was attacked with a knife and injured. He said this happened in last September, 1963.

Next he had purchased a piece of land from R/C Jamalpur Sub-division. All the legal documents showing his ownership of the land were with him. But a Muslim, Md. Ramzan Ali, belonging to Noakhali and staying at Kalakuma, took the land forcibly. When witness started to plough the land, he along with many other Muslims threatened him and told him by showing weapons like ramdao, spears and lathis that they would kill him if he would insist on possessing the land. He filed a suit in Jamalpur S.D.O. Court. But S.D.O. replied that there was no law for border areas. The Witness complained to the Chairman, Union Council but he also took the side of Muslims and refused to judge his case. Being oppressed he left his village with other villagers and crossed the border on February 5, 1964.

Similar acts of forceful occupation of land have been confirmed by the Witness No.MN-1022.

Samuel Marak (Witness No.MN 1205), said that he stood for Union Council membership election. His rival party with the help of E.P.R. Ramchandrakura and Hatipagar Camps put up false case against him and harassed him. He said that local Muslims used to cut bamboos, grass and crop from his field and E.P.R. of Hatipagar and Ramchandrakura Camps used to encourage them by standing beside the miscreants.

Prosanna Kumar Debnath (Witness No.MD 156), said that some miscreants entered the house of Kutashar Nath and looted his house. They abducted his daughter-in-law and raped her. She was seriously injured and died in the hospital at Mymensingh.

Durgesh Chandra Marak (Witness No.MD 2) of Songara said that the E.P.R. of the B.O.P. of Bijoypur Camp used to harass Hindus living in border villages by looting their property.

He said his daughter Parul aged 17 years old was studying in Ranikong mission. When she was coming home she was kidnapped by Muslims, Kabir Sheik and Nurul Hussain. She was rescued by the witness afterwards. He said that his house was also not spared and Muslims looted rice, paddy, cattle and all the household things.

He said another instance where a girl from village Gaimara was abducted and raped. He also mentioned the name of another girl of his village who was kidnapped. The villagers complained to the police but no steps were taken to give protection to them.

Amar Sangma (Witness No.MD 3), Bagh Para, said "the

E.P.R. of Chorapara B.O.P. used to come and beat the villagers making false accusations, if they were not given money which they demanded from the villagers. He said that he himelf was beaten severely by them in March 1964. Because of the harassment from E.P.R. he left Pakistan and came to India. He was not allowed to carry anything with him while coming to India."

Budesh Marak (Witnes No.MD14), Surjyopur, said – "My village was situated near the border area. The police and Ansars used to come to our village and trouble us in various ways. In the year 1963, my wife with two other women of the village were abducted by the border police and were raped. Next day they were taken to the Haluaghat police station and were released after being detained the whole day.

In February 1964, a mob of Muslims along with the border police and Ansars attacked our village. They said 'Leave Pakistan, otherwise you will be killed.' So we had to leave Pakistan."

Ayna Sangma (Witnss No.MD 36), Digolbak, said – "Our village was situated just on the border of Pakistan. Everybody in border belt area knew how terrible it was to live on the border of Pakistan. We were daily troubled by the border police and Ansars.

In about lst week of Falgun 1370 B.S. the border police and Ansars with Muslim villagers armed with rifles, spears and sticks came to our village and shouted 'Go to India or embrace Islam otherwise you would be all shot down.' Saying this they drove each of us out of our house and looted our paddy, rice, cows and other house materials and flew away.

When the day was over the miscreants came again at night and set fire to houses. Five houses were burnt down with everything inside.

Sadari Sangma, daughter of Gobinda Marak, was raped by Muslims. She was eighteen years old and she was my niece, said Ayna Sagma.

This happened at the end of December 1963, the Muslim scoundrels, nearly five in number, entered the room where Sadari

Sangma was. Time was then just evening. They raped her and tried to take her away to their house but in the meantime having heard the shouts others rushed to the place and saved her from the hands of those scoundrels." He also mentioned the names of the miscreants.

Susenrda Areng (Witness No.MD 8), Kalsinder, said – "Our village was somewhat away from the border area so we were not troubled by police or Ansars but Muslims always troubled us. They tried to harass us in various ways. They used to let loose their cattle and damage our crops. They used to occupy our land forcibly and unlawfully.

Suddenly, the Muslims who were our neighbours, armed with spears, sticks and other weapons attacked our village. They were shouting 'You must go to India, Pakistan is not for you.' He said that they looted his paddy, rice, cattle and other household things. They carried away whatever they could carry in their carts and drove the villagers out saying 'Go away'. As they had no place to stay on they came to India."

Noni Sangma (Witness No.MD 26), Sapamari, said - In March, 1964, Mahmad Babar Ali, member of No.8 Haluaghat, with the help of local Muslims came to his village and burnt their houses. All the movable properties were looted and they were driven out of their houses. Complaint was lodged against the miscreants, with the officer-in-charge of Jikna E.P.R. Camp but no action was taken.

Bipin Chandra (Witness No.MD 115), Hajong, said – "In the second week of January,1964, the Muslims of Ranipur threatened us to leave Pakistan. They told us that if we would not leave Pakistan, they would kill us and would abduct our women. When we were leaving Pakistan, on the way the police of Charnapara border camps detained us and snatched away our money. They also snatched my wife and took her to the police camp. After that night they set her free and sent her to India on the 16th January, 1964."

Similar incidents were reported by the various Witnesses

No.MD 60, MD 61, MD 62, MD 63, MD 64, MD 65, MD 66, MD 68, MD 69 and MD 70.

Lalmohan Chiran (Witness No.235), said – "Our village was away from the border area. Our village was surrounded by Muslim villages and we were always harassed by them in various ways. They used to abduct and rape girls from minority class. My daughter and niece took shelter in Bahlu Kaparo Mission when the miscreants tried to abduct them. Kadir Sheikh, Chairman No.3 Dubaura Union Council, was one of the miscreants. He was helped by some of the village leaders and police staff of Durgapur P.S. So there was nobody in the village to whom we could go and complain."

He said the recent disturbances broke out in the first week of March 1370 (February 1964). The Muslims of neighbouring villages with help of police of Durgapur P.S. raided the village and looted everything and forced them to leave Pakistan and came to India.

Similar incident was also described by Witness No.MD 236.

Upendra Chandra Roy (Witness No.MD 93), Dakshin Maij Para, said – The local council members with the help of neighbouring Muslims suddenly surrounded the village on February 10, 1964. They were armed and were shouting slogan "Pakistan Zindabad". They had seen houses burnt in the neighbouring Hindu villages. So being frightened they went to E.P.R. Camp at Charnapara but they were refused help. However, that night passed and they left Pakistan the next day, on February 11, 1964.

Similar account was given by Witnesses MD-89, MD-90, MD-91, MD-92, MD-94, MD-95, MD-96, MD-97, MD-98 and MD-99.

Kero Marak (Witness No.MD 74) , Arapara, said – his house was burnt by Md. Emam Ali, Md. Rakman Ali, Md. Sam Meah of his village on February 21, 1964. He complained to Chairman and O.C. police but no action was taken. He said that a girl, Anjona Rongdi, a daughter of Pahar Mandal, was raped by Md. Momroj Ali in her house. She shouted for help. The villagers went to her house and arrested the miscreant and took him to the Chairman. But the Chairman instead of punishing him, released him. He himself was injured twice by E.P.R. and Muslims.

Belku Hajong (Witness No.MD 154) – said that on 20th Falgun 1370 (March 1964) a great number of Muslims along with border police and Ansars came to his village and shouted "Leave Pakistan". They looted whole village. He said that his house was also looted and paddy, rice, cows, goats and household things were taken away. He left Pakistan on 20th Falgun 1370 (March 1964).

Rajani Marak (Witness No.MD 248), Goberchena, said that local Muslims took away his paddy as also his land by force. On 20th Falgun 1370 (March 1964) a large number of Muslims entered his village shouting "Allah ho Akbar" and looted their houses. He complained to Md.D. R. Mannan, village Suhakipur and to police authorities but no steps were taken to protect them. Being frightened they left Pakistan.

Similar story was told by Witnesses MD-249, MD-250, Md-251, MD-252, MD-253, MD-254 and MD-255.

Peter Marak(Witness No.MD 190), Thowsalpara, said – "Being oppressed by the Muslims and E.P.R. he could not live in Pakistan peacefully. The Muslims used to come every night with danagerous weapons and threaten him and his village people to leave Pakistan. The women could not move freely outside and inside the village because of the rough behaviour of the Muslims.

By the middle of Poush 1370, the Muslims rushed to his house and forcibly took away his reaped paddy from his house. Every year the Muslims used to reap his crops from his paddy field. By the lst week of Falgun 1370, the Muslims set fire to the house of his neighbour. For the security of life he was compelled to migrate to India."

In Sylhet, so far as the border areas are concerned, there were organised and determined efforts to drive out the minority communities. These communities were largely Christians.

The organised efforts took the shape of creating a climate of complete insecurity for the minorities and finally of large scale attacks on villages where looting and burning of houses took place. The unfortunate occupants of those houses were driven out in the bitter cold of January 1964, and were told that there was no room for them in Pakistan as Pakistan belonged only to the Muslims.

Joy Kishor Das (Witness No.S 8), Sylhet P.S. Bishnupur, said that his boat was stolen. He approached the Chairman of the village council but with no result. He finally came away because of the general lack of security.

Kumud Chandra Banik (Witness No.S 9), Sunamgunj P.S. Sunamgunj town, said- "Muslims used to threaten us and extort money from us. We were not permitted to have our religious festivals. One day at the end of May 1964, a Muslim, Gada Mia, drove us out from our house. We could get no assistance from the authorities. When we were fleeing away, we saw a number of dead bodies of Hindus on the way. I, my daughter and my brother-in-law were beaten."

Nripendra Chandra Bhattacharji (Witness No. S 10), Ballavpur, said that the wife of M.D. was raped by four Muslims and was badly injured. The complaint to the police proved futile. Cows of Sullahamoy Das were taken away by some Muslims during the day time. There was a dacoity in the village.

Jayachandra Das (Witness No.S 11) said that in April 1964, there were disturbances in the village and houses were looted and burnt by large mobs of Muslims. One woman was abducted in broad day light. He had given the names of the assailants. He also gave the names of the abductors as Khandan and Gada, among others, of village Rangarchar.

ANNEXURE - 5

NOTE ON THE CONFIDENTIAL CONVERSATION AT DACCA ON 25 MAY 1950 BETWEEN MR. J. N. MANDAL AND MR. T. V. VENKATRAMAN, THE HINDU, CALCUTTA CORRESPONDENT

Mr. Mandal said : "The Hindus in East Bengal to a man are emphatic that they have no place in Pakistan and are determined to leave. I have advised them to wait for a few weeks more and that I too am prepared to accompany them to India. So long I have been claiming to be a representative only of the Scheduled Castes, but after what I have seen and heard, I feel I can speak for the entire Hindu community here.

"I have informed Delhi that it is only a question of time before the last Hindu reaches ;India from East Bengal. You must be prepared to receive us and rehabilitate us, and if necessary throw out enough Muslims to make room for us. If India is not prepared to do this, we shall appeal to the world, become Buddhists, Christians, but we will not submit to a slow process of Islamisation.

"My idea is that there should be no East Pakistan. There is a feeling in Pakistan that the Delhi Pact provides a breathing time for Pakistan; or to put it bluntly, to make Pakistan a permanent and lasting fact. Every Muslim feels lthat there should be no Hindus left inside Pakistan. India should not be foolish enough to believe thatg after driving out the Hindus, Pakistan will live in peace with India. West Pakistan is sufficiently armed land protected. They are now buying arms and ammunition openly in the world markets and it will not be long before East Bengalis also well armed. Orders have been issued to strengthen the defences of East Bengal. If in February there had been an armed intervention in East Bengal from India, it would have been all over with East Bengal, like Hyderabad, in the course of fifteen days. When East and West Pakistan are well armed, surely the Muslims are not going to rest content. They will launch a two-pronged attack on India. I caution India to be on the alert and not to be complacent and think that Pakistan will adhere to the Delhi Pact or any pact.

"One of the leading citizens of East Pakistan, whose counsel prevails with Liaquat Ali Khan (Mr. Anwar, Chief Adviser to the West Punjab Governor) once bosted that it will not be long before Pakistan expended her territory. But the Kshmir affair and the way India not only halted the onslaught by the raiders, but was beginning to reclaim lost territory, made Pakistan sit up and take stock of her situation. You people agreed to a truce. Now the Pakistan leaders (they have lost all interest in Kashmir as far as I can tell – they know, once they violate the truce, they are finished) are being told that the Kashmir affair should be kept burning to keep aloft the morale of the Muslims of Pakistan. The same thing happened in East Pakistan. When Liaquat Ali after his tour of East Bengal found that India was bent upon coming to the rescue of the Hindus, your Prime Minister concluded a pact with him. Believe me, there is no remedy. There should not be an east wing of Pakistan.

"I have undertaken a long tour of East Bengal and shall remain here for a long time helping the Hindus to get away from here. I have asked my followers (I represent about 25 lakhs of Scheduled Castes, mostly Namasudras) not only to resist aggression by Muslims, but to avenge thoroughly any injury done to a Hindu. If Delhi will realise our plight, we will to a man be led by Pandit Nehru and act according to his instructions. They want to drive away the Hindus from here and enjoy their property without allowing a single Muslim to enter East Bengal from India. They know that if East Pakistan is lost, Pakistan loses 12 Annas in the rupee. And they know that so long as Hindus continue in East Bengal they cannot get all that 12 annas for themselves.

"After the Delhi Pact Muslims are being told that it is just like the Chamberlain-Munich Pact affair (comparing India to Hitler), that it is only a question of time before Hitler is crushed. I am awaiting the lead that Delhi will give the East Bengal Hindus. I am prepared to go toDelhi and plead personally with Pabdit Nehru the cxause of the East Bengal Hindus. My cabinet colleagues have realised that my presence here is embarrassing to them. I have been asked to return to Karachi under various pretexts. They even asked me to lead the Pakistan delegation to the ILO to get me away from East Bengal.

"The Ansars are the greatest culprits in the recent trouble. They should be disbanded without any delay and their arms taken back. They were recruited from amongst the hooligan elements amongst the Muslims and with little or no means of livelihood. So it is no woder they perpetrated all sorts of crimes upon Hindus.

"There is no propaganda by Muslims to uphold the Delhi Pact or any attempt to persuade the Hindus not to leave. The higher authorities are well meaning, but there is limit. If they find that one particular senior officer is taking too much interest in the Delhi Pact, they promptly transfer him. Take the Superintendent of Police of Barisal who is an honest Muslim. The District Magistrate is a great rogue and he has been largely responsible for the greatest amount of mischief. When he and the S.P. clashed, the S.P. was promptly transferred. The lower officials are bent upon frustrating the pact and any amount of orders and instructions from the top will not make them budge. They have to pander to the Muslim mentality.

Mr. Mandal narrated a large number of instances where officialdom and Muslims alike were making life hell for the Hindus. Open threats are being issued to Hindus to marry their womenfolk to Muslims. Money is being extorted in the guise of giving protection to them from hooligans. If Hindus dare report to the authorities, punishment often descends upon them. Houses and crops are destroyed and women molested. Koranic prayers are to be said in every school and every Hindu is to attend standing. Indian history is being tampered with. Maharaja Nandcoomar is being mentioned as Kaffir Nandcoomer. Hindu names of schools are being changed to Muslim names. Without contributing a pie to the funds of the schools, Muslims are being given 50 per cent or more representation in the administrative bodies. In district and union board elections under joint electorates, Hindus are being terrorised not to vote so as to get as many Muslims elected as possible. The situation in Barisal and Khulna continues to be most unsatisfactory and the two districts were the worst affected during the riots.

About the large number of Hindus who are daily returning to East Bengal, he said that the majority of these returning evacuees were from the Scheduled Castes, mainly Namasudras. They were returning with the object of settling down because they have large landed properties here and wanted to look after their agricultural interests. The Caste Hindus who were returning were doing so with the object of disposing of their property and migrating permanently to India. The fact that most of the caste Hindus have left has considerably weakened the morale of the lower Hindus. Ultimately he expects that with no more Caste Hindus left, the wrath of the Muslims will surely descend upon the lower class Hindus.(Sukharanjan Sengupta, Banga Sanhar Abang, p-204-207).

ANNEXURE – 6

An extract
From THE TRANSFER OF POWER, Vol.IX, Letter No.531
Mr. Krishna Menon to Rear-Admiral Viscount Mountbatten of Burma

Mountbatten Papers. Official Correspondence Files : Political Situation in India and constitutional position of Viceroy (2)

INDIA HOUSE, ALDWYWEH, LONDON,W.C. 2
13 March 1947

My dear Lord Louis Mountbatten,

I enclose the last page of my notes, which was inadvertently left out of the copy I gave you. (1)

As I told you, there are a number of matters to be included in it if the basic idea appears to be of any use. If you need me, I shall be glad to see you again before I leave. Your ADC apparently knows how to get in touch with me. I recognise the importance of hastening slowly, but it appears that in India things will not rest as they are. There is a great threat of famine also, which may add to complications, but at the same time makes effective central authority essential.

I was glad to see you and to have had our talk. Perhaps you will let me know sometime what you think of what I have said.

Yours sincerely,

V. K. Krishna Menon

1. The complete notes were reproduced here. It is evident from this and an earlier letter on the file that Mr. Krishna Menon had had an interview with Lord Mountbatten on 13 March.

Section I.

. The Problems are :-

1. The crisis in the Interim Government.
2. The Machinery for taking over.
3. The Princes.
4. Indo-British relations.

(1) and (2) are obviously closely inter-connected, and (4) is closely connected with (1) and (2), both severally and jointly.

Section II. The crisis in the Government.

1. The decision of the Congress to force the issue of a genuine coalition or the dismissal of the League members is in suspense *for the moment*, pending (a) the arrival of the new Viceroy and (b) the slight hopes of response from the League to a further approach.
2. The resolving of the crisis, in my view, *rests basically*, on the relation of the Ministry to the Viceroy – that is British power.

The assumption of a new role by the Viceroy quite obviously (not merely willy willy) is essential to a change for the better in the present situation.

3. The Attlee declaration apart from all other causes, makes it both logical and incumbment on the British side that its power (as distinct from its influence) should not only rapidly diminish (to vanishing point in 1948) but that *immediately there should be a change in thi relationship whereby the entire onus of administration is in the hands of the Interim Government.*

It is the failure on the part of Lord Wavell to accept this position, and his unfortunate excursion in the contrary direction since the middle of the last September, that is largely responsible for the present crisis.

4. When the Viceroy assumes this new role (analogous to that of the King in England or the Governor General of a Dominion) certain consequences follow :-

   a) Leaderhip (as distinct from multiple leadership) emerges in the Government.

   b) If the Government contains Moslem Leaguers, they will either tend to merge into a *genuine* coalition or be reduced to impotence.

   c) If the League is in opposition within the Government or a constitutional opposition outside, the Congress, which has the leadership will be forced at every step into behaving as though it were a partner in a *genuine* coalition.

   d) If on the other hand the League (or indeed any group) are in unconstitutional opposition, relying a violence and anarchy, there would be a Central Government strong and resolute enough to deal with the situation.

5. (i) The result of the step thus suggested is to bring right into the fore-front the main long term issue both in the way of (a) the future Constitution and Unity of India, (b) the authority for taking over, and

   (ii) to render the problem of 1(4), Indo-British relations, capable of approach by the British side in more practical terms and in a friendly atmosphere.

6. Failing the assumption of this new role by the Viceroy, a crisis of some kind or another will be precipitated within the first few weeks of his arrival. This is inevitable, and if this happens 1(2), 1(3) nd 1(4) become far more complicated, and the economic, political and administrative situation in India will approach disaster.

7. A strong Government, capable of enforcing its authority centrally and of co-operating with the Provinces, is

indispensable for dealing with the economic situation which in the next 12 months threatens to be disastrous (famine included).

8. In the new situation, the role of the Viceroy is by no means a negative one. His influence would be very potent and his assistance sought. His role would be historic and would make the regime not one of a new leadership.

Section III. Taking over.

1. In July 1948, it is obvious there must be machinery for taking over. This machinery may well be –
   (a) that which is established under a new constitution by a Constituent Assembly with or without Moslem League particiation; or
   (b) the Interim Government (under Dominion Conditions) or
   (c) the de facto repositories of Power and Power relationships, or
   (d) some machinery arbitrarily decided by the outgoing authority.

I do not propose to deal with the question of what constitution may emerge by one process or another.

The immediate problem is what has to be done for obtaining comparatively stable conditions for (a), (b), (c) and (d) above, or some combination of these.

In hard reality this poses the question, *what about the Moslem League* and, in a lesser way, the Princes, and what solution or way out can be found by the Viceroy using his great influence as contemplated in II above?

2. What I propose here is intended as a realistic approach rather than a crystllised formula, and I think aloud in this way.

Recognise, if the League so desires it, its claim for "Moslem homelands" – Pakistans.

This recognition is possible only on the basis that the homelands are to be limited to those areas where at present the Moslem population is predominant, and where the League holds an appreciable majority of elected seats.

In other words, it is impossible to think in terms of homelands on the basis of British provinces. This is not a question of whittling down Pakistan or driving a bargain on it, but of seeking the only method which would enable a Pakistan to be created at all.

Therefore, I propose the following :

(a) A Western Pakistan in the North-West, to include the Moslem majority districts of the Punjab together with the Moslem districts of Sind, with an approach to the sea at Karachi irrespective of the composition of the population on this boundary. Any attempt to provide a homeland which is boxed in all four sides is an unfair offer from the League point of view.

The port of Karachi, irrespective of its predominant non-Moslem population and all-India importance, to be included in Western Pakistan, thus giving the League a first-class sea and air port and great city.

The remainder of the Punjab to be constituted into a separate province of all-India.

The question of the remainder of Sind has to be thought out.

(b) Eastern Pakistan in the North-East, to include the ditricts of Eastern Bengal which are predominantly Moslem, and certain areas of Assam, thus partitioning Bengal (Shades of Curzon).

The problem here are (i) the comparatively strong opposition in Bengal to partition and (iii) Calcutta.

I believe that Partition is the price that will have to be paid for any stability in Bengal.

With regard to Calcutta, any solution which hands over Calcutta to Pakistan will be unstable and impractical. The reasons are well known.

On the other hand, the League has to be given a port on the East, and the solution is that as part of the compromise settlement India should build large-sized city and port in Chittagong, that is, provide the money for it however many millions it may cost.

(c) *Question of powers and status.* The Pakistan shall be styled as autonomous states, and not provinces. They should have all the attributes of statehood except foreign relations and defence. These two cannot in any event, before 1948, be made available to any Pakistan, because any new state created would have no foreign relations by that time even if it succeeds in getting recognition, except with the co-operation of the rest of India. This is therefore a problem of the future, and it is dealt with further below.

Defence is equally not capable of being vested in any Pakistan at the time of its creation. Even if it were, it would confer little power on Pakistans, as the heavier defence of all-India would reduce the defence power of the Pakistans to impotence.

On the other hand it is proposed that the Pakistans as here contemplated should have vaster powers than for the groups under the Cabinet plan. Therefore they should be given not merely the title of autonomous States, but all the competence except the two mentioned above, that is to say all tariffs, currencey, control of communications, including posts and railways, flag, external trade, control of resources and independent heads of States. They should also be accorded the right to secede from India and establish themselves as independent States when they are in a position to obtain foreign recognition and to build up their defences sufficiently effective(ly) for the independent protection of their homelands. This right of secession must be genuinely conceded, irrespective of whether it will be used. All these rights and functions can obviously be made amenable to any agreements of give and take with India.

(d) The Pakistans would, as different from the Provinces, maintain a High Commissioner or Agent General, or some such functionary of the semi-ambassadorial level at New

Delhi, who would be the links on the problems of defence and foreign relations and be a general liaison in the neighbourly relations contemplated. Obviously no taxation will be levied in the Pakistans, except by their own Governments. They would make an agreed contribution annually to the Government of India in respect of defence and foreign policy, which shall not be varied with consent.

(e) The inclusion of areas other than those mentioned here need not in principle be ruled out. For example, if the League is able to make terms with the rest of the Punjab and bring such areas into its Pakistan, it should be permitted, but such consent must be a matter of plebiscite in which at least 75 per cent of the population votes in favour of such incorporation.

(f) It should be pointed out here that in this arrangement the Pakistan receive a far higher status of independence and considerably more powers and functions than the present provinces claimed for Pakistan would receive if power were handed over in July 1948 on the basis then likely to exist in the absence of any agreement of this kind. For provinces, in spite of autonomy, have much less power than contemplated for the Pakistans as herein.

Section III. (IV). The Princes.

1. It is too late now to challenge or refute the stand unfortunately taken by the British Government on the question of Paramountcy. I myself think that the position so taken is a preposterous one, but the purpose of these proposals is to deal with the situation as we find it. Therefore we have to take as starting point the fact after July 1948 the States will be relesed from feudatory allegiance.

   At the same time, their economic and military dependance on India and their geographical encirclement are hard facts which no argument about paramountery can dispose of.

2. Therefore in the absence of a Constitution emerging the

following relationship and arrangements may be contemplated at the change-over.

3. The Viceroy in the next 15 months will still be the representative of the paramount power. At the same time as Governor General he has become a Constitutional head. He cannot exercise his relationship with the Princes except with the aid of the economic, administrative and political power, which, as head of British India, is with him.

Here is a context where influence rather than power can forge a solution, and if nothing better can be obtained within the next 15 months, the States can be brought into relation by agreement with the all-India Government, which alone will have competence in foreign affairs and defence. If the States resist, they would have to be allowed to retain their competence in all other matters, but equally they cannot expect out of their relationship with the all-India Government any support for the maintenance of their autocracies as hitherto under British rule. The problem of popular freedom in the States will have to be amenable to the forces of popular awakening. The all-India Government should undertake, for the sake of peace, non-interference in matters of dynasty etc.

The Viceroy's role and the favourable terms which he can obtain for the States by his influence with the all-India Government can be hoped to effect (a) grouping of small States; (b) acceptance by smaller and larger States of all-India competence in various matters such as Communications, tariffs, currency, minerals, etc., (c) conversely it would obtain for these areas, most of which are backward, economic, administrative and other assistance from all-India; (d) under the arrangement here contemplated, there will be no danger of anarchy or balkanisation at the time of the change-over.

Section IV (V). Indo-British relations.

It should be said at the outset that any attempt to bring in Dominion status by the back door would create suspicion in India and defeat its purpose. What has to be sought frankly is not any constitutional hegemony of the Commonwealth, or any detraction of India's independence. This would be going back on the Attlee statement of withdrawal. What then can be the basis of Indo-British relations ?

(a) Reciprocity of Citizenship.

(b) Agreements with regard to mutually suitable arrangements concerning the liquidation and re-arrangement of relationships which now exist.

(c) Long term treaty of alliance in all respects consistent with the obligations owing to and the spirit of the United Nations. There is room for the discussion of Most Favoured Nation clauses.

Reciprocity of citizenship rather than a common crown is frankly the hard core of Indo-British relations.

Section V (VI)

The creation of Pakistan and the conferring on it of rights and functions far in excess of the Cabinet plan will evoke protests and opposition from the Congress and other groups. Mr. Jinnh would regard it on the other hand, as a truncated Pakistan. But for either side the alternatives are far worse, and for the British it would involve a repudiation of the solemn to pledges of the Attlee declaration and the prospect of having to deal with anarchy or termination of relationships in such ways as are injurious to both sides.

It may be further pointed out that the proposals here are not based upon theoretical considerations, and are largely, in fact, a planned approach to what would willy nilly be the position if in July 1948 no Constitution has emerged.

Finally, even if a Constitution emerges, the approach in these proposls would *at present* be called or, but it would have to be made clear that this is no substitute for Constitution making which is untouched by them.

It may also be added that these proposals concede to Mr. Jinnah his demand for two Constituent Assemblies.

ANNEXURE 7

PRIME MINISTER,
INDIA.

New Delhi,
28th April 1948.

App^{d} GR

JAWAHARLAL NEHRU presents his humble duty to Your Majesty and has the honour to submit, for Your Majesty's approval, the proposal of Your Majesty's Ministers in the Dominion of India that Sri Chakravarty Rajagopalachari, Governor of West Bengal, be appointed to be the Governor General of India on the demission of that Office by His Excellency Rear Admiral the Earl Mountbatten of Burma, K.G., P.C., G.M.I.E., G.C.V.O., K.C.B., D.S.O.

Jawaharlal Nehru

PRIME MINISTER
OF THE DOMINION OF INDIA.

Bibliography

Azad, Maulana Abul Kalam – *Indian Wins Freedom* (Reprinted June 1967).

Azad, Salam – *Contribution of India in the war of Liberation of Bangladesh*, 2003.

Archive Papers - 1857, Proceedings of the Lt. Governor of Bengal (No.662), Fort William the 10th August 1857.

Adiraju, V. R. – *Netaji Subhas Bose : The Great Revolutionary*, 2001.

Butalia, Urvashi – *The Other Side of Silence*, 1998.

Bhattacharjea, Asit – *Count Down To Partition : The Final Days*, 1997.

Bhattacharyya, Sushil Kumar – *Gandhism in Indian Politics*, 1996.

Basham, A. L. – *The Wonder that was India*, 1967.

Bose, Biswanath – *RIN Mutiny 1946*, 1st published 1988.

Collins, Larry and Lapierre, Dominique – *Freedom At Midnight*, 1978.

Carter, Lionel – *Mountbatten's Report on the Last Viceroyalty*, 2003.

Chopra, P. N., Ed.- *The Collected Works of Sardar Vallabhbhai Patel*, 1998.

Chopra, P. N., Ed. – *Quit India Movement, British Secret Documents*, 1986.

Chakravarty, Sachi – *Quit India Movement : A study*.

Chakrabarti, Prafulla K. – *The Marginal Men*, 1990.

Constitutional Relations Between Britain And India, *Transfer of Power, 1942-47*, 1981.

Calcutta Disturbances Commission of Enquiry, 1946.

Das, Suranjan - *Communal Riot in West Bengal.*

Dutta, Akshay Kumar – *Bengal's Fight For Freedom*, 1972.

Dutt, Guru - INDIA : *In the shadow of Gandhi and Nehru*, 2000.

Ghai, Prem Vati – *The Prtition of the Punjab (1849-1947).*

Gossman, Patrticia A. - *Riots and Victims.*

Gandhi, M. K. – *An Autobiography Or The Story of my experiments with truth*, 1927

Gandhi, Rajmohan – *Patel : A Life*. 1991.

Hasan, Mushirul, Ed. – *India Partitioned : The other face of Freedom.* Vol.II.

Hodson, H. V. – *The Great Divide*, 1969.

Hartog, Rudolf – *The Sign of the Tiger : Subhas Chandra Bose and his Indian Legion in Germany (1941-45).*

Ikram, Dr. S. M. - *Indian Muslims and Partition of India*, 1965.

Indian Annual Register, Vol.I & II, 1942.

Indian Commission of Jurists, New Delhi, 1965 – *Recurrent Exodus of Minorities From East Pakistan and Disturbances in India.*

Kamra, Sukeshi – *Bearing Witness : Partition, Independence end of the Raj*. 2001.

Karlekar, Hiranmay - *Bangladesh : The Next Afghanistan*? 2005.

Kulkarni, V.B. – *Pakistan : Its Origin & Relations.*

Lahiry, Pravash Chandra – *India Partitioned and Minorities in Pakistan*, 1964.

Lohia, Rammonohar – *Guilty Men of India's Partition* (4th Edition), 2000.

Mosley, Leonard – *Last Days of the British Raj.*

Moraes, Frank - *Jawaharlal Nehru : A Biography*, 1956.

Moraes, Frank - *Nehru : Sunlight And Shadow*, 1964.

Moon, Penderel – *Divide And Quit : An Eye Witness Account of the Partition of India*. 1998.

Mathai, M. O. – *Reminiscences of the Nehru Age*, 1997.

Nanda, B. R. – *Three Statesman : Gokhale, Gandhi And Nehru*. 2004.

Panjabi, Kewal L. – *The Indomitable Sardar*, 1962.

Prasad, Bimal - *India's Partition in Historical Perspective : Maulana Azad Memorial Lecture*, 2005.

RGK – *India : A Nation in Turmoil*, 2004.

Ray, Jayanta Kumar - *Democracy And Nationalism on Trial : A Study of East Pakistan*,1968.

Roy, Tathagata – *My People Uprooted : A Saga of the Hindus of East Bengal*, 2001.

Roy, Amarendra Nath – *Bengal's Turbulant Years, 1905-40*, p-7, 1989.

Sarila, Narendra Singh – *The Shadow of the Great Game: The Untold Story of INDIA'S PARTITION*, 2005.

Sen, Dhirendranath – *From Raj To Swaraj*, 2005.

Sherwani, Latif Ahmed – *The Partition of India and Mountbatten*. 1986.

Samanta, Amiya K., Ed. - *Terrorism In Bengal, (1905 to 1939)*. 1995.

Sareen, T. R. – *Indian National Army* (5 Vols.). 2004.

Settar, S and Gupta, Indira Baptista, Ed. – *Pangs of Partition*, Vol.I&II, 2002.

Singh, Dr.(Smt) Anshu – *National Movement and Communal Strife in India from 1937 to 1947*.

Saha, Dr. Meghnad – *Memorandum on the Rehabilitation of Refugees from Eastern Bengal, By the East Bengal Relief Committee*, 1958.

Sen Gupta, S. C. – *India Wrests Freedom, 1962.*

Sen, Mohit - *A Traveller And the Road : The Journey of an Indian Communist*, 2003.

Zakaria, Rafiq – *The Man Who Divided India*, 2006.

Ziegler, Philip – *Mountbatten*, 1985.

Bengali Books

Asoke Mitra – *Tin Kuri Dash*, 2000.

Annada Sankar Roy – *Yukta Banger Smriti*, 1990.

Amalendu Dey – *Banglay Bharat Charo Andolan.*

Asim Roy – *Banga Brittanta*, 1988.

Chattapadhyay, Rudrapratap - *Sir Saiyid Ahmad Khan – A political biography*.2001.

Hiranmoy Bandopadhyay – *Udvastu*, 1970.

Maleka Begum, Ila Mitra,

Sinha, Dr. Dinesh Chandna – *Syamaprasad : Banga Bibhag O Paschimbanga,* 2001.

Sinha, Dr. Dinesh Chandra – *Noakhalir Mati O Manush*, 1993

Subhas Mukhopadhyay – *Bangalir Etihas*, 1999.

Salam Azad – *Ethnic Cleansing*, 2002.

Salam Azad – *Hindu Sampradaya Keno Bangladesh Tyag Kareche*? 2001.

Sukharanjan Sengupta – *Banga Sanhar Ebong (1946-1950)*, 2002.

Satabarsher Aloy Shayama Prasad, Ed. *Dr. Shyamaprasad* Memorial Committee, 2002

Shyamaprasader Diary O Mrityu Prasanga, Ed. Umaprasad Mukherjee, 1997.

News Papers

Amrita Bazar Patrika, 5th April, 1945.

National Herald, December 4, 1945.

The Dawn, 1st August, 1940, 4th October, 1945, 7th October, 1945, 26th March, 1946, 11th April, 1946.

Hindustan Times, 6th October, 1945.

Harijan, 24th May, 1942, 30 May, 1942.